26/03/11

Dear Julie, Knut & Max 4450

Good luck in your new home

love Brett, Jacqui,

Brigitte & Christopher.

GW00471827

SAFFRON WALDEN'S HISTORY :
A CHRONOLOGICAL COMPILATION

by

MALCOLM WHITE
(Town Clerk, Saffron Walden)

SAFFRON WALDEN
1991

*To Daniel and Thomas, the future
generation, from their Dad, the present
generation, so that they may learn from past
generations.*

1st impression 1991
2nd impression 1998

ISBN 0 9517445 0 X

Printed by Hart Talbot Printers
Saffron Walden, Essex

CONTENTS

ILLUSTRATIONS

FOREWORD

A compact history of Saffron Walden has long been needed. Many people will find use and pleasure in Malcolm White's affectionate and painstaking book.

In these pages readers can trace how the physical layout of the town has been shaped through the ages. This should stimulate fresh interest in many of its landmarks and better understanding of their age and development.

The forging of Walden's character is also well documented. No wonder this is a town of concerned citizens. Its history teems with examples of public spirit, good conscience and community involvement. Less good behaviour is not forgotten, but then as now it was confined to a tiny minority.

Certain names shine through the story. Both Walden's early growth and later progress owes a lot to families which at times wielded great influence and often demonstrated sustained philanthropy. This book explains why their names are so widely honoured in the Walden of today.

In a span of history of this scale the full extent of change and adaptation is bound to impress. Yet the author has managed to detect certain strands or themes which suggest why the town seems always to have maintained a special nature. Equally as he reads about the problems of health, employment, education, housing and roads in yesteryear the cynic may be tempted to say that little has changed after all.

The first Member of Parliament for the Saffron Walden constituency hoped when he retired in 1895 that "political battles of the future may be fought with that mutual forebearance and fair play which alone are worthy of the citizens of our great Country." Perhaps readers will conclude that mutual forebearance and fair play have indeed emerged from the mists of time as the hallmarks of this town.

Alan Haselhurst, M.P.
March, 1991

ACKNOWLEDGEMENTS

A work of this nature relies heavily on the goodwill of numerous people and my gratitude to the following is sincere and heart felt.

My thanks therefore to Jill Palmer and all the staff at Saffron Walden Library, particularly Martyn Everett, whose knowledge and interest in the town's history is only equalled by his unfailing courtesy on all occasions; and to Essex County Council Libraries for permission to reproduce pictures on pages 185 and 211; to Colin Moule, Editor of the Saffron Walden Weekly News, for his help and ready assistance in permitting use of extracts from his newspaper; to Doctor Steven Bassett, (a real historian!), for permitting use of his works for the earlier centuries; to Mike Hibbs for kindly and patiently drawing the maps in the book and for taking so much care and time on their accuracy; to Len Pole and the staff at Saffron Walden Museum, for providing assistance and an inspirational museum; to Mike Petty, a former colleague and Librarian of the Cambridgeshire Collection for helping me with the one 'missing' year; to Saffron Studios for their assistance with the prints; and to Jean Gumbrell for help and encouragement.

Particular thanks are due to all those authors mentioned in the bibliography on p.256 many of whom I have not contacted and whom I hope will be understanding in my use of their efforts; to my father-in-law Leonard Lambert for all his assistance in photographic matters; and to Alan Haselhurst for kindly finding the time in a busy schedule to write the foreword.

A special mention should also be made of my history mentor, Fred Thompson, former Deputy Head of Newport Grammar School, who inspired in me a lifelong interest in history for which I shall always be grateful. I hasten to add that any historical mistakes are mine!

Thanks are also due to Saffron Walden Town Council for permission to reproduce diverse pictures from their collection, and to numerous individual Councillors for their interest and encouragement in this book. I am sure that they will understand that tact and political expediency means they do not get mentioned by name!

Finally my genuine thanks to all those people kind enough to buy the first impression of this book and for the many kind compliments paid to me; to Ken Wood the Managing Director of Hart-Talbot for the many hours and insults he has paid to me (!) and for agreeing so readily to a re-print, and last and most important of all to my wife Kate, whose help, encouragement, support, interest, and tolerance of a long drawn out project only rarely wavered!

Malcolm White

PREFACE

I suspect that this history of the town owes it origins to a former geography master at the County High School with whom I used to play cricket. For in about 1978, I suddenly discovered a whole stream of school children entering my office wanting details of the geographical development of the town in the 16th, 17th and 18th centuries and with a message from that particular master saying he was sure I would be able to help them! The fact that I was unable to was largely because I could find no chronological history of the town. This book then, is an effort to fill that gap.

The student of Walden's history should however be wary of trying to find anything startlingly original in this book. I would ask that you look carefully at its title, for with one small exception, I claim no originality. Much though I would like to be called a historian, by profession I am a librarian, a person who accumulates and disseminates information. This book is just that, a compilation of other sources arranged in a chronological form. It therefore follows that I owe a considerable debt of thanks to all those authors from whom I have unstintingly plagiarised! I hope none take offence, for imitation is the sincerest form of flattery, and in copying I only do so in an effort to arrange Walden's history in a logical and hopefully readable format. The numbers in brackets throughout the book refer to these sources which are listed in the bibliography.

I mention one exception, and that is the period from 1889 to 1945, when most of the material is based on reports in the "Saffron Walden Weekly News". I have always felt that there would be some interesting material to be obtained from these old newspapers, and after spending much time at the British Museum Newspaper Library I was delighted to discover that Saffron Walden Library had recently acquired the papers on microfilm, thus both saving me time in going to London, and making the papers available to other students.

The aim of this book is to try and bring together the many and varied parts of Walden's history. I hope it shows that a town like Walden is an amalgam of centuries, involving continual change by degrees. Too often people oppose new ideas simply because they are new and without considering that change does not necessarily have to be wrong. If this book helps to make people realise that continual evolution, and not stagnation, has helped to make Walden, what I consider the finest market town in England, then I shall be satisfied.

Malcolm White – March 1991

Chapter 1
Walden to Domesday

Prehistoric times

North-West Essex has always possessed some of the most fertile land in the country and so it is not surprising that the area showed signs of human habitation from earliest times. The needs of early man for water, good soil for crops and plentiful wild life for food, were all to be found in North - West Essex. The land was watered by the Slade, a tributary of the Cam, and was situated just north of the great forest which covered a large amount of Essex and Hertfordshire. The forest itself was virtually impenetrable and much of the land was swampy, both factors helping to make good cover for game (33).

The earliest remains found were of wild horses and straight-tusked elephants. The abundant source of food from wildlife, combined with the chalk outcrops of the eastern end of the Chilterns, which ensured that flints were available for tools and weapons, made this an attractive and habitable area. It is believed that the first settlers in Walden – it can hardly be called a town at this time – were Neolithic farmers, (18) and in addition to Walden there has been archaeological evidence to suggest their presence at Great Chesterford, Littlebury, Newport and Wenden, all of which are on the main Slade tributary.

Neolithic Man was followed by Bronze Age man. It is thought they entered the region through Cambridgeshire by following the tributary of the local river. Indeed at this time it would have been very difficult for them to approach North - West Essex from any other direction because of the great forest to the south. Again settlement was restricted to the river beds and Beaker pottery typical of the Bronze Age was discovered in this area. Examples of pottery are on display in Saffron Walden Museum. In addition a spear or dagger head found in the Walden area can be seen in the Cambridgeshire Museum of Archaeology. Mrs. Monteith considers that at this time the main route through the town, High Street and Windmill Hill, was established, the Slade being forded at the lowest point of the High Street.(33)

The question of what contribution the Iron Age made to the period is raised by the presence in and around the town of three great defensive areas; Ring Hill (near Wendens Ambo), the Grimsditches (N.E. of the town flanking the Slade near Byrds Farm) and the Battle Ditches. Ring Hill is about 1,100 yards in circumference and signs of occupation at the eastern end have been discovered. The Grimsditches are described as being similar in shape to other Iron Age hill forts. They are now however very badly damaged and the area is largely covered by woods. V.C.H. (53) mentions that traces of earthworks defences also exist around the Castle. The Battle Ditches, although for many years considered to be of this period (See Chambers (12)) are in fact almost certainly 13th or 14th century. (See Bassett(3)).

Roman Times

So where exactly was Walden at this time? Although that may seem a peculiar question to ask, the town has gradually evolved and its centre has moved. From the attached map it can be seen that the 'town' was roughly in the area of Audley Park. This has been substantiated by a number of Roman finds to the west of the town. Additionally some Roman finds have been made in the grounds of Audley End Mansion. As far as Walden was concerned the Romans had very little influence on the town. Their two chief forts in Essex were at Colchester and Great Chesterford (Cestreforda). The evidence that does exist suggests they passed through Walden rather than settled in the town. During the 19th Century, Wyatt George Gibson, who lived in Hill House at the southern end of the High Street, discovered in that general area, a samian bowl, an urn, a basin and also a paddle-shaped mount and a brooch thought to be of 1st century age. Roman remains have also been discovered in Little Walden, and include a samian bowl, a glass unguentarium 3½" high, an iron lamp holder, part of an iron spear head barbed on one side, a spear shaft, a pair of iron hinges, part of an iron staple and hasp, pieces of lead, and six iron headed bronze studs each with a central iron rivet and a groove with attachments (probably for a leather thong). According to VCH (53) the hinges and hasp fittings suggest the goods were originally buried in a chest.

Pottery and coins have also been found at Byrds Farm, Audley End Village, Copt Hill, Almshouse Meadow, Swan Meadow and Walden Place. Two coins, one of the Emperor Nero and one of Phillipus 1, were discovered on the maze on the Common. Other Roman finds include part of a stone moratium, a platter, three fragments of lava mill stones and two pudding stone querns, all found at Hunters Well Field near Roos Farm. The little amount that has been found suggests lost equipment, although there may have been a small settlement at Little Walden. Bassett (4) feels that it was very likely that there was an early Roman military site in or close to the town, possibly in the area of the Gibson Estate.

Archaeologists have suggested there is a possible Roman road from Colchester to Great Chesterford, and aerial photographs show an ancient road about a third of a mile in length running approximately north-west to south east across a large field north-west of the old SW to Bartlow railway line.(53) Strategically Great Chesterford was much better placed for the Romans, than Walden since it not only occupied the high land, but was also at the junction of at least two important roads. According to Mrs. Monteith (33) the straight stretch of road through Sewards End is also part of a possible minor Roman Road running from Stane Street at Dunmow through Thaxted to Great Chesterford.

The Anglo - Saxon Period

After the Romans left, this area continued to be occupied until the Anglo Saxon invasion. This is partly supported by the town name, Walden, which is thought to be a derivation from 'Wealadena', meaning Valley of the Britons or the serfs, a name undoubtedly given to the town by the Saxons. It seems apparent therefore that the town was continuously occupied from at least Iron Age times and was not merely a Saxon settlement.

With the fall of the Roman Empire, a Germanic invasion of the country took place. It is known that there was a Germanic settlement around Cambridge and probably also at Great Chesterford, but Bassett (4) feels that on the evidence of archaeological finds Walden remained relatively unaffected by the Germanic influence. So what was the town like at this time? Some idea can be obtained from the excavation of a Saxon cemetery in the area of the modern Gibson Close. These excavations were carried out by George Stacey Gibson in 1876-78, when some 200 graves were found. Objects found on the skeletons, and the position they were buried, suggests a substantial Christian community lived here from about the 7th to the 11th centuries, either late Saxon or Danish. The few grave goods that were found included a beautiful late Saxon necklace, which is on display in the museum, and 22 Romano - British bracelets. (A full account of the discovery, a list of the finds, and a plan of the cemetery, have been documented by H. Ecroyd Smith.(23) It is believed that the majority of the bodies found in the cemetery were of the 7th century or later, but at least fifty of these may have been from Roman times. The cemetery continued in use until at least the 9th and probably the 12th centuries. The cemetery probably ceased use with the building of the first Church on Bury Hill.

The site of the town gradually moved during the Anglo - Saxon period towards what is now the area of Abbey Lane.

The Saxon burial ground at Gibson Close.

The area of the town was effectively bounded by what is now Abbey Lane and Hill Street; Fairycroft Road and a line parallel to Audley Road. As will be seen this was the probable line bounded by the Battle Ditches in the 13th or 14th century. Although the Battle Ditches have now been proved conclusively to be of 13th century origin by Stephen Bassett (4) it would nonetheless seem an appropriate spot to speculate on their history and importance to the town, since almost certainly as long ago as the Iron Age the line of the Battle Ditches marked the western boundary of the town. Earlier excavations on the site revealed foundations of huts above Bronze Age remains, and this seems to suggest that it was a permanent settlement from about the early Iron Age through until the Saxon invasions. This is further evidenced by pottery finds on the site. Entry into the town would have been by way of a north and south gateway - the outlines of the remaining ditches suggesting the northern gate was in Abbey Lane/Hill Street and a line south of Audley Road being the southern gate.

An interesting paper written by W. J. Chambers (12) made various suggestions for both the use and the age of the Battle Ditches. Mr. Chambers notes that there is a mound visible at the join of the existing south and west portions of the ditch. Other references have suggested a similar mound existed in the High Street (approximately where the War Memorial now stands.) The general theory seems to be that they were a kind of earthern fort. Evidence has been discovered of a skirmish of some sort being fought near here. Lord Braybrooke (8) as early as 1836, talks of a 'sanguinary conflict' and mentions a skull found with a long and distinct cut obviously made by a sword or axe. (This skull is on display in the museum). Mr. Chambers suggests that the most valuable article on the subject of the Battle Ditches is in the 1904 Transactions of the Essex Archaeological Society, by Chalkley Gould. This article suggests that there was once a palisade or stockade of timber running along the top which was possibly Celtic in origin. On the strength of this, Mr. Chambers suggests that the Battle Ditches were probably built in a period between late Neolithic and early Iron Age (1800 B.C. to 500 B.C.).

Until 1959, these dates were accepted. However an excavation carried out in that year proved conclusively that the earthworks had no connection with the Anglo-Saxons and was constructed at a later date in the middle of the 13th century. A section cut across the western arm proved it to be of a single period construction, and the earliest pottery discovered was only about 700 years old. It is thought the ditches may have been built in connection with some medieval town planning scheme.

Further investigations were carried out in an archaeological excavation on the old cinema site at the junction of Gold Street and the High Street between 1972 and 1980 by Doctor Steven Bassett, Professor of Archaeology at Birmingham University. In his preliminary report, he said:-

'There can be little doubt that the ditch extended originally for some appreciable distance to the East. Its former line is mirrored by a series of

The Battle Ditches in about 1800.

property boundaries and ancient wall lines for a distance of almost eighty metres beyond the eastern limit of excavation . . . furthermore, that length of Gold Street onto which the site fronts to the north can be seen as the development of a new road immediately to the rear of the bank or rampart. The ditch is an obvious continuation to the east of High Street of the line of the early 13th century Battle Ditches. This extant earthwork runs southward from near Abbey Lane to an almost right- angled corner and returns at present as far as Gibson Gardens. Within the past two hundred years, apparently, it extended as far as High Street, where the Cucking Stool Pond marked its eastern butt end, (now beneath Margaret Way.)'

However Doctor Bassett feels that there are two objections to certain identification of this site as a continuation of the Battle Ditches. The first is the conspicuous absence of any reference in charters or conveyances dealing with land to the east of the High Street. It would have been normal practice in medieval times to have used such a prominent feature as a basis for location and identification. The second objection related to the differences between results of the 1959 excavation on the remaining ditches, and the 1972 excavation on the old cinema site. It is felt, overall, however that there can be little real objection to accepting that the southern line of the Battle Ditches ran across the cinema site parallel to Audley Road.

Whilst the site bounded by the area of the Battle Ditches was probably the original town, it almost certainly had disadvantages. Being the lowest part of the town, it probably flooded quite regularly and so thought would have been given to moving the town to higher ground. It is probable that a new site was chosen in Saxon times, the site being adjacent to the Battle Ditch site, but on higher ground. We know that the site used was roughly within the area now bounded by Castle Street, Church Street and High Street. This site had the advantage of natural defences on three sides – the Slade to the north and south and marshland to the west.

In 1982, Doctor Bassett published the authoritative account of his excavations in Saffron Walden (4). This excellent work should be consulted by anybody interested in a detailed history of the town to the 13th century. There are some recorded references to Saxon landowners. In the 'Chronicles and Memorials of Great Britain and Ireland', vol. vi. the following reference is made:-

'I, Ethelred, procarator of the Mercians, hand over and grant to my faithful minister Wulfgar, with the consent of my bishops, a certain portion of land. There is of land about the space of XV houses in a place called Waldene, to have for his obedience as long as he lives, and to his heir with all appurtenances, meadows, pastures, waters, etc. . . .'

Ethelred was the ealdorman of Mercia. The land was later given to St Alban's by Wulfgar. (2)

According to the Domesday Book, the Manor of Walden, until the Conquest, belonged to Ansgar, the Master of Horse under Edward the Confessor, and an Ealdorman of London. Guy Maynard, writing in the Saffron Walden Almanac of 1905 says that Ansgar owned 2000 acres of wood, arable land and meadows sufficient to pasture a thousand hogs. The marshland to the west referred to above as the third side of the towns defences was known as Hogs Green and is shown by that name in a map of the town of 1758. It was also often used in old title deeds to refer to land covering the area now bordered by the High Street, Abbey Lane and Freshwell Street, presumably obtaining its name from its use. This land would of course provide an ideal defence. It is believed that a wooden fort was probably on the fourth, unprotected side, approximately where the castle remains now stand. Mrs. Monteith (33) considers that the curved shape of Freshwell Street was possibly due to a wooden palisade placed at the edge of Hogs Green. Maynard suggests that the fort was:-

'probably a low timber house built on an artificial mound of earth, surrounded by deep ditches and strong palisades, with large court-yards and outbuildings for the accommodation of a great Thane's numerous household.'

Local field names mentioned in other medieval charters also show Saxon origins:-

COCK BUSH FIELD, shown on the 1845 Tithe Map as being to the east of Windmill Hill was derived from the Saxon name Coppid Bush Field which in turn was derived from the Saxon word 'coppede' meaning having the head cut off or pollarded. (Pollarding trees was a favourite method for producing strong straight stems for bows.)

DODDEN HILL, shown on the 1845 Tithe Map as east of Little Walden Road, came from the Saxon 'dodden' meaning to lop branches; and

LEIGHTON STEDLEYS, a field approximately where London Road and Borough Lane now meet, is derived from the Saxon for a town clearing.

Freshwell Street pond in about 1900 before the road was forded.

Field names also suggest that isolated dwellings may also have been founded by the Danes. The field shown on the 1845 map as DAINES MEAD, adjacent to Duck Street in Wendens Ambo, was probably originally the field called DANES BOTTOM. Two other names also suggest Danish settlements, ERICHSHAMSTALL and GUNNORES-HAMSTEALL, the first part of each name being common Danish names, and the second part 'hamstall' being Saxon in origin and meaning a farm or smallholding.

So after the Romans left the area, the settlement of Walden between about the 7th and 10th centuries appears to have moved further north and formed both a central dwelling area as well as a few small farmhouses in various scattered clearings. Not many features of the present landscape however date from Saxon times.

Domesday and Walden

The only written record for this period is also probably the most famous, the Domesday Book. According to the Anglo-Saxon Chronicle a Council was held in mid-winter in 1085 in Gloucester (10) and after discussing with his Earls, King William sent his men into each Shire to enquire in great detail about its resources and who held them. A contemporary account by Robert Losingu, Bishop of Hereford, says that 'other investigators followed the first; and men were sent into provinces which they did not know, and where they themselves were unknown, in order that they might be given the opportunity of checking the first description' (50). This is important because it emphasises that as a record of the Norman period, the Domesday Book can be relied upon as being both accurate and factual. The object of the book was 'to discover the quantity and value of every man's fee [i.e. land holding], to fix his homage, and to obtain precise information as to the services which were due or might be exuded by the Sovereign.' (13)

The Domesday Book is in fact two volumes, the Great or Exchequer Domesday Book and the little Domesday which covers Norfolk, Suffolk and Essex. Written in medieval Latin, various translations have been made. There are three entries relevant to Walden; two relate to Manhall, a manor to the west of Little Walden, the third to Walden. The first Manhall entry reads thus:

LXX HERVEUS DE ISPANIA
(Uttlesford Hundred. Manhall in Walden)
Hundred of Udelsforda - Monehala is held by the same
Hervey of the Earl; it was held by Siward for i hide.
Always ii villiens, then i serf, now none; now i bordar;
always half a team; vii acres of meadow, and ii parts
(ii thirds) of a mill. It is worth xx shillings

To transcribe:-

Monehala is held by the same Herveus of the Earl:-

Manhall was a manor somewhere to the west of Little Walden. Morant (34) says 'The manor house [of Manhall] hath been down from time immemorial.' The manor was held by Herveus of Ispania (Spain) from the Earl. According to Morant (34) Herveus' family came from Spain but it is more likely they were a Norman family from the parish of Epaigne near Pont-Audemar in France. All land was technically owned by the king - Earls owned it 'Of the King' and in turn other subjects would own it from the Earl. In this instance the Earl was Alan, Earl of Bretagne.

It was held by Siward for i hide.

The land was held at time of the Conquest by Siward and measured one hide. A hide was a measurement which has been variously described as 80, 100 or 120 acres. It consisted, theoretically, of 4 virgates, a virgate being 30 acres, but measurements would vary from place to place.

Always ii villiens, then i serf, now none; now i bordar

There were in 1066, and still were in 1087, two villiens on the land. A villien, or villager, was a class of person in possession of 'yardland'. This would vary between 15 to 30 acres. (52) They were tied to the land and could not leave the land except to fight in wars. The villien was without legal redress for any civil injury received at the hand of his Lord, and as if this was not bad enough, had to render services such as ploughing, reaping and sowing on the Lords lands.

The serf, of which there was one in 1066, was even worse off and his condition was little better than that of a slave. It can be assumed that this particular serf improved his lot and by 1087 had become a bordar. A bordar was a smallholder and was considered slightly less superior than a villien. He would have rendered menial service in return for a cottage; perhaps Herveus was a benevolent landlord in this respect and wished to improve the lot of his serf.

Always half a team

The land required half a team to plough it. A team was four oxen.

vii acres of meadow and ii parts (ii thirds) of a mill. It is worth xx shillings.

The land comprised of seven acres of meadow and a further two acres on which a mill stood. The remaining third of the mill was owned by a socman or freeman. In early medieval documents a mill called Faryngworth is said to be the mill of Manhall manor. This is the first documentary reference to a mill in Walden but no doubt there was a mill in Walden from then onwards. Mills were extremely important in both the economics and trade of the town. Whoever owned the mill had a powerful monopoly over his neighbours whose farming activities were useless without access to the mill. The 1514 charter mentions a mill, but it is highly unlikely this was the same mill as the poor methods of working wood and the rigourous forces of nature meant mills would only last twenty or thirty years at the most. The whole land was deemed to be worth twenty shillings but any method of trying to relate this to present day values would be unreliable.

The second entry relating to Manhall reads thus:-

CXXIV
(Manhall in Walden)

In Munehala a certain Englishman holds of Geoffrey iii Virgates, which were held by a freeman in the time of King Edward; and in the time of King William he became Tenant of Geoffrey of his own accord; and the tenants of Geoffrey say, that afterwards the King granted it to Geoffrey in exchange. But neither does the man himself, nor the Hundred bear testimony in favour of Geoffrey. In this estate there was then i team, now one half, always iii bordars; vii acres of meadow. It is worth x shillings.

This is an unusual entry as it relates to corrupt practices at the time of the Conquest. 'A certain Englishman' who is unfortunately unnamed held 3 virgates or approx 90 acres of land of Geoffrey de Mandeville. This land was held before the Conquest by a free man (i.e. a man holding land who was not tied to that land and was free to roam.) However during Williams reign he 'became a tenant of Geoffrey of his own accord' although neither the man himself or other residents of the hundred support this claim. A footnote in the translation (13) says 'A good illustration of the ordinary course of events. This wretched Saxon, by violence or through fear, was driven to become (of his own accord!) a vassal of the Norman Lord of the neighbouring estate. When this survey took place, he perhaps conceived a hope of ridding himself of his tyrant. At any rate he gladly confirms the hundreds testimony that Geoffrey had no title from the King and that the pretence of exchange was a pure invention.'

The third entry relates directly to Walden and transcribes thus:-

Geoffrey holds Waledana in lordship, which Ansgar held before 1066 as a manor, for 16 hides. Then and later 8 ploughs in lordship, now 10. Always 22 men's ploughs. Then and later 66 villiens [villagers], now 46; then and later 17 bordars [smallholders], now 40; then and later 16 serfs, now 20.

Woodland then and later 1000 pigs, now 800; meadow, 80 acres, always 1 mill.

Attached to the manor before 1066, were 13 freeman, now 14, who hold 6½ hides. Then and later 8½ ploughs, now 8.

Then and later 10 bordars [smallholders], now 14.

Woodland, then and later 50 pigs, now 30; meadow, 20 acres; then a third part of a mill. Then 6 Cobs, 11 Cattle, 200 Sheep, 110 pigs, 40 Goats, 4 Beehives; now 9 Cobs, 10 Cattle, 243 sheep, 100 pigs, 20 Goats, 30 Beehives.

Value then and later £36 Value; Value now £50.

Of this manor, Odo holds 1 hide and 1 virgate, and Reginald 1 hide less 12 acres, 2 ploughs. 13 bordars [smallholders].

Value 50s. in the same assessment.

From this we can see that Walden was held until the Conquest by Ansgar as a manor and was 18½ hides, or about 2,200 acres. In 1087 it was held by Geoffrey de Mandeville as a manor and farm . Within this area stood a mill, and a name mentioned in medieval documents 'Castelmela' coincides with a mill shown in a 1750 map as standing opposite the site of what is now Audley End Mansion. The name suggests it is the manorial mill – (the 'castle mill') and could provide the site of the mill mentioned here.

According to Barker (2) this entry shows that the manor was the personal estate of Geoffrey who farmed part of it as a home farm, with 10 plough teams of 8 oxen each, and 20 slaves (or serfs). Living on the estate were 46 villeins, farming about 30 acres each, and 40 bordars holding about 15 acres each. (Both these classes were unfree, and belonged to the estate.) There were also 14 freemen (or socmen) farming about 60 acres each, paying rent to Geoffrey. On the freemens' land, there were 14 families of bordars, woodland for 30 pigs etc. Two free Norman Knights, Odo and Reginald (or Renard) also lived on the manor with about 120 acres each, held on condition they carried out military service for Geoffrey. They had 13 families of bordars under them.

Museum Street and Castle Street. Note the sweep of Museum Street follows the outline of the castle bailey.

Chapter 2
12th and 13th Century Walden

We know from Domesday that the Manor was held by Geoffrey de Mandeville (or Goisfridi de Magnavilla). According to Morant (34) he was 'one of the valorous Chiefs who attended [William the Conqueror], and so distinguished himself in his service that he rewarded him with no less than 118 Lordships.' Geoffrey built a Castle at Pleshey in Essex and became the first Constable of the Tower of London, the power base of William the Conqueror. Both his son, William, and grandson were also Constables. The grandson, also called Geoffrey, was created the first Earl of Essex in about 1120 and married Rhoasie-de-Vere, the sister of Alberic the first Earl of Oxford.

Earl Geoffrey 1 also inherited the 118 Lordships, forty of which were in Essex. He decided to chose Walden for his residence. At this time the town would have been centred around the end of Abbey Lane and it would have taken Geoffrey little time to realize the importance of a high vantage point. His first move would almost certainly have been to build the castle and although no accurate date can be given for this work, it is probable that it was built between 1125 and 1141. The castle consisted of a bailey , the outline of which can still be seen in the present line of Museum Street and Castle Street, and a keep. A pamphlet produced by the Saffron Walden Museum (54) gives a detailed history of the castle in as much as it can be established. The earliest reference to the castle was in the Empress Maud's first charter of 1141 (of which more later). However during the Civil War of Stephen's reign Geoffrey changed sides at least once finally finishing up on the losing side. As a result Walden Castle was given first to Turgis d'Avranches and then to Reginald Fitz Count. In 1156 the castle was returned to the third Geoffrey de Mandeville but it was at least partially demolished in 1157 or 1158 because Exchequer records show a receipt of £9. 12s. 4d for 'throwing down of Earl Geoffrey's Castles in Essex'. For the subsequent history of the castle the reader is referred to the Museum pamphlet (54).

Much of Walden's history from the 12th century to the 16th century was inevitably closely linked with that of Walden Abbey from its original inception between 1136-1139 until its removal during the reformation period of 1536 - 1540. The site of the abbey was roughly in the area of the present Audley End House.

The historian of Walden is very lucky in this respect as two manuscripts survive which tell the story of the Abbey. The first is the B.M. Arundel MS no.29, The Book of the Foundation of the Monastery of Walden (6). This was apparently copied from an earlier manuscript by Lord William Howard in 1595, Howard having been born at Audley End in 1563. As its title suggests, it relates the history of the first 100 years of the monastery.

The second manuscript is B.M. Harlein MS 3697,(43) and called The Register of Walden (Cartulary of Walden Abbey). This acts as diary of major events occuring in the life of the Abbey. Both documents were transcribed and translated by C.H.Emson in the early 20th century and the information here is taken from that translation. However, both these sources should be treated carefully as they are known to contain chronological errors.

In 1136 (although possibly later) Earl Geoffrey 1 de Mandeville decided to build a monastery for monks of the Benedictine order. The exact date is not clear, as Geoffrey is described in the two manuscripts as Earl of Essex, a position he did not attain until 1140. According to the Arundel MS (6) he considered a monastery would be useful as he could summon his people together more frequently to celebrate festivities and to promote and transact business.

The site chosen was at the intersection of four roads in an angle made by two streams, and approximates to the present position of Audley End Mansion. It was described as 'flat and four sided fairly free from filth with healthy air for those dwelling there watered by streams which rise and flow there perpetually.' It is probable that the monastery occupied three separate sites prior to its creation as an abbey in 1190. (See Bassett p.95/96 for a discussion on the various locations (4)).

The consecration of the monastery took place in 1136 and was attended by three Bishops, Robert of London, Nigel of Ely and Walter of Norwich. In addition Geoffrey de Mandeville, his wife, Roheim, and the chief men and townsfolk attended.(53) The priory was dedicated to the honour of God, the Virgin Mary and St. James and was called the monastery of Walden.

To finance the monastery, Geoffrey endowed it with the revenue, tithes and property of the Church of Walden; 19 other churches; 120 acres of arable land in Walden; 100 acres of woodland; a meadow called Fulefen; a mill at Walden; another mill at Enfield; the hermitage of Hadley in Middlesex and common of pasture in the park there, as well as pannage for pigs. The grant was confirmed by King Stephen, who in addition granted the monks a fair at Walden on the vigil and feast of St. James.

The first Prior of the Abbey chosen by Geoffrey was William of Luffield. A man who lived in the style of a hermit, rather than a monk, William had previously been Prior at Bradwell, near Buckingham, and Geoffrey was impressed with his integrity and humility. However, because of Earl Geoffrey 1's downfall and the difficuty of finance, the first buildings erected were only small houses for a few monks. Initially, there was a chapel situated near what is now Audley End between the river and the road. Soon, however more substantial buildings were erected on higher ground to the east, probably just at the back of Audley End House where extensive foundations have been found. However Braybrooke (8) says that 'the walls of the new monastery were of stone, but neither high nor substantial'.

A chapel of wood was provided by the first prior, with a hall and cloister, and a large garden and fishpond. The priory did not at first assume the character of a religious house, the few monks devoting themselves to literary work, and the entertainment of travellers. They were however presently instructed in the observances of the Benedictine order by monks from Evesham Abbey. (25)

Meanwhile the most important thing to happen to the town during this period was to be the creation of the market in 1141. The market was to be a significant factor in the town's growth and was a result of Geoffrey de Mandevilles' machinations in the Civil War with the Empress Matilda (usually called Maud).

The civil war occured following the death of Henry I's eldest son at a young age. The succession was not at all clear. Both Henry's daughter, Maud, and Stephen, his nephew made claims to the throne – Stephen on the grounds that he was the nearest male relative. Both looked to the nobles for support and Geoffrey de Mandeville, who was already considerably powerful, owning lands in 11 counties and being Constable of the Tower of London, saw an opportunity to play one off against the other. A series of charters followed as first Stephen, and then Maud tried to win his support. The first granted to Geoffrey in 1140 gave him the Earldom of Essex. Maud retaliated by granting him a second charter in 1141 which confirmed him as the Earl of Essex and Constable of the Tower of London.In addition Geoffrey was granted a licence to fortify his castles at the Tower and Walden, and given large grants of land worth £100 p.a., a tremendous sum in those days. Most importantly, however for local history, Maud agreed to the removal of the market from Newport to Walden. This benefitted Geoffrey considerably as the grant of a market ensured his home town of an important role.

The charter said:-

'I [i.e. Maud] grant to him and his heirs custody of the Tower of London . . . and similarly grant to him and to his heirs as free domaine from me and my heirs in lordship, namely Newport, for as much as it was customary to give in return on the day in which my father King Henry was living and dying; and to remove the market from Newport to his castle of Walden with all the customs which belonged to that market and toll bridge . . . and that they shall be directed on the roads from Newport which are near the banks of the river according to custom, to Walden; and the market shall be on Walden on Sunday, and a fair shall be held at Walden, and shall begin on the evening of Pentecost, and last the eight days of Pentecost . . .'

It is probable that the market was held to the west of the castle bailey somewhere between the area of Church Street and Castle Street and would have stretched across the High Street to about Myddyleton Place. Bassett (4) feels the market probably remained there until its move to the south of Bury Hill in the early 13th century. The reason for the move was probably for several reasons. The original site was restricted by houses to three sides, and the castle to the fourth. Additionally the relocation of the

Market day in about 1854.

market helped provide the church with a site for its cemetery. It is probably from this period that the town came to be known as Chepynge (or Chipping) Walden, Chepynge meaning Market.

Meanwhile, in December 1141, Geoffrey received a third charter, this time from Stephen's wife. It was undoubtedly beneficial although its contents are unknown, the charter merely being confirmed in later charters.

Geoffrey de Mandeville received two further charters, one in 1141, again from Stephen, and another in 1142, again from Maud. However the process of playing the one off against the other was always a dangerous game and when Stephen eventually put Maud to flight at Oxford, Geoffrey's last attempt to change sides and support Maud was discovered. He was arrested at St. Albans while attending the King's Court and given the choice of being hung or surrendering his castles at Walden and Pleshy. Angered at this Geoffrey gathered a large army and attacked a number of places in the Fens. However whilst defending this area he was wounded by an arrow at Burwell and died in about 1144.

Having been excommunicated for his attacks on church property he was denied burial at Walden Abbey, but other members of the order of Knights Templar 'carried the body to London where they hung it in a lead coffin upon a tree in the old Temple Church garden, until the ban was removed, where it was buried in the porch of the west door of the New Temple Church.' His heirs were forced to give up his property including Walden Monastery.

For several years the monastery remained in the hands of the King, and the Prior, William, was often exhorted to ensure the money owed to the throne was raised. On Stephen's death, in 1154, the new King, Henry ll, returned Walden Priory to Geoffrey's son (also named Geoffrey) as well as other properties. However the second Geoffrey was not to remain in favour for long either, and the Chronicler reports:-

> 'Since for some time he [i.e. Geoffrey] did not cohabit with her in such natural union as was fitting the wife complained that what was due from a husband was by no means rendered to her, at which the King became greatly angered; after a divorce had been effected and two manors had been taken from him, namely Walden and Walthen a (new) husband, Anselm de Campdanene with these two manors.'

Henry later relented however, and restored the manor to Earl Geoffrey 2, although keeping Walden Monastery and its revenue for himself. Meanwhile, William was very concerned for the future of his abbey and wished for a period of stability.(5) He appealed to the King in vain, for the reinstatement of the priory to the de Mandeville family. But, after much labour and expense he managed to persuade the Pope, Alexander III to absolve Earl Geoffrey 2 in 1163. Not long after, on returning from a long journey from Dunstable, William was found dead in his sleep with his arms 'placed in the manner of a cross'. At length, 'since he was a very stout man, corpulent and with a protuberant belly' he was quickly buried in December 1164.

A new Prior was appointed, Reginald, a former monk at Reading Abbey. He had been Keeper of the Great Seal, but had been banished and decided to enter the Church. On his appointment he found the priory in a decayed condition, with only 11 monks but he was a keen and talented man, with a competent knowledge of secular affairs, and so the priory flourished. (25) He succeeded in obtaining a large source of revenue from a number of wealthy individuals. With this additional income he repaired and improved the abbey, widened the mill pond and made new ponds, and altered the road so that it no longer passed through the monastery. Finally an orchard was started. Reginald also probably made the road from the monastery to Walden which is now known as Audley End Road. Until then the main road had in fact run from Abbey Lane and through what is now Audley End Park to the monastery.

The village which grew up around the abbey became known as Brookwalden and by 1400 we know from the court rolls for the manor of Chepyng Walden that there was a shop and 51 houses situated on two streets. Brookwalden was to remain a fairly substantial settlement until the dissolution of the Abbey.

With the death of the Earl Geoffrey 2, in 1167, the priory became the scene of his burial. The Bishop of London, Gilbert de Foliot, and the Abbots of St. Edmundsbury and Titley together with Prior Reginald officiated, the Bishop celebrating the mass 'And plentiful entertainment, and alms given to all who attended'. (25)

DE MANDEVILLE & DE BOHUN FAMILY TREE

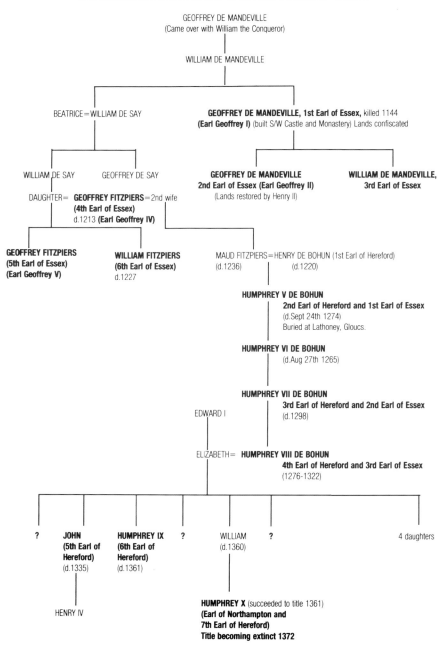

GEOFFREY DE MANDEVILLE
(Came over with William the Conqueror)

WILLIAM DE MANDEVILLE

BEATRICE = WILLIAM DE SAY

GEOFFREY DE MANDEVILLE, 1st Earl of Essex, killed 1144
(Earl Geoffrey I) (built S/W Castle and Monastery) Lands confiscated

WILLIAM DE SAY   GEOFFREY DE SAY

**GEOFFREY DE MANDEVILLE
2nd Earl of Essex (Earl Geoffrey II)**
(Lands restored by Henry II)

**WILLIAM DE MANDEVILLE,
3rd Earl of Essex**

DAUGHTER = **GEOFFREY FITZPIERS** = 2nd wife
(4th Earl of Essex)
d.1213 **(Earl Geoffrey IV)**

**GEOFFREY FITZPIERS
(5th Earl of Essex)
(Earl Geoffrey V)**

**WILLIAM FITZPIERS
(6th Earl of Essex)**
d.1227

MAUD FITZPIERS = HENRY DE BOHUN (1st Earl of Hereford)
(d.1236)   (d.1220)

**HUMPHREY V DE BOHUN
2nd Earl of Hereford and 1st Earl of Essex**
(d.Sept 24th 1274)
Buried at Lathoney, Gloucs.

HUMPHREY VI DE BOHUN
(d.Aug 27th 1265)

**HUMPHREY VII DE BOHUN
3rd Earl of Hereford and 2nd Earl of Essex**
(d.1298)

EDWARD I

ELIZABETH = **HUMPHREY VIII DE BOHUN
4th Earl of Hereford and 3rd Earl of Essex**
(1276-1322)

?   **JOHN
(5th Earl of
Hereford)**
(d.1335)

**HUMPHREY IX
(6th Earl of
Hereford)**
(d.1361)

?   WILLIAM
(d.1360)

?   4 daughters

HENRY IV

HUMPHREY X (succeeded to title 1361)
**(Earl of Northampton and
7th Earl of Hereford)
Title becoming extinct 1372**

His estates passed to his brother, William de Mandeville, 3rd Earl of Essex. Initially there was a short peaceful period, but Prior Reginald lost favour with William, when he went to Ireland without his lord's permission, to assist in attempting to establish a monastery at Labnon. On his return he had to appease the Earl with a cup of gold and silver, and 100 marks. William became a great benefactor to the priory bestowing upon it part of his lordship of the manor of Walden, with the park and mill, and after a pilgrimage to the Holy Land he presented the monks with rich vestments and hangings for the church. On his arrival in Walden he was received by the whole convent body in procession, and conducted to the High Altar, where he offered various precious relics obtained in the Holy Land. (25)

On William's death two people made a claim on his estate. The first claimant, his cousin Geoffrey de Say was favoured by both King Richard and the Prior, Reginald; the second claimant, Geoffrey Fitz-Piers whose claim was the weaker, was however both extremely wealthy and extremely powerful – indeed King John was to later regard him as a threat to the throne.

De Say sought to strengthen his claim by confirming large bequests made by William de Mandeville, and Prior Reginald sought to assist by sending a monk to King Richard in Normandy to obtain a Royal confirmation of these bequests. However it may well have been that Reginald's real reason was to persuade the King to make the priory into the raised position of an abbey. Whatever the reason, Reginald was successful, and in 1190 Walden priory became Walden Abbey, a position it was to retain until its dissolution in 1537. Prior Reginald was made Abbot by the Bishop of London in a dignified ceremony in St Pauls Cathedral. By this time there were 26 monks. (25)

However de Say's request of King Richard had its price, a sum of 7000 marks to recognize his position. The King required such a sum urgently because of his expenses in connection with the Crusades. Although de Say tried, he was quite unable to find such a sum and so he had to surrender the property. Geoffrey Fitz-Piers offered to pay the sum in total and so succeeded to the estates as the 4th Earl of Essex.

In helping to convert the Priory into an Abbey, Reginald had unwittingly further antagonised Fitz-Piers, since the appointment of the Abbott was in the hands of the King, unlike that of a mere Prior. This, allied to Reginald's open support for Geoffrey de Say, meant Fitz-Piers was to treat Reginald very harshly. Arguments ensued over the right to cultivate the lands bequested to the abbey by William, and Fitz-Piers kept the lands himself, and had them cultivated by his own men. Reginald appealed to the Bishop of London who sent the Dean to investigate. Finding Fitz-Piers men on the fields he 'forbade their proceeding with the audacious deed; but he was assailed with insults and held in contempt; he at the same time excommunicated all his insultors and cursed them all in the name of the Lord; and withal he gave instructions that the Parish Church of Walden should be deprived of divine service'.

The Bishop however, fortunately for the innocent congregation, felt excommunication too severe and he reinstated the right to hold Communion. The problem of the land was still not solved however. Abbot Reginald therefore appealed to the Bishop of Ely, and he reinstated the disputed lands to the Abbey.

Fitz-Piers' anger with the Abbot merely increased. He deliberately and systematically started to harass and torment the abbey and its inhabitants. An appeal to the Pope by Reginald and consequent letters of censure were ignored by Fitz-Piers. He even succeded, by threat and bribery, in preventing an inquiry by the Archbishop of Canterbury from reaching a conclusion for over seven years. Eventually, however, one of the monks from the abbey, having been sent overseas to the King was succesful in obtaining from him a letter ordering the Archbishop to reinstate the lands.

This was more than Fitz-Piers could take. The following graphic description of his drastic actions, taken from Rowntree (45), shows his anger:-

'Sir Geoffrey was transported with rage . . . and the myrmidons of satan who were at the head of affairs in Walden . . . raged with unheard of cruelty, . . . forbade us the use of all the lands of their Lord, . . . they kept watch on our doors, and the ways leading to the public market, by placing ambushes on all sides, lest any sustenance should be brought in for the use of the brothers, or even wood for the purpose of cooking the vegetables, in order that by these means . . . famine might do to death the starving brothers.'

Fitz-Piers also herded many of the abbeys animals into the castle and demanded a ransom for their return. The monks turned to their monarch for his support, but Fitz-Piers' influence at Court was sufficiently great for this to fail. Indeed when John came to the throne, he confirmed Fitz-Piers as the 4th Earl of Essex, and gave him certain rights over the abbey which had previously been the sole prerogative of the monarch. This included the right to appoint the Abbot. Later when John visited the abbey, he conferred on the monks the right to hold an annual fair, which continued to be held long after the abbey itself had disappeared.

The Abbey did not always have a good relationship itself, with the town. There was often a feeling that the monks did little for the community whilst living there at its expense, the abbey having been endowed with, amongst others, the income from Walden Church. In fairness in 1174 they returned one-third of it and permitted the Church to retain monies collected at their Sunday services. Even that though was reclaimed in 1365 when extensive repairs had to be undertaken at the Abbey. (9)

Reginald died in 1203 and was succeded by Roger. A list of all the Abbots can be found on pp. 68 - 70 of Braybrooke (8).

13th Century Walden

With the development of the two sites, Brookwalden (now Audley End) and the town of Walden situated around the castle, the town's roots became more firmly established. So by the start of the 13th Century with the de Mandevilles having established Walden on the national map the town began to play an important role to its region.

Earl Geoffrey 4 died in 1213 and was succeeded by his son Earl Geoffrey 5 who was killed in a tournament near London in c. 1220. The title passed to his brother William, the 6th Earl of Essex who died in 1227.

The 6th Earl left no successor and the estates passed to his sister Matilda, (or Maud), who was the widow of Henry de Bohun the Earl of Hereford. On Matilda's death in 1236 the land passed to her son Humphrey V de Bohun and remained with the de Bohuns until 1373. Two further Humphreys' succeeded Humphrey V, Humphrey VII in 1275, and Humphrey VIII in 1298. (See the chart on p.18 to show the confusing relationships!)

The most important action of the de Bohun family for Walden was the granting of the town's first charter. Recent controversy concerning its date has finally been laid to rest by a pamphlet produced by Dr. Jennifer Ward (55). Although the hand writing style of the charter suggested the charter was of mid 13th century origin, the seal and witness list prove conclusively that the charter was dated c. 1300. This authorative work also gives further detail about the witnesses to the charter and should be consulted by those wishing to find more about the town's first charter.

The charter, which is in Latin, reads in translation:-

'Know all men, present and future, that we Humphrey de Bohun earl of Hereford and Essex, Constable of England, have given, granted, and by this our present charter confirmed for ever to all and singular our burgesses of the burgh of Walden, in the County of Essex, that when any of the said burgesses shall die, that his heir or heirs may have and hold his burgage freely and quietly without making any relief and heriot of his burgage to us and our heirs or assigns for ever, just as they and their predecessors have had and were accustomed to hold of us and our predecessors. We have also granted to the same burgesses and their heirs and their assigns, all liberties and free customs which they and their predecessors have had and at any time were wont to have of us and our predecessors. In witness whereof we have put our seal to this our present charter. These being Witnesses, Lord Robert de la Rokele, William Poucyn, John de Thonderle, William le Enueyse, John de Westlee, Henry, son of Michael, John son of Robert de Wymbiss, John Michel of the same and others.'

The significance of the charter to the town is that it represents the first break from the feudal system. Burgesses' of Walden no longer had to pay relief or heriot. Relief was the payment made by a freeman on taking up a holding. Heriot was normally the payment by a villien's heir of his best

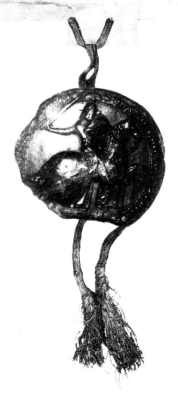

The town's earliest existing charter given by Humphrey de Bohun in the 13th century.

beast to the Lord. Thus this represented an important concession to the townsfolk.

The names of the witnesses are interesting, as they reflect local names which still exist – Thonderle is now Thunderley Hall; Westlee – now Westley Farm; Wymbiss – now the village of Wimbish, and Poucyn – now Pounce Hall. From this list it seems that Sewards End originated in the 13th century as a settlement for workers from the two smaller manors of Pounces and Mattens. The Cartulary of Walden Abbey (43) says that Abold Poucyn inherited these manors from his grandfather, Siward, in 1124, from which the name of Sewards End developed. Pounce Hall still survives, but Mattens was swallowed up and now forms part of the present village. The old Manor House was near Redgates Lane.

Mrs. Monteith (33) gives examples of several other large houses or sub-manors which existed during the 13th century. Bowlesgrove, a large house to the north of Pounces, was mentioned in an Inquisition Post Mortem of 1286. Westley is mentioned as existing in the 13th century, and the two farms on Ashdon Road, Butlers, which originated in the 12th century, and St. Aylotts, are mentioned in the Calender of Charter Rolls dated 1248.

In religious terms the most significant happening of the 13th century was the establishment of a church adjacent to Bury Hill (the present location of the Parish Church.) It is believed that parts of this building have been incorporated in the present church when it was rebuilt in the 15th century. In a booklet written by the Rev. G. Montagu Benton in 1889, based on transcriptions from a manuscript notebook, he suggests that the chancel arcade, and the western arches of the north and south chapels are part of the building of 1300. (5) Bassett (4) points out that there is no conclusive evidence that there was a church on this site until the 13th century. Certainly the earliest datable work of the present church is of mid 13th century. However Braybrooke (8) says that evidence from digging of graves in the early 19th century suggests the present site may have been the home of a smaller earlier church. According to the 1882 Saffron Walden Almanac it is believed the original church was a small one and was rebuilt between the years 1237 and 1268. No parts of the original church were left except the lower part of the tower. It is likely to have been of richly Norman character.The earliest written record refers to the consecration of the church on the feast of St. Mark in 1258, but this of course does not refer to the present building which is of 15th and 16th century origin.

The 13th century also saw the first planned development of the town. This took two forms, the so-called magnum fossatum (perhaps better known although not accurately, as the Battle Ditches) and the development of the rectilinear street plan. Extensive and detailed work on both of these were carried out by Doctor Stephen Bassett and others between 1972 and 1980 and have been excellently documented. For a much more detailed examination of this aspect of Walden's history the reader should consult Bassett's work (4): what follows is only a resume.

The regular layout of Walden's streets suggests deliberate planning. This seems to have occurred in two phases, the first in the earlier 12th century, the latter approximately 1227 to about 1240. The first phase probably occurred at the time that the castle was being erected. It was probably then, that the line of High Street, Church Street and Castle Street were established, as well as the shape of Museum Street, (following the outline of the inner bailey). The second phase saw the creation of what Bassett calls the magnum fossatum (or Great Ditch) which involved the destruction of the southern and eastern arms of the earlier outworks. It appears that in fact the magnum fossatum did not surround the town since the marshy area of Swan Meadows to the north west of the town, and the escarpment surrounding the northern edge of the castle made a northerly extension unnecessary. The magnum fossatum served to clearly delineate the boundaries of the town and it becomes clear that within this area, particularly to the south of Church Street, a clearly defined street layout was made. Bassett, who made this discovery, bases this on the fact that the land to either side of High Street south of the junction with Church Street divides up regularly into square parcels of land measuring 12 perches (or 60m) square. However it appears that this planned expansion was too ambitious and many of the planned 'squares' were not immediatley developed. This was probably for three reasons. First, until, the c. 1300 charter the payment of relief and heriot did not encourage people to the town. Secondly, entry fines (money paid to the Lord for the benefit of his protection) were very high, and thirdly, potential traffic was probably lost to the abbey on the main London to Cambridge road.

The use of Walden as the main home of the de Bohun family meant that the town would have been the centre of events such as tournaments. The chronicler Matthew de Paris, states that a notable tournament was held in Walden, possibly on the Common in 1252. During the tournament, 'Roger de Leeburn encountered Ernauld de Mounteney, a valiant knight, and unhappily ran his lance into his throat under the helmet, it wanting a collar, whereupon Mounteney fell from his horse and died.' (8) It was suggested at the time that Roger in fact deliberately killed Ernauld because of a broken leg he had received in a previous tournament.

A Tuesday market was granted to the abbey in 1295 as an additional source of income, and it was probably this market, which gave the town its medieval name of Chepyng (or Chipping) Walden, Chepyng meaning a market. Certainly the town was called this by 1328. (7)

Chapter 3
14th Century Walden

In 1400 a detailed land and rent survey of Walden was made (10). An analysis of this was made in 1966 (16). The survey gives a detailed account of farming life in Walden in the middle ages. The abbey not only held the land immediately surrounding the abbey, but also owned over 1000 acres within the parish. The land was subject to a three-course rotation of seasons, Seisona Warecte or fallow, Seisona Frumenti (probably winter sown grain) and Seisona Quadragesimae (lent or spring sown crops). This rotation would have applied to all the 7000 or so acres of land being farmed in Walden, and areas of varying proportions, known as 'quarentas', lying within the bounds of larger fields, would in turn be subject to this rotation.

Individual land-holdings would have been small, some not more than two acres, and peasant holdings would have been considerably smaller. However, the parcels of land belonging to the abbey close to the town had, by 1400, been almost entirely leased to local men, and Walden was becoming an established farming community with produce to be sold – hence the importance of the market.

The soil, as now, was productive, and considered too good to be used only for grazing. The number of sheep was strictly controlled to about 3 per acre. It appears that the abbey tenants were prevented from keeping sheep themselves, so leaving that much more grazing land available for the abbey's use; however other landowners may have kept flocks of 200 or more. (32)

During the 14th century, Walden continued to expand. In addition to the market and a prosperous abbey, the chief courts for all the extensive lands owned by the de Bohuns was in Walden and this inevitably encouraged trade. The modern-day town centre was begining to evolve at this period – title deeds of that time included references to Gold Street, Abbey Lane, Castle Street and Hoggs Green (now Walden Place).(21)

It was during this time that many wool towns in Suffolk began to flourish but there appears to be little documentary evidence to suggest that Walden gained much trade from this. (33) The 14th Century Court Rolls for the Manor of Chepyng Walden make references to two dye rooms and there was a large number of sheep for a town of its size. Mrs. Monteith (33) suggests that the wool may well have been taken to nearby Suffolk towns.

A further article by Mrs. Monteith in the Essex Journal (15) gives a marvellous account of the social and legal organisation and the daily life of the town in the 14th century. It appears from the Court Rolls of that period that there was a significant development in the role of the market. Prior to 1391 many of the butchers and fishmongers trading in the market came from outside the town. By 1400 this number was considerably

The Woolstaplers' Hall which stood near the Market Square.

reduced and Mrs. Monteith feels that this suggests that the burgesses had won from the Lord of the Manor the right to exclude strangers from the market, thus ensuring that local people had the best opportunity for trading. The Court Rolls list an interesting selection of occupations being practised at the time – brewing, malting, shoemakers, carpenters, tanners, tinkers and woolmongers all had shops in the town.

It was during the 14th century, that many of the town's streets began to acquire their names. Many were named after the trades being practised in them. Some have since been lost although others continue to this day. Thus there is Le Clothrowe first recorded in 1336, ffisheresrow, and le Cornmarket in 1372, Chapmanrow in 1378 and Pultrehill in 1453. (42)

Walden was even playing a part by this time on the national scene. During Edward III's great invasion of France, Essex was called upon to provide 200 archers for the campaign which was to culminate, in 1346, at the Battle of Crecy. The towns of Essex had to also find a number of foot soldiers, and Walden was expected to provide six of these.

During the 14th century the manor remained in the hands of the De Bohuns. In 1347 the 4th Earl of Hereford (Humphrey VIII de Bohun) obtained a licence from Edward III to embattle his Manor House at Walden. Probably the outer walls of the castle would have been repaired. However the project seems never to have been carried out, probably owing to the advent of the Black Death, which from the records of Walden Abbey, we know to have devastated the district.

The line of De Bohuns came to an end with Humphrey X de Bohun, 7th Earl, and his titles and vast estates were divided between his daughters; Elianor married to Thomas of Woodstock, Duke of Gloucester, 6th son of Edward III, and from whom the Staffords, Dukes of Buckingham descended; and Mary who married Henry Bolingbroke, Earl of Derby, who was later Henry IV. By this marriage the Walden estates became vested in the Royal House of Lancaster. They were owned successively by Henry IV, Henry V, his widow Katherine of France, and Henry VI, and upon his deposition, the manor of Walden was vested in the Crown, where it lay until 1538 when Henry VIII granted it to Sir Thomas Audley the Lord Chancellor.

The ill feeling which had long existed between the residents of the town and the monks of Walden Abbey flared up again in the 14th century. By 1365 extensive repairs to the abbey were necessary. The Abbot, John, appealed to the Bishop of London, who gave permission to override the 1174 agreement that one third of the income from Walden Church could be kept by the Parish. The resultant loss of income meant that Walden could only have a lay priest. The Vicar, Peter Pawe, appealed, initially unsuccessfully to the Pope. However when a new Pope, Gregory XIII was appointed, a second appeal was successful. A counter appeal was launched by the Abbott, but documents in the Town Council archives show that this appeal failed.

It was during the 14th century that the first guilds were formed. As we shall see the guilds were to have an important effect on the history of the town, eventually being the bodies to which self governing powers were attached. The fraternity or gild of All Saints was founded by John Auncell and John Adams at some time in the 14th century; and then, in 1379, the gild or fraternity of Corpus Christi was founded by Simon, Adam and John Chaumpeneye.

Famous Persons

The 14th century produced the first notable native of the town, Roger Walden. He is said to have been of humble birth, being the son of a butcher of Walden, from where he took his name. However the Dictionary of National Biography (19) suggests that this 'statement comes from sources not free from prejudice, and cannot perhaps be entirely trusted'. Whether or not he was born in the town will probably never be known. In 1391, he was made Rector of Fordham, by the Patron, Richard II. In February 1392 he became Rector at St. Andrews, Holborn, and then in quick succesion became Treasurer of Calais, Secretary to the King and then on 30th Sept, 1395, Lord Treasurer of England. At the same time he continued his clerical career, obtaining the prebend of Gillingham, in the Church of Sarum, a stall in Exeter Cathedral, and in 1396/7 the Bishop of London gave him the Prebend of Willesden. Then in 1397/8, at the King's request he was appointed Archbishop of Canterbury, although Thomas Arundell had been elected by the Chapter of the Cathedral. Arundell had been banished from the realm by the then King, Richard II, but on the accession of Henry IV in 1399 he returned to resume his Archbishopric. Roger Walden lived in poverty for five years , but then, in 1404 through the kindness of Arundell he was appointed as Bishop of London. He died in January 1405/6 and was interred in the Priory Church of St. Bartholomew, Smithfield, where his monument can still be seen. (22)

The practice of using the name of the native town was also adopted by Thomas Netter. Born in Walden in about 1367, his parents were John and Maud Netter, but Thomas soon became known as Thomas Waldensis. He is said to have grown up in London and obtained his degree at Oxford. Returning to London he became a Carmelite monk and went on to become a favourite of Henry IV. He was appointed the principal champion of the Church against the heretics. In 1409 under the King's instruction he went to the Grand Council at Pisa and on returning was made a member of the Privy Council of Henry IV's successor, Henry V as well as his Confessor. In 1419 he was involved in peace negotiations between the King of Poland and the General of the Teutonic Order. In 1422 Henry V died in the arms of Waldensis, and he was then appointed Confessor to Henry VI, uniquely enjoying the confidences of three successive monarchs. Waldensis died in Rouen in 1430. He showed excellent talents in the classic languages, and wrote 'Doctrinale Antignum fidei Ecclesiae Catholicae'.(22)

Chapter 4
15th Century Walden

In 1400 the Guild of our Lady of Pity was created in Walden. As Rowntree (45) points out it is a charter in which Walden can take special satisfaction because the benefactors sought no personal advantage from it, and because its charitable objects have continued until the present day. The Guild was constituted by letters patent from Henry VI following a bequest of £40 from John and Eleanor Butler. The purpose of the Guild was to provide an almshouse 'for the succour and sustenance of XIII poor men such as be lame, crooked, blind and bedridden, and most at need.' The secondary aim of the Guild was religious and it provided for a house to be built in the churchyard as a home for a priest who was to act as chaplain to the almshouse. The money remaining after the building was to be given towards constructing another house in Clavering. Many local in-habitants, perhaps inspired by this generosity, gave other gifts in the form of land and money and these included the famous Mazer bowl, which was donated by the Butlers' daughter and was, years later, used by Samuel Pepys.

The priest had to give free house room to two other priests who were to assist in saying Mass. In return for this they received the sum of two shillings per year. To supplement this a school was started by the priests.

The 1400 Almshouse in Park Lane.

However in 1423 the Abbot of Walden Monastery, John de Hatfield, summoned the two priests, John Bernard and William Brynge, before him. They were accused of teaching young boys without the authority of the Abbot. At that time the Abbot had the sole right of nominating schoolmasters and, not unnaturally, this was jealously guarded. The two priests relented and were granted a licence to teach one child of every inhabitant the Greek alphabet. With such restrictions the post of assistant became more and more difficult to fill and by the end of the 15th century it had ceased to exist. This fact was to have an important part to play in the 16th century history of the town.

By 1402 the Manor of Walden was in Royal hands. Humphrey VIII de Bohun had been a notable warrior, having fought at Bannockburn and being captured there. He had later been exchanged for the Queen of Robert the Bruce. Later, however, he turned against his King and was killed at the Battle of Boroughbridge, 1322, when fighting the King. Edward III had subsequently confiscated his lands for this act of treachery, and when he made his son, John of Gaunt, the Duke of Lancaster, he endowed him with lands in Essex, Hertford and Northampton, including the Manor of Walden.

John's son succeeded to the Throne as Henry IV in 1399 and to celebrate his elevation to the monarchy he issued a charter, in 1402, to all the towns in his Duchy. In addition he gave a special power to Walden to appoint a Clerk of the Market, and the right to retain all the fees levied in the Court of Pie Powder (the special market Court). In addition the charter gave the residents of Walden freedom from a number of tolls.

The charter was confirmed by Henry V in 1422. Both of these charters are in the Town Council archives.

Little is known of the town in the 15th century although Braybrooke (8) suggests that with the creation of the Guild in 1400 and the expenses involved in rebuilding and ornamenting the church, the town must have been very wealthy, for there is no evidence of the need to borrow money for the financing of this work.

We do know that wool was playing an increasingly important part in the economy of the town at this time. By July 1419 over 2,700 sheep were held according to returns from local landowners and Walden Abbey, and the industry supported the magnificent Woolstaplers' Hall in the Market Square.

However one valuable source of information for the 15th century has survived, the Churchwarden's Accounts, giving receipts and payments for the period from 1439 to 1485. These are available at the Essex County Record Office, having been originally part of the archive collection of Audley End. This account book is mostly in Latin although the early part is in Norman French. Most of the entries relate to the purchase of Ecclesiastical things, such as candles, bellropes, communion clothes etc. In addition there are a large number of references to building work, in particular of the south aisle of the church. The records give details of money paid in 1465 for the digging of the foundations of the buttresses, and other building work.

The Churchwarden's Accounts also record a Royal visit of 1452, when Margaret of Anjou visited Walden. She visited the abbey and the church, and the accounts record the fact that the church ringers were fined 2 shillings for failing to welcome the Queen with a merry peal. It is believed that she was on her way to Norwich at that time.

The accounts also record the five different side altars and chapel that existed in the church in the 15th century. These were dedicated to St.Nicholas; St. Mary; the Holy Cross; and the Holy Trinity. In addition there was also the rood altar. Numerous pictures and images of saints existed, including those of St. John, St. Peter, St. Catherine, St. Mary Magdalene, and St. George, this according to the records being painted on the clock face. Payments were made for a 'Miracle Play' to be performed and the accounts also show that money was collected for Church Ales. (29) Other aspects of the accounts are very interesting for giving an indication of monetary values. To whitewash the church porch and paint an image thereon cost 4d. The Vicar was paid 2 shillings for his easter offering and the bell ringers received 4d for a peal of bells.

Some of the things paid for were very interesting:- 'for dressing up of ye Churche on Crystmas Heve' and a payment for straw 'browte on Good Friday' so that people could prostrate themselves upon it during the service. (29)

Other records of the 15th Century include the early rolls of the Court Leet. This was a court held by the Lord of the Manor of Cheping Walden. The Court had power to hear minor case. There is a record of a person being fined for 'videlicet Le Tenys' (i.e. playing tennis). In 1441 Robert Bate was fined for putting improper materials into a torch to be used on the Festival of Purification or Candlemas Day – 'Qd. Robtus Bate fec unam torchiam ad usum ecclie ad festum Pur le Marie Virgin ult. ptit in qua posuit rosyn et cepu nimis multu in decepcoem ppli.' And in 1452 Roger, the Parish Chaplain, was fined twice for playing at handball, and for tearing somebody's clothes. (29)

Henry VIII's charter of 1514 granting the town the market, a malt mill and a windmill.

Chapter 5
16th Century Walden

Because of the restrictions placed by the Abbey on teaching, the posts of assistant priests to the Guild of Our Lady of Pity had proved impossible to fill. This fact was to prove important in Walden's history.

When Henry VII came to the throne in 1485 being of a frugal nature, he determined to place the finances of his household on a sound footing. He particularly wished to ensure a regular income. On reviewing all previous charters granted by his predecessors he realised that these could be important. It was far from automatic for monarchs to renew their predecessors' charters, and Henry, given his relatively parlous financial state, felt that this was an excellent chance to renew a regular source of income. He therefore sent out commissioners to investigate whether tolls and customs which had only been annulled by charter could be renewed.

A memorandum in the Town Council archives show that in 1494, Commissioners visited Walden, and found that 'of old time there was wont to be paid certain tolls and customs'. Examples of these are:-

'every brewer should pay to the King for every quarter of Malt that he did brew to sell, a farthing . . . every chapman that did stand market in his own freehold or otherwise should for opening of every shop window on the Market day pay to the King a farthing. . . .'

However the effect of the tolls was crippling on the town. According to the memorandum there was:-

'great annoyance to all the inhabitants of this town and like to have brought it to great decay and ruin, for chapmen forsook the market and maltmen forsook the town and went to other towns, because they were so troubled with paying such tolls and customs.'

This had a devastating effect on the town, and, in 1513, to try and counteract these effects six of the town's residents decided to petition the new King, Henry VIII. The six concerned were all notable residents, John Leeche, the Vicar; Dame Jane Bradbury, James Bodle, Nicholas Rutland, William Bird, and Thomas Strachey. First they attempted to buy the King out, by offering 'great sums of money' to retain the customs and tolls but they were advised to attempt another method, as the King still was not prepared to be seen giving way to a bribe. So it was suggested by lawyers, that were a religious Guild to be formed it could be then used to attach certain local government type powers to it at a later date. Whilst a Guild did already exist in Walden at that time, (the Guild of Our Lady of Pity), it was felt better to create a new Guild. Rutland, Bird and Strachey had already agreed in 1510 to act as trustees to the will of Katherine Semar and so it was suggested that the new guild be in her name.

Henry VIII agreed to this, and on March 24th 1514 he granted Walden the charter which created the Guild of the Holy Trinity. The Guild was permitted to hold land to the value of twenty marks and to provide for a chaplain who was to say mass for the trustees, Katherine Semar, and the King and Queen. The reason that the King included himself on the charter was because he saw the possibility that at a later date, the Guild could provide a useful source of revenue. The Guild was also authorised to hold a four day fair on the feast of St. Ursula.

To meet the original requirements of the petitioners, another charter followed just two months later, on May 12th 1514. This charter, arguably the town's most important, gave the Guild local government type powers. It allowed the Guild to run the market, the Court of Pie Powder (a special market court), the windmill, and a malt mill. (The latter two were important since the Guild had a monopoly right on their use and could therefore charge any sum they chose.) However Henry, a notoriously spendthrift character, was not going to miss this opportunity for additional income, and so a rent of ten pounds – a considerable sum in those days – was levied. Henry obviously thought it better to have a regular annual income than the lump sum offered in 1513.

To meet the cost of obtaining the charter John Leech and Katherine Semar each contributed £20, while various tradesmen paid sums equal to four years' dues for opening their shops on market days, in return for which they would pay no further dues.

As a result of this, in 1514, Katherine Semar revised her will to leave her property to the Guild, and in 1517, John Leech, the vicar, gave the Guild additional lands which he owned in Newport and Widdington to provide the Guild with a second Priest to say Mass for the benefactors of the Guild, including himself and his sister, Jane Bradbury.

Shortly after this Leech died. But before his death, his sister had persuaded him that the second priest should be freed from some of his duties so that he could act as master of a school which she proposed to endow. She did this by obtaining from Henry a charter, dated August 24 1522, giving her power to give to the Guild, at her own cost, lands to the value of ten pounds.

It was necessary also to receive the consent of the Abbot, John de Thaxted, since the Church still retained its monopoly on teaching, and a tripartite agreement was signed between Jane Bradbury, the Abbot, and the Guild on May 18 1525. The agreement provided that Jane would give an additional £4 a year to engage a priest who would also be a 'profound Grammarian'. In addition, she agreed to substitute a single annual charge of £12 from her lands in Willingale, (near Ongar) in return for the many and diverse lands which John Leech had given in Newport and Widdington – thus saving considerable time in collecting rents.

This act on Jane Bradburys' part represented the first step towards a formal education service in Walden and was a monumental step for the town. The first Master to be appointed, in 1525, was Sir William Dawson who had already acted in this capacity for Jane Bradbury and it was agreed that future Masters would be chosen by the Treasurer and

Chamberlain after being interviewed by the Abbott and Vicar. Children born in Walden, Newport, Widdington and Little Chesterford were eligible for free places in the School. The Master was to have 'his dwelling in a Mansion called the Trinity College . . . against the north door of the Church'. It was decided that the curriculum was to be based on the schools of Winchester and Eton and details of the curriculum eventually adopted can be found in Rowntree(45) and the VCH(53). Boarders were accepted, but they had to lodge in private houses in the town. (A full and complete history of the school can be found in the VCH vol. 2 pp 521-525.)

In 1542 Henry VIII granted the town the right to hold an additional four day fair in Mid Lent in a further charter.

But in 1547, by an act of Edward VI, all chantries and their lands and endowments were made available for the Kings disposal. Chantries were bodies whose single aim was to pray for the soul of the departed benefactor. Parliament did not stand in the way of the act, since any additional income for the King would prevent the necessity for further taxation. Both Walden's Guilds were chantries, and as a consequence their possessions fell to the King.

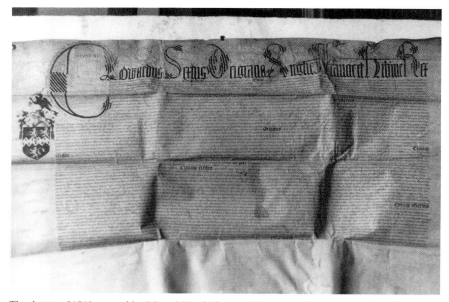

The charter of 1549 granted by Edward VI which created the town's first commonalty or Council.

Considerable negotiations followed between the town and the Monarch since the loss of income from the chantries meant the inmates had no income on which to survive. The exact details of whom was involved in the negotiations are not clear as two conflicting accounts exist (45). The first account says that the King sold the property to John Smyth, a wealthy Walden man, for £600. Smyth was supposed to have lived in a house in the north-east corner of the Market Square, and was High Sheriff of Essex and Hertfordshire. The second account says that the properties were sold to Smyth's son, Sir Thomas, a man who was later to become Secretary of State to Edward VI and Queen Elizabeth. This account alleges that he brought the Guild for £531.14.11. But whichever account was correct, it was a second son, also John Smyth who took the lead in the negotiations with Edward VI, and succeeded in the restoration of the towns incorporation. This was achieved with the grant of a new charter on February 1 1549 which created 'a commonalty of 24 assistants of the most honest and discreet men', effectivly the first 'Council' of the town. The charter also named 'John Smyth the Younger of Walden . . . the first and present Treasurer, and William Strachey, the Younger, and Thomas Williamson of the same town, the first and present Chamberlains'. The charter also granted to the town, the market, two mills, the right to hold a Mid-Lent Fair, the Court of Pie Powder and the right to hold a court once in three weeks for the recovery of small debts.

In addition the charter gave the new corporation power to administer and maintain the almshouse and the grammar school, provided they included the name of Edward VI in their titles.

The corporation celebrated the new charter by purchasing two new silver maces, which have been retained by the Council to this day. The purchase is recorded in the following entry from the Guild of Holy Trinity Accounts for 1549 (28):-

'For 2 new maces, weying 18 ownces on quarter, and half at 8s. the ownce, 7l.7s'.

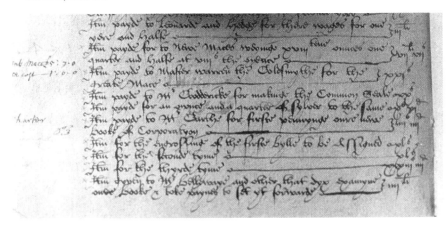

Two more charters were to follow in quick succession, the first from Mary, on 16th November 1553, being a grant by letters patent confirming Edwards charter; and the second from Elizabeth also being a confirmatory charter on May 6th 1558.

It is interesting to look at the further details of the almshouses which King Edward gave power to create and which the King insisted should bear his name. Letters Patent for the almshouse were granted on February 18th 1550. The almshouse was to be for 13 people and their diet was laid down for them:-

'for their sustention and living every week one bushell of wheat to make bread, 2 bushells of malt to make drink and in money for cates (sic) two shillings and twopence; in Lent to buy fish six shillings and eightpence; and for winter 6 lbs of candles every fortnight, one peck of oatmeal every month and one peck of salt; and in Lent six bushell of peas; and in Summer six gallons of butter; and every year 700 faggotts of wood.'

Arrangements were made for a matron or 'Dame'. The letters patent said that one of the thirteen:-

'. . . should be a discreet and sober woman who shall dress their meat, make their bread, brew their drink, and keep those that are sick, and wash and govern them as she shall be able and shall be called 'Dame of the House'.'

Even their day was rigorously laid down for them. Rising at either six or seven there were first of all prayers in the chapel. This was followed by breakfast and from that to church for Divine Service, 'there sitting in the north side of the church in the almshouse stalls and there to remain till all the service be done.' This was followed by dinner, with grace and more prayers, and then they were allowed to go about their work until the time of Common Prayer when it was back to the church. Finally, it was back home for more prayers, supper and last of all more prayers in the Oratory. (56)

The King Edward VI almshouses still survive to this day, providing accomodation for those in need.

Closure of Walden Abbey

Perhaps the major event in Walden in the 16th century was the closure of the Abbey. Henry VIII had had a long running battle with the Catholic Church following its refusal to grant him a divorce from Katherine of Aragon. His ultimate solution was to break the country away from the Roman Church and its inevitable consequence was the dissolution of the country's monasteries.

The suppression of Walden Abbey appears to have been carried out without any serious opposition. William More, the Abbot surrendered the abbey to the King on March 22 1537, became the Vicar of Walden, and eventually died in 1540. The abbey was valued at £372 18s. 1d. according to Dugdale. Henry decided to grant the estates of the abbey along with the £10 rent due from Walden Corporation to his Chancellor, Thomas Audley, for his 'good and faythefulle servyce'. This was done, by charter, on 12th January 1540. But complications about the charter were ultimately to lead to the town purchasing its market. This apparently unrelated incident was caused because the charter by which Henry granted the estates to Thomas Audley also made three other grants. These were:-

i) the 1514 grant of the market, mills etc. to the treasurer and chamberlains of the town for a rent of £10;

ii) a lease made in 1524 for 21 years of the Manor of Walden to one James Williamson, in return for a rent of £21;

iii) a grant in 1529 of 'our park of Walden in the hamlet of Little Walden' and all the deer in the park, for a rent of £6.6.8 and certain shooting rights for a rent of £1.

This complicated agreement meant that by 1584, there was confusion as to whom the corporation should pay the rent of £10 for the market. On the one hand there was the 1540 grant to Thomas Audley of the rent from the market, and on the other side, there was the act of Edward VI of 1547 confiscating the properties of all chantries, which included the Guild of Holy Trinity, to whom the market had been granted.

To try and resolve this problem an appeal was made to Queen Elizabeth. Her view was expressed in a document which reported that she had inspected a Court of Westminster record of the 23rd year of her reign. She noted that Walden had paid the rent of £10 in full to the Crown.

The corporation's position was complicated. Their attorney, William Hunt, relayed the chronological sequence:-

i) Henry VIII had granted the rights to receive the market rents to Thomas Audley on March 31 1539/40.

ii) In 1545, Audley had died and his widow, Elizabeth, retained the right to receive the £10. After her death the right was to pass to her daughter, Margaret.

iii) In 1547, Edward, by Act of Parliament abolished all chantries (including the Guild of Holy Trinity) and the properties reverted to the Crown.

iv) In 1549, a new Corporation was established in Walden, (the old Corporation disappearing with the abolition of the Guild in 1547).

v) In 1566, Margaret, (Audley's daughter) died having married Thomas Howard, Duke of Norfolk. She left all her property to her husband – including the right to receive the £10 rent.

vi) In 1571, Howard was executed for treason, having conspired with Mary Queen of Scots. His property was confiscated to the Crown.

vii) in 1583, the property was restored to Thomas Howard, Junior, as Lord Audley.

1618 charter granting rights to the Market.

One could understand the confusion as to whom the £10 rent should be paid!!

The Queen's view was that 'The receivers will be the Baliffs and other officers of the aforresaid Lady the Queen'.

Thus Lord Audley lost out. But in 1603, when James came to the throne he decided to reward those supporters of his mother, Mary Queen of Scots, and Audley was made Earl of Suffolk. In 1618, the King granted him the market rights in Walden as well as the malt mill, windmill and courts. Audley, in desperate need for money for the maintainance of Audley End Mansion, agreed to sell the rights, except for the windmill to the town for £300 and so Walden finally owned its own market.

The Parish Church

Physically the most notable change to the town during the 16th century must have been the building of the Parish Church, St. Marys. A church had stood on the site of the present church, probably from Saxon times and it was rebuilt between 1250 and 1258 (27). It is believed it was then built in the 'decorated' style, and was probably of a cruciform plan with a central tower. However the building was comparatively short-lived, because according to the Annals of John Stowe, on Candlemas Eve, 1445 there was a 'great wethering of wind, hayle, snow, rayne and thunder; with lightening whereby the churches of Baldock in Hertfordshire, Walden in Essex, and others were sore shaken, and in the same storm St. Pauls Cathedral was set on fire'.

As a result it was decided to put in hand a rebuilding work and, largely under the hand of John Leche, the vicar from 1489 to 1521 the church was completely rebuilt. The work was carried out between 1450 and 1526, mainly by two masons, Samuel Clerk and John Wastell. Wastell was one of the country's leading stonemasons of his time, and it was said that he used Walden church to practice many of the techniques incorporated into Ely Cathedral.

The first stage in the rebuilding was the erection of the tower, and this was completed about 1470. The nave was next built and is believed to have been completed by about 1510. Finally the two side chapels were virtually rebuilt and the church was completed in about 1526, although Lord Audley carried out further alterations to the south chapel in 1544.

It is also known that an organ had been installed in the church as early as 1451, having been built by John Hudene. Thus music played an important role in Walden church from a very early time, a tradition continued to the present day.

The church would have been beautifully decorated with painted walls, stained glass, carpets, candlesticks, gold and silver, for at this time Walden was a prosperous town, and the efforts of John Leche, the Vicar, and his sister, Dame Joanne Bradbury had ensured a secure financial footing for the church. Sad, therefore that it was completed only just before the dissolution and the protestant reformation. In 1553 a body of special commissioners arrived in Walden. They compiled a list of everything in the church, the list of which still exists, and then confiscated everything except a cope, a chalice and patten and a cover for the communion table.

According to VCH (53) the sale of plate brought in £85 19s. 6d. which was used for the relief of the poor, the maintenance of a free school and other charitable deeds. Among the few items not taken was 'A egle or lectorn of latten'. In addition the commissioners returned to the churchwardens 'a little rounde box to carry the Sacrament in with a purse to putt it in'. The VCH (53) comments that this is believed to be the only instance known throughout the kingdom, where the commissioners made any provision for reserving the Sacrament for the sick.

The church is fortunate in retaining all the registers of baptisms marriages and burials from 17th November 1558, one of the earliest collections in the country following the passing of Hardwicks Marriage Act in 1556 which required compulsory registration. The records are now kept at the County Record Office at Chelmsford.

Famous People

It was during the 16th century that Walden saw its first religious martyr. Following Henry VIII's move towards Protestantism, greater freedom was shown towards religious views. One of the King's chaplains, John Bradford took a particular interest in Walden church, visiting and preaching in the church in a number of occasions, but on the accession to the throne of Queen Mary, the country was forced to return to

The stake at Smithfield where Bradford was burnt.

JOHN BRADFORD

Catholicism. Bradford was one of a number of clergy who refused and was subsequently burnt at the stake at Smithfield.

Whether or not Bradford had a following of support in the town is not clear, but possibly he did, because during Mary's reign John Newman, a travelling preacher from Kent was arrested in the south of Essex. Rather than sending him to the stake at Smithfield, however, he was burnt in Walden market place, on 31st August, 1555, possibly as a warning to the residents of the town. Whether or not it had any effect is a moot point. Walden still practised nonconformity an act which resulted in 1574 in an Information being laid against the congregation (53).

Probably Walden's most eminent person in the 16th Century was Sir Thomas Smyth (or Smith). He was born on December 23rd, 1513, the son of John Smyth, described as a gentleman, who was himself to become Sheriff of Essex and Herts in 1539. Thomas was first educated at Walden Grammar School, then at the age of 14, at Queens College, Cambridge, becoming a Fellow there in 1529/30. He was obviously a hard working

Sir Thomas Smyth – Principal Secretary of State to Edward VI, born in Saffron Walden.

scholar, for he was soon called upon to deliver the Greek public lecture, and it was said that senior members of the University would attend his lectures. He was noted for introducing an improved pronunciation of the Greek language.

In 1538 he was elected University Public Orator, but he relinquished the office in 1539 so that he could go abroad for study in order to improve his languages. He visited Paris and Orleans and then attended Padua where he obtained the degree of Doctor in Civil Law. Returning to Cambridge he took his LL.D. and was made Vice Chancellor in 1542-43 being considered the best scholar in the University, not only for rhetoric and the classics, but also mathematics, law and natural and moral philosophy (8). With the accession of Edward VI, he entered the service of the Protector Somerset in February 1546/7 and was employed by him in various affairs of state, as well as making him the Master of Requests, Warden of the Stanneries and Provost of Eton. In April 1549, he was made Secretary of State, was knighted and about the same time married Elizabeth Karkek. Sadly she died in 1553 and on July 24th 1554 he married Philippa Welford who brought into the marriage, as her jointure Hill Hall at Theydon Mount in Essex. However Somerset was to fall out of favour at this time and Smyth was committed to the Tower on suspicion. Whilst there he wrote many religious works and translated the Psalms of David into English verse. On regaining his liberty he was reinstated as Secretary of State and was sent on a mission to France to try to arrange the marriage between King Edward and the eldest daughter of the French monarch.

During Mary's reign, he was deprived of all his appointments, and was charged not to leave the Realm. Being a protestant, his life was in constant danger, but in 1555 he found a powerful supporter in William Smythwick of Bath who, having obtained a Papal Indulgence, was able to name any five friends he wished, to receive the protection the indulgence offered. Smythwick named Sir Thomas, and so he became exempt from risk of excommunication and other ecclesiastical measures.

On the accession of Elizabeth, he assisted in revising the Prayer Book. In 1562 he was sent as Ambassador to Paris to negotiate peace with France. He was employed on various other missions on behalf of the Queen, and in 1576 he was made Privy Councillor and Chancellor of the Order of the Garter. For the last few years of his life he again held the office of Secretary of State and assisted the Universities by obtaining an Act of Parliament enabling them to receive one third of their rents payable under their leases in corn if they so wished. Sir Thomas Smythe died in August, 1577 and was buried at Theydon Mount in Essex. (20) During his life he was very much attached to his place of birth. He assisted in obtaining the almshouses for the town, gave a silver cup and cover to the Corporation, in 1567, and occasionally lived at The Priory on Common Hill.

Gabriel Harvey was born in Walden in about 1545, as were his brothers, Richard, John and Thomas. Their father was a master ropemaker, and an entry exists in the records of Stortford Church for 1579 which reads 'Paid to Harvey of Walden for a rope for the bell, 2s 3d.'. Circumstances suggest that the family were reasonably prosperous. The Harveys were said to be related to Sir Thomas Smyth and like him they were educated at Walden Grammar School and Cambridge. Gabriel obtained his B.A. Degree at Christ's College and was elected a Fellow of Pembroke Hall. He later became Proctor of the University and in 1580 was created Doctor in Civil Law at Oxford. Gabriel's brothers were also achieving academic success – Richard obtained his degree in 1577 and John after that.

Gabriel soon became a don of some repute, and the author of a number of books, becoming an important literary figure. He was a close friend of Spencer, who honoured him by allowing Harvey, under the pseudonym of Hobynoll, to introduce his famous poem 'Faerie Queene' in 1596. However Harvey appeared to be an arrogant man and was certainly less than modest. He claimed to have been responsible for a new literary technique in adapting the metre of hexameter verses to the English Language, and this, allied to his dabbling in astrology, was to lead into a literary argument with a number of noted figures, most notably Thomas Nash and Christopher Marlow. The controversy gradually became very acerbic, each side issuing several pamphlets including Nash's 'Have with you to Saffron Walden'. But the arguments became very scurrilous so that Whitgift, the Archbishop of Canterbury, stepped in to stop the argument by ordering all copies of the pamphlets to be seized and burnt.

Although studying at Cambridge, Harvey did not forget his home town. During the visit of Queen Elizabeth to Audley End in 1578, he composed 'Gratulationes Waldenses' in the Queen's honour and presented it personally. During his later years Gabriel lived in Walden at a house situated in Market Street, where the Saffron Walden Building Society is now situated. As well as being a writer he was also something of a gardener and he developed the Harvey apple, described as 'A big apple; whitish green in colour, and generally marked with black spots'. It was much favoured as a cider apple and is still grown for that purpose.(32) Gabriel died in 1630 and was buried, on February 11th in Saffron Walden Parish Church. (8)

Richard Harvey took Holy Orders, and became much interested in astrology. At the age of 25 he published a pamphlet entitled 'An astrological Discourse upon the Conjunction of Saturn and Jupiter which shall happen the 28th Day of April, 1583, with a Declaration of the Effects which the late Eclipse of the Sunne is yet hereafter to worke'. The pamphlet which was written in Walden in December 1582 ran into two editions caused widespread alarm at a time of considerable belief in astrology, for Richard predicted that gales and floods would devastate the country. The failure of this prediction however was to add to the ridicule heaped on the Harveys.

John, the third brother became a physician and also dabbled in astrology. There was a fourth brother, Thomas, but of him, little is known.

Visits of Monarchs to Audley End

On the 19th August 1571 Queen Elizabeth visited Audley End, and the Corporation Account Book recorded the visit thus:-

'The Progress and comynge of the most excellent Prynces and our moste gratious and Soveraygne Ladye Elyzabeth, by the grace of God, Quene of England, France and Ireland . . . to Awdlens the 19th of Auguste . . . 1571, James Woodhall, Treasorer of the Towne of Walden, Will'm Ayleward and Thomas Turner, Chamberlyns, . . . [and others listed in the account book] . . . rode . . . to the furthest parte of their bounds, there all knelynge, the Recorder made an Oracion w(hi)ch ended, the Treasorer delyvered hys present as foloweth, and afterward, mounted upon his horse, he rode before her Ma(tie) with his mace to the Hall dore: there the Quene extended her hand to the Treasorer to kysse, gave hym thanks for hys payns, and soe he toke hys leave'.

Then follows a list of the expenses occasioned by the event amounting to £29.6.6d. and including this entry:-

'To the Quene's Majestie a cupp of silver doble gilt, with a cover, weying 46 ounzes, at 8s. the ounze, and a case to put it in, given to her Maj(estie) a presente .... £19.3.0.'

The Queen again visited Audley End on the 26th July, 1578. She was welcomed there by a deputation from the University of Cambridge, including the Chancellor, vice Chancellor, and Heads of Colleges. The Vice Chancellor presented the Queen with a 'paire of gloves, perfumed and garnished with embroiderie and goldsmithes wourke, price 60s.'

Again, in honour of the visit the Corporation were required to make the Queen another gift and the following payments were authorised:-

'Imprimis, given the Quene's maiestie a Cupp of Silver doble gilte, with a cover, waying 40 ounces at 7s. the ounce .... £14. 0. 0.'

Apparently the Queen did not warrant as large a cup a second time around!

Industry

Several major industries existed in Walden by the 16th century. Cloth was made and there are numerous records of wool-staplers in the town records. Rope and twine were being made in Walden at this time. Indeed Gabriel Harvey's father was a rope maker and part of the over-mantel of his house, now retained in the Museum, has a representation of the operation of ropemaking. Other important industries at this time included dying and malting – by 1600 there were six maltings in the town, one of which was the property of Katherine Semar at the southern end of the High Street. Emson (21), records a deed of 1st November 1574 whereby the 'Commanalitie' of the town let to Hammond Carter, a miller

'All that their maltmyll in Walden with all the moulter of the same town for a rent of 53/4d pere year plus £20 paid by him in hand for sealing'. (38) Other malt mills in the town at this time almost certainly included the building at the corner of Myddlyton Place and the High Street now used as the Youth Hostel. The old hoist to lift the barley to the first floor can still be seen.

Another major industry was tanning, from which Tanners Row was probably named. A house which stood in Cross Street belonged to John Parker, and he was a shoemaker, tanner and tallow chandler. (38)

Myddlyton Place at the turn of the century showing the old barley hoist.

Chapter 6
17th Century Walden 1600-1659

The 17th century is probably as good a place as anywhere to look at the crop from which the town derived its name, as it was at this time that the crop was at its most productive. However its influence on the town was felt much earlier than that. The Crocus Sativus was extensively grown in the area throughout the 16th and 17th centuries and by 1582 the town had acquired its prefix. According to Reaney (42) it was then known as 'Saffornewalden'. In 1594 it was then referred to as 'Walden called Safron Waldon' (sic). In John Norden's Survey of Essex, also in 1594, his description of Saffron also included a saffron flower drawn in the margin. He described the flower as being of 'watchet, or pale bleue' with chives 'of a fiere couller'. There is even evidence of its influence during the 15th century, as representations of saffron flowers can be seen on a spandrel of the south aisle of the Parish Church. (49)

According to Hollinshed, Saffron was first planted in Walden at the time of Edward III (i.e. 1327-1377), and it is mentioned as a titheable commodity in a deed entered into by the Abbot and Vicar of Walden in 1444. This deed gave the vicar the tithe of saffron, pepper, and all spices grown in gardens outside of the abbey.

There is also a legend that the first crops were brought to Walden by a pilgrim. According to Hakluyt in his 'Voyages' (1599):-

'It is reported at Saffron Walden that a Pilgrim, purposing to do good to his countrey, stole an head of Saffron and hid the same in his Palmer's staffe, which he had made hollow before of purpose, and so he brought this root into this realme with venture of his life; for, if he had bene taken, by the law of the countrey from whence it came, he had died for the fact.'

Its growth was certainly extensive by the end of the 15th century. Geffrey Symond left in his will two houses, two saffron gardens, and a field all at Walden to provide funds for a priest, on 19th September, 1481, and in 1497 Edward Barker of Walden left his son William 'iij acres of lond sette with safferon heddis, lying in my safferon gardyn in a feeld there leding to Sewards Ende ward'.

By the end of the 16th century, Braybrooke asserts(8) that the crocus was being extensively cultivated in the parish.

Walden's saffron was highly prized. During the 16th and 17th centuries English saffron always fetched the best prices on the continent. It was said in 1577 that:-

'as the saffron of England is the most excellent of all other . . . so . . . that [which] groweth about Saffron Walden, on the edge of Essex, surmounteth all the rest and, therefore, beareth worthily the heigher price by six pence or twelve pence most commonly in the pounde.' (53)

The industry was obviously run on a very large scale. It was believed that 'as many as 128 bushels of bulbs were needed to plant an acre.'(14)

According to Braybrooke (4):-

'. . . the saffron near Walden was usually grown on fallow land after barley, a dry mould lying over chalk being deemed preferable, and enclosures varying from one to three acres. The land was ploughed about Lady-day, with furrows drawn exceedingly close, each acre requiring from twenty to thirty loads of short dung, and being planted in July with about three hundred and ninety thousand roots. From this time no further labour was necessary, weeding excepted, till the flowers were ready for gathering, and this operation took place at sunrise, when the three yellow chives or stigmas were picked with the style or string attached to them, and the rest of the flower was thrown away. The stigmas were then dried between two sheets of paper placed on a kiln, by which process their weight was diminished four fifths.'

However it was an uncertain crop, and its price varied wildly. Braybrooke (8) gives the following prices for a pound of saffron:-

1548	£0.12.0	1653	£1.17. 0
1561	£1. 5.0	1664	£3.10. 0
1614	£3. 3.4	1665	£4. 1.10
1631	£0.18.0	1689	£3. 0. 0
1647	£1. 2.0	1717	£1. 6. 6

The reason for this fluctuation were varied; failed crops; vogues of fashion in medicine; foreign imports; and fluctuating markets all contributed towards making saffron an economically unreliable crop. Such was the situation, that by 1790 the crop had disappeared entirely.

But the townsfolk were obviously proud of the crop which by the middle of the sixteenth had given the town its distinctive name. During the 16th and 17th centuries, the corporation made several presentations to successive monarchs, when they visited Audley End:- Elizabeth in 1571, James in 1614, Charles in 1631, Charles in 1665 William III in 1689 and George III in 1771.(49) Entries for all of these gifts are recorded in the Guild of Holy Trinity Accounts in the town's archives. Perhaps the most interesting entry is that relating to the visit of William III:-

'In October A.D. 1689, our Sovereigne Lord William the IIId came to Audley End, where Mr. Reynolds, and other gentlemen and inhabitants of Walden met the King, and there presented to his Majesty a silver plate, which cost 4l. 6s. 6d. and fourteen ounces of saffron, which cost 3l. 11s. 8d.; and at the same time the gentlemen and inhabitants made an address, which Mr. John Morgan read before his Majestie, whom God grant long to reign.'(28)

The practice of presenting saffron to monarchs was a good early example of civic pride for we find that by the time George I visited Audley End the saffron was actually purchased from Bishop's Stortford as it had ceased to be grown locally.

A.F.J.Brown in 'Essex at Work 1700 - 1815' writes:-

'One local crop, saffron had been discontinued by 1730, when it had almost disappeared around the town that bore its name. Saffron Walden had, in 1696 been 'the chief market for it as well as the principal place of its growth' but by 1726 Littlebury was the only place in that area still growing it; in 1770 the saffron sold at Newport Fair came from Cambridgeshire.'

According to the Saffron Walden Almanac of 1880, the last of the saffron growers was an old farmer named Knot who lived at Duxford. He grew about half an acre, and would go once a year to London to sell the crop. After his death in about 1820, no more was apparently grown locally.

Saffron itself was used in cooking to colour and flavour dishes; as a dye, a remedy for pimples and as a precaution against plague.(49) An excellent article on saffron can be found in Morant's History and Antiquities of Essex (34) and a Bibliography in Stacey's Article on Walden and its Saffron. (49)

Gifts to visitors to the town were fairly commonplace, and one such entry may have recorded the visit of William Shakespeare to the town in 1606. The entry reads:-

'Item, given to the Kinges plaeirs 6s.8d.'

The entry is in 'the accompte of Mr. Benedicte Growte later Treasorer of the town Corporate of Walden aforesaid, Mr. Robert Newton and Mr. Robert Baker then allso Chamberlaines of the same towne, taken and allowed the seaven and twentith daie of December Anno Domini 1606.'

According to Dr. J.O. Halliwell Phillips in his book 'The visits of Shakespeare's Company of actors to the provincial Cities and towns of England' (1887):-

'From December, 1594 to the end of his theatrical career, it is certain that Shakespeare was one of the Lord Chamberlain's actors.'

As apparently it was not the practise to put on play-bills or to advertise the names of the actors, it is not possible to state with certainty that Shakespeare did appear in Walden, although as a prominent actor there is a likelihood that he did.(37)

The building of Audley End

It was at the start of the 17th century that Audley End Mansion was built. Braybrooke (8) says that there are few documents relating to the actual building and therefore much of what follows has to be speculative. Following the dissolution of the monastery on 22nd March 1537, the lands fell to the Crown. In turn, Henry VIII granted the abbey to Sir Thomas Audley, the Lord Chancellor, together with the title of Lord Audley of Walden, on 14th May 1538. Audley obtained an additional 200 acres by licence in 1540, (SW Almanac,1890). The lands subsequently passed to his grandson, Thomas Howard, 1st Earl of Suffolk.

It appears that the Earl of Suffolk was determined to erect a mansion which in size and magnificence would surpass anything in the land. To that end he had a wooden model made, in Italy at a cost of £500. There is some confusion over who the architect was - Horace Walpole suggests it was Bernard Jansen, but Braybrooke (8) believes that based on the type and style it was probably the work of John Thorpe, who built many houses of that period for the nobility. The earl named the mansion Audley House after his grandfather.

The building work is believed to have taken about 13 years to complete, having started in 1603. It would have been considerably advanced in 1610, when James I visited Lord Suffolk. James again visited Audley End in 1614, and it was probably on one of these visits that the James made his remark that the house was too large for a King though it might do for a Lord Treasurer.

The actual cost has to be speculative since no record exists. The Earl was overheard to have remarked to the King that the complete cost including furniture was £200,000, a collosal sum when Hatfield House, built about the same time only cost £8,000. Certainly it left Suffolk in some debt, and he had to sell various other properties then in his ownership including an estate worth £10,000 a year. The clerk of works was Henry Winstanley, of whom more is written later. The cost of its upkeep was also huge – after Suffolk's death none of his predecessors could keep a full establishment of staff.

The original completed house consisted of buildings around two spacious quadrangular courts. Braybrooke (8) describes the buildings thus:-

'That (Court) to the westward was the largest, and was approached over a bridge across the Cam, through a double avenue of Limes, terminating with a grand entrance gateway, flanked by four circular towers. The apartments on the north and south sides of the principal court were erected over an open cloister, and supported by pillars of alabaster; and on the eastern side, a flight of steps led to the entrance porches, placed on a terrace running parallel to the great hall, which formed the centre of the building; beyond the hall was the inner-court, three sides of which only remain, and constitute the present house.'

With the accession of Charles II to the throne, the House was to change hands. Charles visited Audley End in 1665/6 and again in 1668. He was obviously attracted with what he saw, and purchased the estate from James, the third Earl Suffolk on the 8th May, 1669. The conveyance of the estate says:-

'. . . that the King, upon his own personal view and judgement, had taken liking to the mansion called Audley End, with the park, outhouses, courtyards, orchards, gardens, stables, water-mills and appurtenances, as a seat fit for his majesty's residence; the ancient houses of the crown having been in a great measure destroyed and demolished during the late times of usurpation, and therefore fit to purchase the same at the price of £50,000.'

Audley End from the south in its original form.

AUDLEY END FAMILY TREE

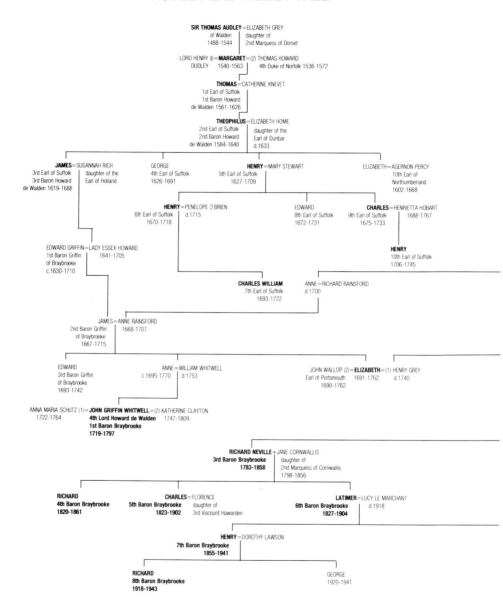

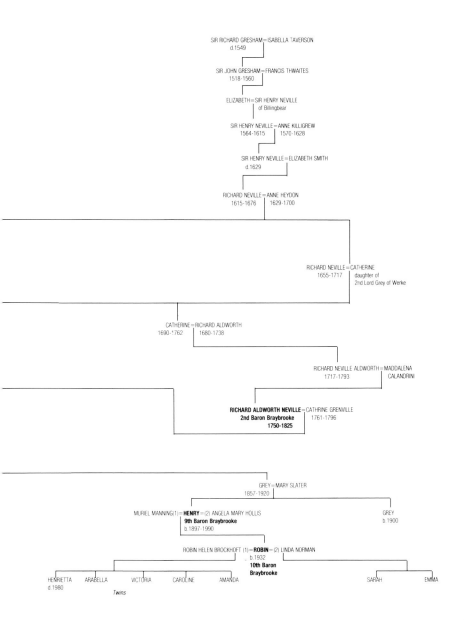

SIR RICHARD GRESHAM = ISABELLA TAVERSON
d.1549

SIR JOHN GRESHAM = FRANCIS THWAITES
1518-1560

ELIZABETH = SIR HENRY NEVILLE
of Billingbear

SIR HENRY NEVILLE = ANNE KILLIGREW
1564-1615   1570-1628

SIR HENRY NEVILLE = ELIZABETH SMITH
d.1629

RICHARD NEVILLE = ANNE HEYDON
1615-1676   1629-1700

RICHARD NEVILLE = CATHERINE
1655-1717   daughter of
2nd Lord Grey of Werke

CATHERINE = RICHARD ALDWORTH
1690-1762   1680-1738

RICHARD NEVILLE ALDWORTH = MADDALENA
1717-1793   CALANDRINI

RICHARD ALDWORTH NEVILLE = CATHRINE GRENVILLE
2nd Baron Braybrooke   1761-1796
1750-1825

GREY = MARY SLATER
1857-1920

MURIEL MANNING (1) = **HENRY** = (2) ANGELA MARY HOLLIS
9th Baron Braybrooke
b.1897-1990

GREY
b.1900

ROBIN HELEN BROCKHOFT (1) = **ROBIN** = (2) LINDA NORMAN
b.1932
10th Baron
Braybrooke

HENRIETTA   ARABELLA   VICTORIA   CAROLINE   AMANDA
d.1980

Twins

SARAH   EMMA

The mansion was renamed the New Palace, which perhaps gives some idea of its original grandeur. Charles would often hold Court here during his visits to Newmarket. It remained in the hands of the Crown after Charles' death even though a large portion of the purchase money had not been paid. Lord Suffolk and his successor the fourth Earl, moved to Chesterford Park, but in 1701 the estate was reconveyed to Henry, the fifth Earl of Suffolk, provided he made no claim on the outstanding mortgage on the property. (8)

In 1721 the cost of the upkeep simply proved too much. Three sides of the great quadrangle were pulled down; the fourth side is the remaining building seen today. Subsequently the estate was sold to the Countess of Portsmouth in 1747. She was succeeded in 1762 by Sir John Griffin Griffin, who began a complete reconstruction of the house. 'Capability' Brown was hired to redesign the grounds, and the house was refaced and partially rebuilt (24). In 1784 Lord Braybrooke came into possession of the house and it remained with the Braybrooke family until shortly after the last war when it passed into the hands of the Ministry of Works and, lately, English Heritage.

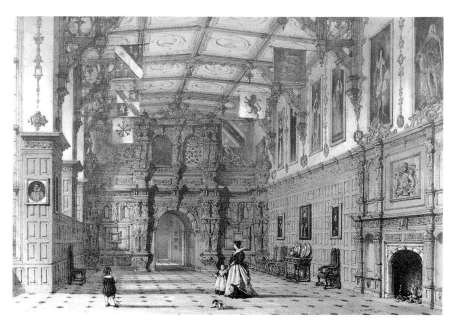

Interior of Audley End Mansion.

Saffron Walden Parish Church circa 1800.

The Parish Church

The established church occasionally found Walden somewhat rebellious. In August, 1610, William Bayley, the Vicar of Walden, and Thomas Dawney were engaged in discovering recusants. A William Atkinson was called upon to assist, but refused, using threatening language. He was reported to the Council for his actions but no record exists of what happened to him. During the 17th century there was considerable controversy about the administration of Communion at the altar rail. A document issued to Jane Leader concerned 25 woman who refused to take Communion at the altar rail. The document stated that one of the woman, 'Goody' Taylor was a modest and sober woman who had not opposed their minister out of any undutiful disposition, but that she had not come up to the altar because she was a weak woman and the Communion table was situated on 'lofty and bleak stairs'.

The local church often disagreed with the High Church view, and annoyed the ecclesiastical authorities by performing services without wearing a surplice. Much of the opposition to the High Church was led by George Burdett the Clerk of Yarmouth. Over a period of time he preached a series of remarkable discourses at Walden. He was later suspended from office. His use of the church at Walden suggests the town was at the forefront of opposition to the High Church. (22)

The Vicar of Walden, from 1607 to 1634 was William Bayley and he was succeeded by Nicholas Grey. Grey was a learned man who was also Master of Eton School and it was perhaps this dual role which led to his dispute with Mr. Burges the headmaster of the Grammar School, in 1636. Grey tried to eject Burges on the grounds of his puritanical beliefs, with a view to obtaining the office himself. The charges against Burges were that 'Burges practised physic, and left his pupils to the care of an usher, who neglected them'.(8) Burges countercharged that Grey had refused to employ a curate, unless the town bore the expense, and that he was ambitious to obtain as boarders for the school, the sons of great men. The case was referred to the Archbishop of Canterbury for a decision but the outcome was not recorded.(8)

During the 17th century new bells were provided in the church. The church accounts contain many records of payment in connection with the bells, including the following:-

1623 - 1624 Pd. to Wm. Perkin for worke about the Bells xxs.vjd.

1624 - 1627 Paide for casting of the bell £viij 0 0
Paide for xxij pounds of pewter to put into the bell £0 viij iiij

1629 Paide to Graye the Bell-Founder for casting of the greate bell £xv 0 0

Paide more to him for mettal for the same bell £0 xv vj

Paide more to him for casting of brasses £0 xvi vj

Paide for expence there given to his man for
fetching the waytes and carrying them back £0 j 0

Paide to Mr. Cole (the Attorney) for making the
covenant between the town and the bell founded £0 j 0

Paide for craving a day £0 0 iiij

In 1632 there is payment for setting the chimes in a new tune, which shows that there were eight bells at the time.

The records show a large number of payments throughout the 17th century for ringing the bells on special occasions. Often payments were made to local publicans for 'Bread and Beare' for the ringers. These occasions included, the visit to 'Audliend' of King Charles I in 1635; the day the Lord Protector was proclaimed in 1658; Gunpowder Treason Day; when parliament began to sit in 1660; When Charles II was proclaimed King in 1660; the defeats of the Dutch in 1662 and 1665; the coming of King William and his crowning in 1688 and 1689; and 'on ye good news from Ireland' on the victory of the Boyne in 1690.

Charities for the poor

With the total absence of any state support for the poor or the needy, life could be very hard in the 17th century. Saffron Walden was lucky in having a number of wealthy and philanthropic people.

Between 1612 and 1776 the poor of Saffron Walden were remembered in the wills of thirteen people. Of these thirteen persons Thomas Turner, Edward Leader, and Anthony Pennystone were tradesmen. Dr. Bromfield and Joseph Sparrow were professional men. William Turner, Edmund Turner of Walden and Edmund Turner of Audley End, Thomas Adam and Elizabeth Erswell were landowners. James, Earl of Suffolk and the Countess Falkland were of the aristocracy. Nothing is known of Matthew Rand however.

Each of these left bequests either of money, to earn interest, or land to produce rents. The interest and the rents were to be spent in providing benefits for the poor, sometimes in specific ways. Bread was to be distributed for 'cherishing the poor people' and for 'the increase of their

Copy of the will of Lady Falkland leaving a sum to be paid on 'Old New Year's Day to twenty poor men and nineteen poor women'.

diet'. Clothing was to be purchased and distributed, 'the garments fitting their necessities'. Certain groups were expressed to be especially deserving. 'Housekeepers' and those 'who behaved themselves honestly and conscientiously', 'children of such poor and indigent parents as were not able to maintain their families', 'the industrious poor aged or overburdened with children or who shall accidentally meet with other evident misfortune'. All these were to receive special consideration. Some bequests were made for the specific purpose of enabling children of the poor to make their way in the world – 'for clothing, putting out and binding apprentices to some trade, art or manual occupation'.

Inevitably perhaps, certain bequests contained restrictions. Elizabeth Erswell exempted 'common swearers, drunkards or adulterers' and those 'who live scandalously in their conversation'. Anthony Pennystone would deny benefit to 'stealers of corn, hedgebreakers or to any that are in the least suspected for witches and wizards'.

These bequests were administered locally by senior figures in the town. Ultimately the value of the bequests fell and in 1871 the charities were merged as the Saffron Walden Amalgamated Charities. In 1958 a new scheme was approved and the charities and their original general charitable intent continue to this day. (31)

Walden in the 1630's – Hayward's Survey

In 1630, William Hayward made a survey of the town. By now the rows of the town centre were fully developed forming shops with living quarters over and lean to's at the front forming the market stalls. Butcher Row had the largest number of shops. The remains of a typical shop can still be seen in the 'Hoops' shop in King Street.

The survey also shows that numerous inns existed at this time. Brewing was a very popular home industry, particularly for elderly people, who could trade from their own homes as their health failed. According to Plumb,(38) 'The inns provided a vital economic function in Walden as in most market towns, for they were the hotels, banks, markets and offices of the private trader. Four are shown in Market End in the 1630 survey, The Bell, The Rose and Crown, The Angel, and The Dolphin, whilst the White Hart was considered the principal inn in Elizabeth's time'.

The town at this time would have had a strongly based agricultural economy. Cattle were still sold in the streets until the 19th century, and complaints about the cattle obstructing openings are numerous in the Court Rolls. Yet even as early as the 17th century Walden's relative proximity to London meant a much larger market place for the town's traders, particularly for corn, malt skins and meat. According to Plumb, by the middle of the 17th century Walden was at the height of its economic strength (38)

The Civil War and Walden

It cannot be accurately stated whether Walden inhabitants were actively involved in the Civil War. An entry in the Commons Journal of Nov. 7th 1642 records an order 'That the Chamberlains, and other officers of the town of Walden, together with the inhabitants, do presently put themselves into a posture of defence, in providing all things necessary for the safety of the said town, according to the directions of the Militia'.

However the town's one major role on the national scene occurred with the events of the civil war and its aftermath. With the end of the first civil war, in 1647, the Parliamentary army, under General Fairfax, had marched from Nottingham heading for London. It halted at Saffron Walden, where, allegedly, Cromwell stayed in the Sun Inn. According to legend the army's horses were stabled in the Parish Church, and it was probably during this period that the stained glass was removed from the church. Certainly there is only one very small piece of stained glass left in the church from this period.

Cromwell's officers had a problem – they had won their major battles but still had a large expensive army to maintain, and still had problems in Ireland. The army itself was restless – they had three major demands of their Commander – the arrears of pay, – 18 weeks in the case of the infantry, and 43 weeks for the Horse; they required indemnity for acts carried out during the war; and a clear discharge from the army according to their original contract.

The Sun Inn – a contemporary etching.

In February 1647 Parliament approved a scheme to reduce the army to 10,000 soldiers and 6,600 horse whilst a volunteer force of 12,600 was to be raised for Ireland. No mention was made of the large sums of monies owed to the troops. Parliamentary Commissioners under Sir William Waller, were sent to visit Fairfax at Walden, where they discovered the Army furious at the proposals, particularly over the pay issue.

The soldiers rejected the terms of the Parliamentary Commissioners, and, in turn, drew up a petition to Fairfax. However Cromwell disapproved of the petition as inconsistent with army discipline, and the Commons lost its temper and passed a furious declaration against it. This was deeply resented by the army at Walden, and although a second Parliamentary Commission was sent to the town, it could not pacify the troops. The soldiers started to appoint agents to state their grievances directly to the Generals, and as a result Parliament sent four of its members, Skippon, Cromwell, Ireton and Fleetwood to negotiate. (29)

On May 8th this new deputation, all leading Generals, assembled in the Parish Church in Walden to meet the representatives of the soldiers. Cromwell tried hard to act as peacemaker, but would not tolerate indiscipline. Following that meeting on the 17th May they wrote the following to the Speaker of the Commons:-

Walden, 17th May, 1647
Sir, We having made some progress in the business you commanded us upon, we are bold to give you this account. . . .

The Officers repaired to us at Saffron Walden upon Saturday last, according to appointment, to give us a return of what they had in charge from us at our last meeting; which was to read your Votes to the Soldiers under their respective commands for their satisfaction, and to improve their interest faithfully and honestly with them to that end; and then to give us a perfect account of the effect of their endeavours, and a true representation of the temper of the army.

At this meeting we received what they had to offer us. Which they delivered to us in writing, by the hands of some chosen by the rest of the Officers and of the soldiers under their commands. Which was not done till Sunday in the Evening. At which time, and likewise before upon Saturday, we acquainted them all with a letter from the Earl of Manchester, expressing that an act of Indemnity, large and full had passed the House of Commons; and that two weeks pay more was voted to those that were disbanded, and also to them that undertook the service of Ireland. . . .

We must acknowledge, we found the army under a deep sense of some sufferings, and the common soldiers much unsettled; wherof, that which we have to represent to you will give you a more perfect view. Which, because it consists of many papers, and needs some more method in the representation of them to you than can bedone by letter, and forasmuch as we were sent down by you to our several charges, 'to do our best to keep the soldiers in order,' – we are not well satisfied, any

of us, to leave the place nor duty you sent us to, until we have the signification of your pleasure to us. To which we shall most readily conform; and rest, your most humble servants
Ph. Skippon
Oliver Cromwell
H. Ireton
Charles Fleetwood (11)

After a fortnight's negotiations, they returned to London, where Parliament voted for 'eight weeks pay in ready money, bonds for the rest.' A committee of the Lords and Commons were then ordered to go to Walden to ensure that the army was disbanded. However the army was already in revolt. It refused to accept only eight weeks pay, and the commissioners were greeted as enemies. Fairfax, torn between his loyalty to his men, and Parliamentary authority had virtually lost control of the army. Cromwell recognising the need above all to maintain military discipline and so prevent another Civil War decided to act. Cornet Joyce, once a tailor, was ordered to prevent the removal of the artillery train, (then in Oxford) and to proceed to Holmby in Northamptonshire, to secure the King. This he did taking the King, at his request to Newmarket. Cromwell marched his men from Walden to Newmarket to meet Joyce and the King. Ultimately further negotiations at Newmarket and later in London resolved the problems of the troops' pay, but not before the possibility of another Civil War became very real. (9)

The Mazer Bowl from which Pepys drank whilst in Saffron Walden.

Chapter 7
17th Century Walden 1660-1700

Pepys and Mazer Bowl

Little is known of Walden during the period of Cromwell, but we do know that the famous diarist Samuel Pepys visited Walden. His diary for 27th February 1660 contains the following entry:-

'Up by four o'clock. Mr. Blayton and I took horse and straight to Saffron Walden, where, at the White Hart, we set up our Horses and took the master of the house to show us Audley End House, who took us on foot through the park, and so to the house, where the housekeeper showed us all the house, in which the stateliness of the ceilings, chimney pieces and form of the whole was exceedingly worth seeing. He took us into the cellar, where we drank most admirable drink, a health to the King. Here I played on my flagelot, there being an excellent echo. He showed us excellent pictures; two especially, those of the four Evangelists and Henry VIII.

In our going my landlord carried us through a very old hospital or almshouse, where forty poor people were maintained; a very old foundation; and over the Chimney-piece was an inscription in brass: 'Ornate pro anima Thomae Bird,' etc. They brought me a draught of their drink in a brown bowl, tipped with silver, which I drank off, and at the bottom was a picture of the Virgin with the Child in her arms, done in silver. So we took leave, the road pretty good, but the weather rainy to Epping'.

The bowl to which Pepys referred was the famous mazer bowl which was then in the possession of the almshouses. The mazer bowl had ancient connections with the town and when it was eventually sold in 1929, there were protests even in the national press. One protester was Henry Llewellyn Bird, the last lineal descendant of Thomas Byrd who was one of those responsible in 1400 for the founding of the Almshouses. The Byrds were a prominent family in the area whose land it was alleged was dispossessed in Cromwells time. The earliest reference to the mazer was in an inventory dated 29 Henry VIII (that is the year from 22 April 1537 to 21 April 1538.) The entry reads 'in ye Botre a maser wt sylver gyltt'.

The parchment bound ordinances of the Almshouses, which is undated, also mentions the mazer bowl.

The bowl itself is approximately 7½" in diameter, and just over 2" deep. It is made of maplewood with a plain silver gilt rim and a circular silver plate at the base of the bowl. The plate is engraved with the Virgin and Child and is fastened to the bowl by a nail. The silver mark is for the year 1507/8 and an additional mark, the fleur-de-lys was probably the maker's mark. Despite considerable opposition at the time the bowl was eventually sold in 1929, as the money was required to repair the roof of the Almshouses. It sold for £2,900 to a Mr. Percy Oliver. He later sold it to the American banker J. Pierpoint Morgan for £6,000 and it was most recently sold again, at Christies on June 23rd 1971, fetching £22,000.(32)

The Town's charter of 1685.

Charters

In the same year that Pepys visited Walden, Charles II came to the throne, and in 1665 he visited Audley End. As usual he was provided with the traditional gift of saffron, but was also given a 'chased cuppe and cover of plate wayd 56 ounces & 4dr' at a cost to the corporation of £16.6s.0d.

Katherine, Charles' Queen, is supposed to have visited the town, incognito. In September, 1671, along with the Duchess of Richmond, the Duchess of Buckingham, and Sir Bernard Gascoigne, the Queen went disguised in what they imagined to be the costume of country people. However they were soon recognised and '. . . as many of the country people as had horses, straightway mounted with their wifes or sweet-hearts behind them to get as much gape as they could'. (51)

The philanthropy and gifts of saffron were insufficient to overcome the Catholic views of Charles' successor, James II. Shortly after coming to power, he decided on 29th July 1685 to form a corporation of the local gentry, men with no Local Government experience whatsoever. James issued a new charter but also provided himself with a new clause in confirming his predecessors powers. This clause permitted him to remove any members and order the election of new members. The size of the corporation was also reduced from a treasurer, two chamberlains and 24 common Councillors, to a Recorder, a deputy Recorder, a Mayor, a Town Clerk and 12 Aldermen. He appointed the Duke of Albemarle as Recorder. A new mace, still used to this day, was acquired probably to commemorate the new charter.

James was not afraid to exercise his new powers. The Council proved to be less sympathetic than James had hoped for – it showed little Catholic sympathy, and so on 13th January 1687/8 James removed the Mayor, five Alderman and the Town Clerk from office.

The following is the letter sent by James to the Mayor. The original is kept in the Town Council archives.

'Att the Court att Whitehall
the 13th of January 1687
By the Kings most Excellent Majesty & the Lords
of his Majs. most Honourable Privy Council.

Whereas by the Charter granted to the Towne of Saffron Walden in the County of Essex, a power is reserved to his Majesty by His order in Councill to remove from their Imployments any Officers in the said Towne; His Majesty in Councill is pleased to order, and it is hereby ordered, that Sr. John Marshall Mayor, Sr. Edward Turnor, Sr. Richard Browne, Richard Derbyshire, John Turnor, & Richard ffolkes Aldermen, Joseph Sparrowe Towne Clerke, be, & they are hereby removed and displaced from their aforesaid offices in the said Towne of Saffron Walden.

Wm. Bridgeman.'

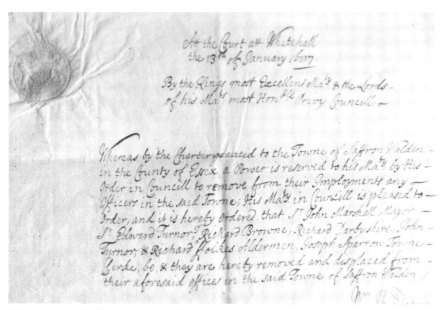

Letter removing the Mayor and Council.

The following day, James issued a note actually stating the names of the seven people to be 'elected' in their stead!:-

'. . . We have thought fit hereby to Will and Require you forthwith to elect and admit Our trusty and wellbeloved Richard Reynolds to be Mayor and one of the Aldermen, Francis Williamson, [?] John Kemp, Henry Cornell, John Potter and William Staines to be Aldermen and Thomas Cobb to be Towne Clerke of our said Burrough . . . without administring unto them any oath or oaths but the usuall oath for the execution of their respective Places, with which We are pleased to dispense in this behalfe. And for so doing this shall be your Warrant. . . .'

However this appointment of a Mayor and Aldermen produced problems later because he had made no mention of the length of time they were to hold office, as well as giving no instructions for the election of their successors.

This problem, and continual interference of this kind, as well as the trend towards catholicism, were to lead to the so called English Revolution of 1688. It was the same Richard Reynolds who had been appointed Mayor who was to welcome the new King William when he visited Audley End in 1689.

The accession of William and Mary to the throne resulted in much celebration in Walden. The accounts record that the Corporation provided £2.5s.0d at the Rose and Crown for a hogshead and a half of beer which was distributed free in the Market Square. (45)

As shown by difficulties over the appointment of the Mayor and Corporation the meddling with the charter by James had resulted in confusion. It was felt that only a new charter could resolve the difficulties. In due course this was granted on December 26th 1694 and provided for a corporation of Mayor, Recorder, Deputy Recorder, twelve Alderman, Town Clerk and Coroner.

Walden received a number of charters over the years and they generally make tedious reading. But the 1694 charter was of considerable importance as it was the charter which controlled the town for nearly 150 years. It established stable government in the town, at a time of change. The following are the salient points of the transcription:-

'Wheras James, the late glorious King . . . hath incorporated . . . the village of Saffron Walden . . . and . . . hath set up . . . one corporate and politic body . . . and hath granted to the same divers liberties, franchises, and other priviliges. But no election of a Mayor and Alderman, nor Government hath been had or exercised . . . for divers years . . . Know therefore (that) We graciously desiring and willing the bettering of our village of Saffron Walden, in our County of Essex, that for the future for ever, there may and shall be in the same village one certain and undoubted manner of and for keeping our peace and a good government, and ruling the same village, and our people inhabiting there . . . ; and that the aforesaid village may be, and remain for ever, a village of peace and quiteness, to the fear and terror of the bad, and to the reward and support of the good; and that our peace and other acts of justice and a good government may prevail, and be able to be better kept and done there: hoping also that if the Burghers and Inhabitants of the village aforesaid may have by our grant, greater and larger priviliges, then may then think themselves more especially and strongly bound to services which they shall be able to exhibit and lay out for us, our heirs and successors. We . . . confirm that the aforesaid village of Saffron Walden . . . may be and remain for the future for ever, a free village of itself; and we . . . confirm that the Burghers and Inhabitants . . . for the future and ever, may and shall be, . . . one corporate and politic body in effect and name, by the manner of Mayor and Aldermen of the village of Saffron Walden . . . truly and fully one corporate and politic body in effect and name, and that by the same name they may have a perpetual succession. And they themselves and their successors, by the name of Mayor and Aldermen of the village of Saffron Walden . . . may and shall be at all times, personable and in law capable of having, demanding, receiving, and possessing lands, tenements, liberties, franchises, jurisidictions, and heriditaments, for themselves and their successors, in copyhold and perpetuity, or for term of life or lives, year or years . . . and also goods and chattels, and all other things of whatsoever kind, nature, sort or quality; and to give grant, and discharge and assign the same lands, tenements, and other hereditaments, goods and chattels and all other deeds and things to be done and executed, . . . by the same name of Mayor and Alderman of the village of Saffron Walden in the County of Essex.'

James Robinet was appointed Mayor, the Earl of Suffolk the Recorder, and Joseph Sparrow the Town Clerk and Coroner. This was to be the towns last charter before the passing of the Municipal Corporations Act in 1835 which established democratically elected Councils.

Nonconformity

It was during the 17th Century that nonconformity in religious matters began to expand in the town. Much of East Anglia was a non-conformist area, and as early as 1555 John Bradford, the minister of Walden church from 1551 to 1553, had been burnt at the stake at Smithfield, because of his puritanical teachings. With the restoration of the Monarchy in 1660, and particularly during the reign of James II (1685-88) Roman Catholics began to take over high offices of state. Many local clergy found such a return to the old faith unacceptable, and in these instances, Parliament by legislation, such as the Act of Uniformity and the Five Mile Act, forced the Clergy out of the living and out of the community. Such a person was the Revd. Jonathan Paine, the Vicar of Bishops Stortford who was forced to live five miles from either Bishop's Stortford or Saffron Walden. Although laws prevented him holding meetings, support for his view was widespread in Walden, and once the Toleration Act, which allowed free religious worship, was passed in 1689, he was almost immediately able to

The Baptist Church in Audley Road/High Street, as built in 1774.

establish a church in a barn in Abbey Lane. His following, initially calling themselves the Independents, and later the Congregationalists, were able, by 1694, to purchase land and erect a building on a plot of land 'Whereupon five tenements did sometime stand commonly called Frogs Orchard in Abbey Lane'. This site of the first Congregational Church in Saffron Walden is still in use by that body today.

The 1694 Abbey Lane Church

On June 12th, 1774 the main body of the church, consisting of the Minister, the Rev. Joseph Gwennap, the Deacon and 67 members of the church broke away from the Abbey Lane church and held an emergency meeting in Myddleton House, having previously worshipped in the adjoining barn. Myddleton House was owned, in 1731, by Thomas Fuller, a Master Weaver and passed on his death in 1752 to his daughter, Elizabeth. The Minister and company decided to establish themselves as Baptists, and it was Elizabeth Fuller who provided the money for the purchase of the land at the junction of Audley Road and the High Street, on which the present day Baptist Church was built. It is believed that there had been Baptists locally as long ago as 1653, and there were also meetings in Gold Street in 1708, and a meeting House in Hill Street by 1711.

The Quakers also first appeared in Saffron Walden during the 17th Century. The earliest reference to them was the imprisonment of a Quaker in 1656 and the setting in stocks of another in 1659. (45) Whilst the congregation met in private houses, until 1676, it was still an offence to do so, and records exist of goods being confiscated in lieu of fines.

The Quakers purchased a cottage in what was then Cuckingstool End Street (now the High Street) in 1676 for £20 and used a room at the rear for their meetings. They continued to meet here in contradiction of the Test Act, and as the Quakers had no Minister it was impossible for the authorities to stop the services by removing him. So in 1682 it was decided to nail up the door of the building to keep them out. The Quakers therefore met in the street, where the magistrates were able to require them to take an oath of allegiance. This they were not prepared to do, and as a result of this, Robert Freak and Richard Mansfield of Ashdon and Thomas Trigg of Littlebury were gaoled. Such punishments continued throughout the 17th century. Later the Quakers were to purchase the two adjoining cottages and, eventually, in 1879, all three were pulled down to make way for the new existing building. Like the Congregational Church, the Quakers continue to meet on their original site. (45)

Famous Persons

One of Walden's most famous citizens, Henry Winstanley was born in the town in 1644. It is believed he was actually born at what is now known as Winstanley House on Market Hill. He was educated locally and achieved a reputation as an artist, a conjurer and an entrepreneur. But it was his reputation as an engineer that was to give rise to his national fame. As an artist and engraver he produced a portrait of Audley End House, which can still be seen, and also designed a pack of playing cards which were produced in 1670. He was undoubtedly an eccentric – 'Winstanley's Waterworkes' were erected in London near to Hyde Park Corner and filled the area with fire and water effects.

He quickly made a considerable sum of money, and decided to purchase six ships. However two were to founder on the Eddystone rocks, and it was this which made him determined to design and build the first lighthouse on the rocks in 1699. Whilst the building work was underway, he was kidnapped by a French privateer and then released by Louis XIV, who, impressed by his work on the lighthouse, offered him a position in his court. Sadly however he was to die in November, 1703. Critics had suggested his lighthouse was not of sufficient strength to withstand a severe storm. Winstanley determined to misprove them and arranged to be on the lighthouse during the winter. Unfortunately he chose the night of the worst ever storm to hit southern England, and when the storm abated both the lighthouse and Winstanley had disappeared.(32)

Winstanley's Uncle, was William Winstanley who was born in Quendon in about 1628 and was eventually made a freeman of Walden. He was a writer of reknown, his most famous work being a parody of Don Quixote called 'The Essex Champion – The Famous History of Sir Billy of Billericay, and his Squire Ronaldo'. He died in 1698 and was buried at Quendon. (32)

Another author of this period born was Hannah Wooley who was born in Walden in 1623. She wrote five books between 1661 and 1675 specifically aimed at women of which the most famous was 'The Gentlewoman's Companion'.(19)

Crime

Saffron Walden is fortunate in retaining all its Quarter Sessions records from 1657-1950. The entries make fascinating reading, with such varied punishments as use of the stocks, the pillory and the ducking stool as well as the more savage whippings, brandings and transportations. It is probable that the court also had power to order hangings – although there is no actual record of such a sentence, there are references to the cost of the erection of the gallows and other similar entries in the Guild of Holy Trinity Account book.

Listed below are typical examples of entries for these various punishments:-

Stocks:

The stocks were situated at the Market Cross until 1818 when the Cross was demolished. They were then moved to the junction of Museum Street and Castle Street, and later placed in the grounds of the castle. The stocks themselves comprised of a double row of ten holes, designed to house five people at a time. 1657 'Vasti Rush was adjudged to sitt in stocks 6 owers and then acknowledge her fault to Mr. Chamberlain Leader.'

The town's stocks.

Pillory:

The pillory was a T-shaped post to which the accused man was strapped for general public mockery. There is no mention in the Quarter Sessions of the pillory, but an entry in the Guild of Holy Trinity Accounts Book says:- 1551(?) Itm. 'For the tymber and workemanshippe of the pyllory iiis iiiid.'

Ducking Stool:

The Ducking Stool was a common punishment for minor offences usually involving women. The victim would be tied onto the stool and dipped a number of times in an appropriate pond or river. In Walden the site of the pond was close to the present day junction of Margaret Way and the High Street.

(In this entry the unfortunate victim appears to have been pregnant when sentence of a ducking was passed upon her – the punishment was not therefore carried out until after the birth.)

1672: 'It is ordered by ye Court yt. after two months Susann Crudd ye wife of Robert Crudd is delivered of her child she now goes withall she should be putt into ye Ducking Stoole and dipt.'

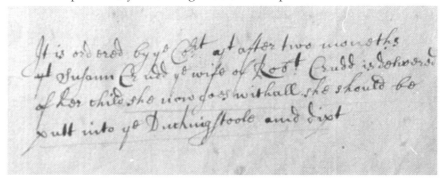

Whippings:

Whippings usually took place in the market place at the Market Cross, a building on the north east side of the market square which was pulled down in 1818. The stocks were also kept in the Market Cross. Rowntree (45) says that in the 181 years between 1669 and 1851 there were 113 whippings in the town.

16th January 1735(6) (The accused Mary Wittare was charged with 'Felloniously stealing . . . three pair of Leather Gloves of the value of ten pence.') The Sentence:-

'It is ordered by the court that she be on the Morrow the seventeenth day of this instant month of January between the hours of twelve and ten of the clock of the day stripped naked from the waste upwards and wipped by the Comon Cryer of the said Town till her body shall be bloody.'

The Market Square in about 1790 showing the market cross and stocks.

Whipping at the Cart's Tail :

A variation on whipping was a 'whipping at the cart's tail'. Here the victim was tied by his wrists to the rear of a cart and towed around the town to be whipped in each street through which he passed. The idea was to let all the towns inhabitants see their fate should they break the law.

'The King agst. Joseph Bird.
   On an Indictment for felony to be publicly Whipt on Saturday next at the Carts Tail from thence by Church Street High Street, & Market End Street [Now King Street] & return to the Market Place being whipt in each street & on going to & from the market place & then discharged.'

Gallows:

There almost certainly was power for the court to pass the death sentence, but if such a sentence was passed there is no record of it. However the following entries, and the names on early maps of Walden of Seven Devils Lane and Gallows Hill suggest that such sentences were passed. These extracts are from the Guild of Holy Trinity Accounts Book:-

1596 'Itm. payd to Mr. Lyn(?) ye carpenter for framing and setting upp the Gallowes...3s.'
'Itm. payd to Groutt of Wimbish for tymber for the gallowes, 3s 8d.
Itm payd to Stammer(?) for two gallowes 3s.'

1609 'for horse hier and charges fetching Robinson from Northampton £2.6.0
for taking of the bolte from his legge 6d
for 7 foote and a halfe of tymber, at 8d per foote for ye gallowes, 5s.
for making the gallowes, 3s.
for carrying the tymber and digging the holes, 6d
for watching the prisoner the night before he dyed, 2s.'

1631 'Payd for tymber, and making the gallowes, 4s 4d.'

1654 'Payd 2 men that pursued Moulton when he broke out of gaol, 1s 4d.'
Payd for fetters for Moulton and Douglas, 16s.
For quart of canary at the Rose, when Moulton and Douglas suffered 2s.
Knocking off their rivetts, 1s. 6d.'

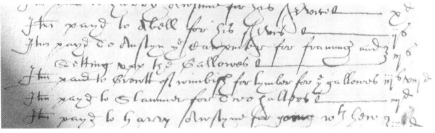

Transportation:

During the late 18th and early 19th centuries the Government encouraged the courts to transport criminals to its colonies and particularly Australia. It was a very severe punishment as the victim was rarely able to return to England and his family. This particular entry of 23rd January 1805, relates to a female convict:-

'The King agst. Jane, the wife of Jn King.

On an indictment for felony. To be transported to such places beyond the seas as His Majesty or his Privy Council shall direct for 7 years and in the mean time to remain in custody in the house of correction.'

Gaoling:

A gaol must have existed in Walden for many years, but its exact location in earlier times is unknown. A building known as the cage was in use in 1633. An entry in the Guild Account Books (28) relating to an inventory of Irons for holding the prisoners, states:-

'Irons Belonging to the prison wch. Timothie Cole Delivered over to J. Parker Treasurer the 11th of October 1633
first one Collar of Iron for the neck of a prisonher
two payers of hand Cuffes
4 Lockes
2 payer of shackls and one single one
1 Iron to brand fellons with
2 Locks for the prison which hange allways on the dore beside the other
4 Locks above sayd
1 Lock on the Cadge Dore.'

Before 1761 there was a gaol in the old guildhall, a building which stood in the south west corner of the present Market Square. When this building was removed in 1761 the gaol was situated in the new Town Hall built in that year. However this proved to be 'not only a nuisance by the people residing in the Market Place but an unsuitable prison from its publicity, the windows being towards the public road. To remove this and provide a secure place for the magistrates to commit prisoners to, a subscription was entered into and a gaol etc. was erected (1818) at the cost of £400 . . . upon the parish property against the Workhouse'. This was at the top of the High Street. (45)

However this did not prove a very suitable site particularly for prisoners arrested during the night as a more central location was required. In consequence a new cage was provided and in use between 1818 and 1840. Subsequently a new lock up house was purchased at the end of Mercers Row joining together the two parts of the Town Hall, and the new gaol was to remain there until the merger of the Borough and County Police Forces in 1857 when new provision was made in the Police Station.

The Recorder was the Chief Magistrate for the area. His house above stood on the west side of the High Street, where Hill House is today.

Chapter 8
18th Century Walden

The 18th century was not without its lawlessness either. A series of newspaper cuttings of that period were reproduced in the Walden Weekly of December 26th 1913, and show that highway robbery was a very real risk. The cuttings give a very good flavour of the period. Two extracts serve to illustrate the risks to travellers. The first from a newspaper of 1736 shows considerable resourcefulness on the part of the victim!:-

'On Thursday . . . Zachariah Whyat, a Quaker of Saffron Walden, going from thence to Sturbridge Fair, at Littlebury he met with on the Road a Brother Quaker . . . so they became very familiar. Whyat [told] his new brother . . . he had . . . 50 guineas in his pocket; upon which his Friend told him he must have it and immediately acted the complete Highwayman. Whyat told him . . . he should not have it without taking some Pains for it, and immediately took his Purse and Gold and flung it over the Hedge; the Rogue jump'd off his Horse and went to fetch it, and in the interim, Whyat dismounted a poor, sorry Scrub of his own and rode away with the Villain's Horse, which proves to be a fine Bay Horse with four white feet and of great value; which if nobody claims it will go a great Way towards his loss.'

The second cutting was from a newspaper of 1741:-

'The roads about Saffron Walden are much infested with robbers; a Farmer returning home from that Market on Saturday last, was stopp'd by a Highwayman, who demanded his Money, the farmer being much in liquor refused it, and began to strike him on the Head with his whip, upon which the Rogue pull'd out a Pistol, and swore he'd shoot him dead if he did not deliver immediately; but still he did not comply; the Farmer's wife being behind him flipp'd her Hand into his Pocket, and took out a purse in which was 4l.15s and gave it to the Highwayman; the Farmer seeing this was much enraged with his Wife, and imputed the Loss of his Money to her Fearfulness.'

Rewards were often made available. Following the escape of a horse stealer from Walden Gaol, in 1753, the following was advertised:-

'Town of Saffron Walden in Essex.
BROKE out of the Goal of this Town in the Night Time of the 30th January last GEORGE KEMP, committed for horse-stealing; a young man of the age of twenty three or thereabouts, pitted with the Small-Pox, has a Scar on the tip of his Nose, occasioned by the Small-Pox, of a fair Complexion, reddish Eye-brows, Weak Eyes, about Five Feet five inches high; born at Chevington near St. Edmunds Bury in Suffolk. He

had on when he went away, a light coloured Fustian Frock, brown Plaid Waistcoat, a short light natural Wig, Leather Breeches, and light grey stockings. Whoever will apprehend the said George Kemp, and deliver him to the Goal of the said Town, shall have a reward of five Guineas paid by me. EDWARD LEVERETT Mayor of the said Town. February 1, 1753.'

In 1707 a great cock match was held in Walden, cockfighting still being legal at this time. The fact that it was advertised alongside a list of 'horse matches' at Newmarket shows its importance as an entertainment.

The eighteenth century saw the creation of the town's major public building, the Town Hall. Before 1761 a Guildhall, as it was then known, existed and this was situated approximately at the junction of King Street and the Market Square, opposite No. 3, Market Place. It is described as being similar to the Guildhall in Thaxted, and consisted of a ground floor on which the gaol was situated, and upstairs, to the right, over the gaol, two rooms, a large one opening into a small one beyond, probably used as the gaolers quarters. On three sides of the Town Hall there were five lean to shops, about ten feet by seven feet in size. It is known that the Court of Quarter Sessions met regularly there – the Town Council retains Quarter Sessions books dating back to 1657 when the Court met in the Guildhall.

However by the middle of the 18th Century the position of the Guildhall at the end of King Street was causing difficulty and obstruction because of the increase in horse drawn vehicles. This, allied to the poor condition of the Guildhall, meant a new hall was required. As a result the Corporation called a public meeting on 8th February, 1760. The meeting agreed to donate and raise money towards:-

'the charge of pulling down the present Town Hall, and ye tenements adjoyning to the Market Place, [i.e. the site of the present Town Hall] these belonging to the Corporation, now in the tenure of Tho. Campin and John Clark, And for the erecting and building a new Town Hall, Goal (sic) and other tenements upon the spot where Campin's and Clark's houses now stand.'

The meeting instantly raised £476 and included some impressive donations. The Rt. Hon. Charles Lord Maynard, a former Recorder of the Town gave £100, and Sir William Maynard the then Recorder gave one hundred guineas. The Mayor, Thomas Wolfe, gave £50, the Deputy Mayor, James Raymond, £40, and most of the Councillors contributed £20 each.

It was apparent, however, that much more would need to be raised. A further meeting was called at the Rose and Crown on 4th May 1761, and the meeting unanimously qualified and defined its aims. It agreed to:-

'pull down the houses belonging to the Corporation called the Dolphin in the occupation of Thomas Campin and the adjoyning tenant late in the occupation of John Clark, they being very ruinous and out of repair and in no condition of being repaired in a sufficient manner. And as it was apprehended there will be sufficient room in the places where the aforesaid two houses stand, not only to erect two other houses, convenient for habitation the one as a private house, the other as a publick house which are likely to advance rather than defrey the income of the Corporation estate, But also between two such houses to erect a sufficient Town Hall and a goal for the town corporate. . . . It is moreover agreed to pull down the present Guild or Town Hall and erect and build the same between the said new intended house, and in the Row where the said two ruinous do now stand and thereby to enlarge the Market Place within the said town. . . .'

A committee was appointed to contract for the order and to manage it. This comprised of Mr. William Mapletoft (the new Mayor) and Messrs. Henry Archer, Thos. Wolfe (the former Mayor), Philip Martin, William Flower and James Raymond. Mr Edward Leverett Snr. was appointed treasurer and Alderman Mr Henry Archer the 'Receiver or collector of all Moneys'. The committee also had to determine who was to control the work, and agreed to employ Jonathon Parker, a local man,'Who hath made a plan of the intended new buildings'. He was to be paid £30 in addition to his weekly salary. Parker was later appointed as one of the first freeman of the town and was buried in the parish churchyard, where his grave stone can still be seen.

The Corporation regarded this as a good opportunity to tidy and clear up the road which is now King Street. At this time King Street was then divided by Middle Row, a small street comprising of three or four small houses with the Guildhall at the eastern end. At a further meeting on the 1st June 1761, the committee:-

'taking into consideration the convenience and accommodation it would be of to this town and all persons travelling to and from the same to have the Middle Row or alley of houses facing the Market Place, belonging to Mr Wale, the Widow Church and Mr Wooley (late Balls) wholly pulled down and the street there widened to the Market Place, having agreed to purchase the same in order to pull down

Mr Wooley's tenement in front of Market Place	£20.00.00
Mrs Church's two tenements adjoining at the back part	£31.10.00
Mr Wale's two tenements adjoining further end east	£40.00.00
	£91.10.00.'

During 1761 a further 46 subscribers from Saffron Walden contributed towards the new hall, bringing the total raised by the end of the year to £653.8s.6d. Among the many contributions was £20 from 'the Tradesmen's Clubb at the Rose' (i.e. the Rose & Crown). Some of the benefactors contributed materials: Mr Robert Cole, a farmer, gave a hundred bundles of hair valued at £2. 10s.0d., and Mr Garton gave the equivalent of 6 guineas in timber.

A seperate appeal was also made to 'neighbouring gentleman' from local villages and this raised a further £43. 1s. 0d. In addition to this, Mr. Chas. Smith of London, the uncle of Mr. John Fiske (a local Walden man) made a present to the Corporation of seats for the Mayor and Alderman to the value of £10.

The sum total of all this philanthropy came to £717.9s.6d, and on 6th May, 1761 the work commenced on pulling down the various houses in Middle Row, and dismantling the old gaol. The foundations of the new hall were built between the 4th and 11th July and on the 12th work started on erecting the hall. Judging from the accounts steady progress was made and a regular amount was paid out each week to the workman.

By Christmas 1762, the treasurer was able to report that £378. 16s. 1d. had been paid out in wages to the labourers, plus an additional £176. 16s. 6d. to the various sub contractors and to Jonathon Parker, the Surveyor. As it was the end of the year various bills for materials were settled – Mr. P. Martin was paid £35. 18s. 0d. for lime and Mr Lines was paid £12. 11s. 0d. for nails.

The work appears by the accounts to have been completed by the 30th April 1763, although some small additional sums were paid out as late as June 1764. The total bill came to £1075. 15s. 3d.

The surveyor, Jonathon Parker, was paid in total £338, some of which was in kind, mainly old timbers. Materials used on the building included:-

Sand:- 51 loads 2/6d the load
Lime:- 1342 Barrells
Bricks:- 159,700 at about 24s. per thousand
Hair:- 60 Barrels (The hair was used to bind the plaster)
Nails:- (A total bill of £32. 6s. 1d)
Timber mainly for laths:- a total bill of £116. 14s. 8d.
Stone Supplied by Wm. Bell & Co. at a cost of £33. 19s. 0d.

Some of the cost was recouped by selling old materials such as the timber and stone (which was sold to the Surveyor of the Highways) and this raised £19. 4s. 3d.

However it will be noted that the original amount raised was only £717. 9s. 6d. and with other costs it was realised that they would be about £500 short. A meeting was called in the Cross Keys on 4th March 1763, and an appeal was made for a £500 loan by Bonds at 5% interest. In fact, a further £625 was borrowed from seven people of whom James Raymond, Tho. Browne. Tho. Wolfe, Henry Archer. and Philip Martin gave £100 each. The interest on the loan was paid by reducing the Mayor's Allowance for the three Quarter Sessions dinners from 40s. to 20s. and abolishing the annual allowance of £10. At the same time the clerk to the committee was instructed to arrange for the hall to be insured for £800. When, in 1774, the time came for the repayment of the bonds, Thomas Wolfe and Henry Archer both released their bond and made no claim for either the capital or interest, and Messers. Brown and Martin and the executors of the late

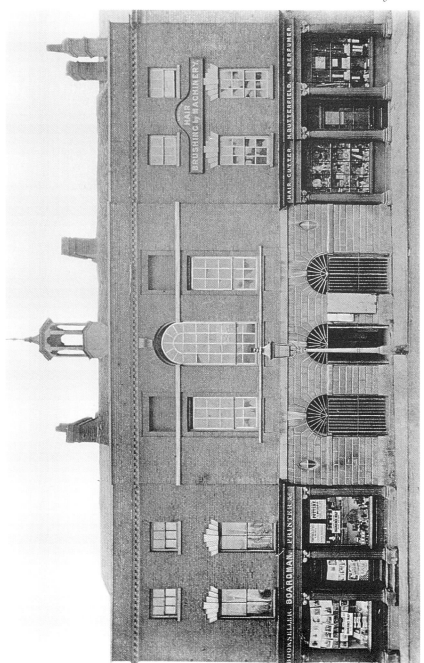

The Town Hall erected in 1761.

James Raymond all waived the interest owed to them. Given the considerable increase in money value since then this was a magnificent gesture.

Work was also necessary on the Parish Church when in July 1769 St. Marys Church was struck by a violent storm. Initially it was believed that the damage done would cost about £200 to repair – even that being a substantial sum to find. However it soon became obvious that in fact the damage was much more substantial. It was not possible to raise the sort of money required and by 1790, the church had fallen into such a state of dilapidation that that it was temporarily closed, with suggestions that it might even become a total ruin.

The Churchwardens called a meeting of the towns inhabitants to consider a report from a London architect, Mr. Brettingham. A second meeting considered proposals from local builders, but it was agreed:-

'At this meeting on Mr. Brettingham's having produced a proposal with an estimate for repairing the Church by putting on new Roofs covered with Westmorland Slate, by which a considerable saving would be made, it was agreed by the inhabitants present (three only dissentient) that his proposal should be carried into execution in preference to repairing the old Roof and covering the same with lead. Mr. Brettingham as architect is directed to supervise the different repairs of the Church.'

The church and castle from Castle Hill in the late 18th century.

The estimated cost of the work was £3,855, (although the final figure actual finished at nearly £6,000), and so in July 1790, an appeal was made to the Patron of the Church, Lord Howard. The letter reproduced in full in Rowntree (45) is a masterly exposition of how to beg for money!!:-

'. . . In this their difficulty the Parishioners take leave to look up to the Noble Patron of the Church, with humble hope and confidence that his Lordship will be pleased to consider the Fabrick of this ancient Church, . . . justly deemed a magnificent Relick of Gothic Architecture, and standing as an elegant Monument of Antiquity in a stile superior to anything of the kind in the Country, as a most valuable part of his Lordship's own Property and Inheritance and well becoming the splendour of his Station and Situation. . . .

They therefore wish to have it made known to his Lordship that they will cheerfully join with him in keeping up the Original Grandeur of this Building, in such a way as his Lordship shall be pleased to have it executed, according to his own taste and Judgement, . . . provided his Lordship shall be pleased solely and singly to take upon himself the Whole Design and Execution of it, and will be pleased to bear One half of the Expence himself, and the Parish the other half, . . .'

But Lord Howard also had a nice line in refusing such an open ended offer:-

'Lord Howard takes the earliest opportunity of informing the Parishioners of Walden that . . . he is not insensible to the Compliment they pay him in their willingness . . . to leave the disposition of the repairs of the Church to his judgement; but his time of life consider'd with the . . . very expensive repair of his own Chancel . . . will not permit him to embark in any additional business; . . . However he will . . . voluntarily contribute one thousand pounds.'

Other methods had therefore to be found of financing the project, and so application was made for an Act of Parliament authorising loans in the form of bonds up to a total of £4,000, which would be repaid out of the rates. Royal Assent was given to the Saffron Walden Church Act on 6th June, 1791, and trustees were appointed to replace the committee.

Another method of raising funds for ecclesiastical matters was called a Brief. This involved the circulation of an appeal approved by the Lord Chancellor, to all places of worship in other parishes, for Walden Church. Two Briefs were issued, the first raising £250, the second £160. In the appeal to the Lord Chancellor for the Brief, the Justices of Peace at the Quarter Sessions held in Chelmsford in January 1791, describe the church as:-

'a very ancient and spacious pile of Gothic Building, by length of time become so ruinous in many parts that the parishioners have not been able for some months past with safety to themselves to assemble therein for divine worship, in particular the south wall of the Nave of the Church, by the total decay of the Wall plates and Timbers under, is

so much out of an upright as to be in great danger of falling . . . the wall
of the South Aile is in great part so much out of an upright as to be
thought necessary to be taken down and rebuilt, and the Roofs of that
and the North Aile are also so much out of Repair as to be thought
necessary to be stripped and to have new timbers worked in; the Tower
Spire and Belfry are . . . in need of new timber, stone and other Work
to support them, . . . the covering of Lead over the whole Church must
be recast. . . . The Inhabitants are not able to raise the sum (£3,853 4s
9d) amongst themselves, being considerably burthened with a
numerous poor.' (45)

On Brettingham's recommendation a Mr. Richard Dyche, of Stretford
had been appointed as stone mason, but this proved to be a mistake. For
whatever reasons Dyche was not a good worker, and on several occasions
Brettingham had to report to the trustees that work was unsatisfactory.
By May 1792, Brettingham was reporting that the work was 'retarded and
neglected in a shameful and unreasonable manner' that the number of
masons had been reduced from six to two, and that fir had been used
instead of oak. Dyche was told that he would not be paid until the work
was properly done, and Brettingham who had recommended Dyche and
was therefore also under pressure from the trustees wrote the following
letter to Dyche:-

'Mr. Dyche, It is very extraordinary that you will not execute your
contract in a good and workmanlike manner, so as to give satisfaction
to your employers and bring credit to yourself. You will replace the
windows in the north Chancel with new, using such of the present
materials as may be found sound and good, and as to stuccoing the
outside of the Church you know as well as I do that it is all to be new,
not patch'd up with common mortar, but stucco'd by some able
Plaisterer, you are therefore to have this properly done or expose
yourself to the expence of doing it twice over, as I certainly shall not
consent to its bein left in incomplete manner.'

The complaints continued, but still the work was not carried out
satisfactorily. Eventually the trustees patience ran out, and they decided
to ask someone else to carry out the work, deducting the extra cost from
that already due to Dyche. Dyche promptly commenced proceedings
against Lord Howard (now treasurer to the Trustees), but Dyche died in
May, 1794. His widow continued the proceedings, eventually succeeding
in obtaining the full amount due. The work was completed by about the
end of the century.

Education

By the 18th century education had been provided in Walden for nearly
two hundred years, at Saffron Walden Grammar School, which had
started in 1525. But a number of people felt there was a need for a more
elementary education and over the years bequests were made for this

purpose. In 1715 the Saffron Walden Charity School was established. Various individuals gave about £40 per annum for the 'instruction of poor children to read and learn about the Church catechism'. In later years further sums of money were left – In 1717 Thomas Penning left £500 to the Mayor and Alderman, which was invested in lands at Steeple Bumpstead; In 1719 Charles Wale left an annual charge on some lands of £5 and later legacies included sums of £50, £100 and £200. There is no indication where the charity school met, although by 1836, pupils were being instructed by the teachers at the National School, which was in Castle Street.

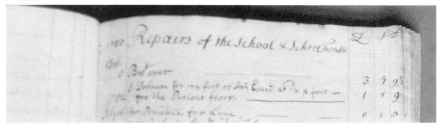

The Grammar School had its own problems during the 18th century. The master had been left a rent free house, plus 40 shillings a year to maintain the school and house. But as time wore on this sum became hopelessly inadequate. Indeed, William Kilborn, who was master in the early part of the 18th century was actually over £35 out of pocket by the time of his retirement in 1714. Kilborn, very generously, waived any claim on this sum. Inevitably the post became difficult to fill particularly as a condition of the post was that the applicant must be ordained. The school in fact had to close for a short while until consent was received from the Charity Commission to waive the condition.

Flooding

In 1792 Walden suffered a particularly severe flood. By the geographical location of the town situated in the floor of a valley, flooding was always a possibility, and in the early morning of July 21st the worst happened. A contemporary report of the flood appears in a newspaper called 'The Star' of 24th July 1792:-

'Saffron Walden, July 21st. This morning, about 1 o'clock the inhabitants of Walden were alarmed by a thunderstorm accompanied with a torrent of rain, which, overflowing the channel and rising to a height neverbefore remembered by any person in the town, made its way down the street filling the cellars and lower rooms of many of the houses in its progress sapping the foundations and carrying away part of the buildings and furniture with irresistable violence. At this moment the stresses of many, particularly the poor cottagers, were truly affecting. One poor women whose cries brought her neighbours to her assistance was taken from her chambers through a passage which they had fixed in her wall being the only means of escape. Several men pressed high in the wall and hazarded their lives by making a breach in the brick wall which resisted the current, but the immense body of water by its weight forced a passage in the lower situation of the wall of several yards in extent and had it not been for this fortunate circumstance the town would probably have exhibited a scene of distress and confusion not to have been described. This calamaty was chiefly if not solely occasioned by an obstruction of the common water course which the inhabitants had very indiscreetly suffered to exixt for many years. The damages cannot at present be precisely ascertained yet are computed at several thousand pounds.'

Following the flood, on 29th August, 1792 a subscription list was started. The appeal said:-

'The several necessitous Inhabitants of this Town, unable to bear the Loss and Distress brought on them by the late Uncommon Flood, after being called upon to make their real Sufferings known, have delivered in their respective Accounts therof, to an Amount of about one hundred & fifty pounds (exclusive of many other Sufferers who have delivered in no Accounts, amongst whom neverless some objects may be found deserving and standing in need of Assistance). A Subscription is therefore proposed to be set on foot to afford some Charitable Relief to those found to be in Distress and Want, under the above Calamity, in such a Manner as to a Committee, at some meeting to be appointed for that purpose & for Investigating the Case & State of each Sufferer, shall be thought right & proper.
N.B. Every Subscriber of One Guinea or more may be of the Committee or have Power to Name one.' (45)

Public unrest

Public unrest was evident in the town during the end of the 18th century, partly due to poor harvests, and agricultural depression, which affected the economy of the town.

The unrest first became evident in 1792, when Christopher Payn, a local bookseller started to sell Tom Paine's 'Rights of Man' which was viewed by the authorities as being seditious. Payn was also the tenant of the Corporation's shop adjoining the Town Hall, and after concern had been expressed to the Council, a public meeting was called by the Mayor and presided over by Lord Howard. The meeting resolved to form an Association for Suppressing Sedition in the town. A copy of the Resolution was signed at the Rose during the following six days by 87 persons.

Although it was intended to take proceedings against Christopher Payn, they were dropped as Payn fled for America.

But major trouble occurred in July 1795 when Walden suffered from probably its only ever riot. Two very poor harvests had resulted in a large rise in the price of bread. As a result a meeting of inhabitants of the town was held at the Rose and Crown on the 10th July 1795. There a number of people expressed their concern at the price of bread and resolved, themselves, to use 'a coarser sort of flour and as small a quantity as possible'.

However well intentioned that aim was, it did little to solve the problem. The chief difficulty was in actually obtaining any flour at all. Farmers were often reluctant to sell to towns since it would then be their own country areas which went short. In an attempt to persuade farmers to sell wheat in Walden, Lord Howard, as Lord of the Manor, offered to pay a premium of two Guineas a load to any farmer delivering wheat to the Mayor.

A committee was appointed by the Town Council, to purchase wheat and flour with monies raised by levies. The wheat and flour was then distributed to over 1000 people at a 1½d. per quartern below the going rate. However, within three weeks the subsidy had had to be raised to 4d. This caused Lord Howard, who was one of the main levy payers to write the following to the Town Clerk:-

'Dear Sir,
I am really uneasy at the measures propos'd for the Reasons assigned and from the Levies already made, if more are to be made, and it must, I am satisfied, create much Uneasiness.

It is our business to get a sufficient stock of wheat and flour in hand to supplie the whole Parish, but none but the Poor ought to be consider'd in its Price, let it be what it may. It would be far better in my Opinion, if necessary, to give a larger number of tickets for the reduc'd Prices of the Quartern Loaves.'

Whether or not the additional premium was successful is unknown. The Mayor, Henry Archer was authorised to buy corn for the Council, and succeeded in obtaining 50 Quarters from a Mr. Horner with a promise of a further 50 Quarters at a later date. The transaction was made through Horner's nephew, a boy called Andrews, but, perhaps due to the rapidly increasing price of corn, Horner cancelled the second order on the grounds that the Mayor had taken advantage of Andrews' youth and inexperience. Lord Howard was asked to attempt to use his influence to induce Horner to sell, but to no avail.

So serious attempts were being made by the authorities to try and feed the townsfolk. But despite these efforts, on Monday 27th July, 1795, rioters succeeded in seizing control of the town, and forcing the shopkeepers to sell food at less than the market price. The organiser and leader of the riots was Samuel Porter, a Cooper by trade. According to Rowntree (45):-

'Porter appears to have collected a crowd in the yard of the Greyhound Inn [at the junction of the High Street and George Street] and himself paid 10/- to supply them with drink, and passers-by had been forced by him and the mob to contribute more for the same purpose. They had then proceeded to climb the ladder leading to the Inn loft, where a

The High Street in the 1860s. Note the Greyhound pub in the bottom left hand corner.

quantity of corn was stored, and having cleared the chamber had carried the sacks off. They had then proceeded to the White Horse Inn, which they appeared to have used as their headquarters, whence parties were sent to various shops, from some of which they took corn, and at others used threats and force to obtain cheese and other food at less than the market price. At the White Horse Inn they had found a luckless carrier from a neighbouring village, and they had insisted that he and his waggon and horses should go with them to Mr. Horner's farm at Sampford, in order to fetch the 50 qrs. of wheat that he had refused to sell to the Mayor. However their attention had been distracted by the plan for raiding the shops, and the carrier had managed to get away.'

On Thursday 23rd July the Military arrived. Several of the rioters, including Porter were arrested, although they were later released on bail. The indictments against the rioters were for attacks on different tradesmen and were drawn up in similar terms. Thus six rioters . . . 'did go to the dwelling house and shop of one John Leverett, shopkeeper and Dealer in Cheese, . . . to compel him to promise that he would sell good cheese at four pence a pound . . . (they made an assault upon him) and did beat and wound and ill treat him so much that his life was greatly despaired of'.

Dispositions taken from various witnesses and reproduced in Rowntree (45) show the extent of the riots. Allegations include taking wheat from Thomas Gardiner and threatening to sell it at 5 shillings a bushel; of Robert Morgan a labourer demanding cheese from his master in 'a stern Manner'!!; and threatening to pull down the house of the Mayor, who was also a butcher.

Whilst there may have been some limited support for the rioters (perhaps witnessed by the ease with which they were able to obtain recognizances for bail), the brief for Counsel was less than sympathetic:-

'It seems necessary to observe that the poor inhabitants of Walden had less reason to complain of he hardships of the time than any of the neighbouring Parishes, and from the very liberal and extensive voluntary Contributions collected and subscribed for their relief, they ought in gratitude to have conducted themselves in a manner very different. The more opulent inhabitants of Walden, with the generous assistance of Lord Howard, have been remarked for the very liberal contributions subscribed annually for the relief of their poor. It has been the practice for several years to keep up a fund by subscription which has been expended in the purchase of coal and other fuel sold out in small quantities to the poor at a very reduced price, and in consequence of the very severe Season in the last year and the high price of bread and corn, these contributions were very largely increased . . . the monies from which were applied . . . to supply the poor with bread at 7d. a quartern loaf and flour at 6d. the Quarter of a Peck. . . .'

'As to the defendant Porter, he is a Cooper carrying on a very considerable business in that line and as a Carpenter and Joiner being possessed of a tolerable property for his situation. It is understood that he means to set up in his defence that his motive for joining the rioters was for the purpose only of fetching from a Mr. Horner, living at Sampford, . . . a large quantity of wheat 50qrs . . .bought by Mr. Henry Archer, the Mayor, for the supply of the parish. . . . But even admitting this to be a justification his Excuse could not avail him in this case, inasmuch as his conduct at Taylors (The Greyhound) is a positive denial of this assertion. The witnesses will declare it as their opinion that the conduct of Porter and others . . . greatly instigated and induced the rioters to conduct themselves in the riotous manner they did, and but for such encouragement and the effects of the Liquor given to them, no doubt is entertained but that the riot would have been very shortly quieted without much disturbance.'

The first cases were heard at the Lent Assizes of 1796. Five rioters, William Church, a bricklayer, Thomas Lord, Charles Ersewell, William Auger, the Younger and William Auger, the Elder were convicted at the Lent Assizes. They received sentences varying from 3 to 6 months imprisonment. At the summer assizes proceedings were taken against Porter. It is obvious that he was regarded as the ringleader. He was found guilty and sentenced to 'pay a fine of £50 and be imprisoned in the Common Gaol one year and until he pay the said fine and also enter into Recognizances with two sureties, himself in the sum of £500, and each surety £250, for his good behaviour for the space of seven years, to be computed from the end of the said one year and then discharged'. (45)

Industries

During the 18th century there is record of several industries. An Essex historian writing in The Gentleman magazine said of Walden that 'the poor are employed in the making of sacks, from whence most of the adjacent parishes are supplied.' The same magazine says that there was 'a manufacture for bolting clothes and for checks and fustians' and obviously cloth manufacturing was an important part of the local economy. Wool played a very large part in this, because of the easy source from local farms. The patron saint of wool-combers was St. Blaize and celebrations of his day, February 3rd, took place for many years. John Player writing in 1845, in his Sketches of Saffron Walden (34) says:-

'The days of Bishop Blaize are still remembered by old inhabitants. We believe the last procession was held in 1778; and, so important was the trade they [the wool-staplers] carried on to the good of the town, that the Mayor and Corporation formed part of the throng which annually proceeded beyond the bounds of the parish – to Newport and Littlebury, for instance – passing Audley End. The feathers, caps, etc., by which the staplers were distinguished were all formed of wool, dyed for the purpose. There was a large band of music, with a bishop, chaplains, shepherds, and shepherdesses. One of the latter carried a lamb in her lap. Orations were made at the places where the procession stopped; and, when it returned, a large party dined at the Rose Inn; the bells rang merrily; while the company that assembled on the occasion, from various parts, led to our informant's intimating that Walden never was fuller than on these days of public animation.'

Probably the most important industry was malting. Certainly by the middle of the 18th century Walden was known as the centre of the malting industry in Essex. There would have been other agricultural related industries – by the end of the century for example over 100 acres were planted with potatoes, and of course wheat and barley would have been extensively grown.

Saffron Walden Castle with the turret built in 1796.

Chapter 9
19th Century Walden – 1800-1850

During the Napoleonic Wars, (1792-1815) the town was undoubtedly aware of the very real risk of invasion. We know that in 1796 a small turret was added to the north-west corner of the castle mound. This is traditionally supposed to have been built as a signalling station in case of a Napoleonic invasion. The turret was built of flint around a core of red brick by Richard Ward, a local bricklayer. (54) Records exist of returns made of the number of waggons available to move troops if necessary, and millers and bakers were required to state their capability of producing enough bread to sustain an army in the field.(32)

In 1800 a local company of volunteers were formed against the possible need to defend the town, should invasion come. The country was ringed with a series of beacons. Should the invasion come the intention was to light them as a method of advance warning. However Lord Braybrooke was not impressed with the system, when it was tested saying:-

'I made and attended the largest beacon at Littlebury, and watched in my neighbourhood the corresponding one at Sewer's End, and notwithstanding a great flame and smoke, our beacon was not seen by our neighbours nor could we distinguish theirs.'

In 1803, with the fear of invasion at its height, the Walden volunteers, were moved to Chelmsford and became part of the 2nd Battalion of the 1st Essex Legion of Volunteers. We know from a plaque in the Parish Church, that the Major Commanding was Thomas Hall, who received his commission on 10th August 1803, the other Officers being Captain Martin Nockolds, Lieutenants William Robinson and Thomas Edwards, Ensigns James Searle and Samuel Fiske, and Surgeon Samuel Fiske. The following year, regular troops were stationed in the town and the volunteers took part in parades and inspections with them. In 1808 the volunteers were formed into a permanent Militia, its members being selected by ballot to receive annual training. (32) In 1887 the Colours were handed over to Major Herbert Taylor, the Officer commanding the Saffron Walden detachment ('I' Company) of the 3rd Cambs. Volunteer Battalion, Suffolk Regiment and placed in the Parish Church.

With the imprisonment of Napoleon at Elba in 1814, it was thought to be the end of the war, and so a massive party for 2,600 people was held on the Common. A contemporary account suggests that, among other sports, there were wrestling, running, carrying weights, balancing, and throwing a ball. Interestingly enough it was also about this time that the towns Cricket Club was founded, when, in 1812, the Gentlemen of Walden played the Gentlemen of Cambridge for a wager of 100 guineas, an enormous amount in those days. Sadly Walden lost both games! (32)

After the Napoleonic wars ended the country settled down to a period of steady prosperity and considerable change. Similar change occured in Walden in the 19th century – affecting its political structure, its population, its industrial and agricultural life, its communications, its size, and through all these, its relationships with the outside world.

As an example of this, the population figures show how the town doubled in size. A national census was first carried out in 1801, and has been held every ten years since then. Thus for the first time we can find an accurate record of Walden's population. It shows a steady rather than a spectacular growth. On two occasions there is actually a dip in the population, but the overall effect is one of sustained growth:-

1801	1821	1831	1841	1851	1861	1871	1881	1891	1901
3,181	3,403	4,154	4,762	5,111	5,911	5,474	5,718	6,060	5,914

The changes that occurred in the first half of the 19th century transformed many of the buildings to the state that we see them today – the Almshouses, the Market Square and the Parish Church are all good examples of these. In addition to this, educational buildings such as schools, the Library and the Museum began to appear, and major alterations were made to structures such as roads, and by the end of the century, pavements.

The almshouses

The almshouses were renovated and enlarged during the 19th century. Since 1694 the almshouses had been situated between what is now Park Lane and the Slade. Six of the tenements had become so dilapidated that in 1782, they had been pulled down and replaced. Unfortunately they faced north, were sunless and provided inadequate accommodation. By 1811, the Trustees felt that the only solution to the difficulties, would be to build a new building on the Almhouse Meadow to the north of the Slade. As this was crossed by a path, an order was obtained to close this in 1818. However work seemed to have proceeded extremely slowly because it was not until 1828, that plans were drawn up. These consisted of a large south facing block, comprising of a chapel and seperate rooms for the inmates. It was also necessary to culvert the Slade, and this work was completed in 1832, with further parts of the Slade being enclosed in 1840. The almshouse block was completed in 1834. In 1840 an eastern wing was added at the expense of Wyatt George Gibson and his family, and the block at the western end was added in 1881 by George Stacey Gibson. Additional almshouses were provided in Park Lane, also by Wyatt George Gibson in 1847.

Other building work was also progressing in Abbey Lane. In 1811 the Congregational Church was built and the Gibsons provided additional housing, the Gibson Free Dwellings in Abbey Lane between 1840 and 1850.

These dwellings were originally provided for former employees of the Gibson family, but were later given to the almshouse trustees.

The Market Square

Redevelopment in the Market Square was partly caused by the unpopularity of the gaol. The gaol had caused difficulties virtually since its erection in 1761. It had windows facing on to the public road and there were often reports of passers-by being spat on. As a result a public subscription was called, and succeeded in raising £400. A public meeting was called on 24th August, 1818, to discuss how these monies were to be spent in improving the market place in general. At this time the Market Cross, which stood in the north east corner of the Market Place and had been used as a central point for the stocks, pillory and whipping post, was in a very poor condition. It had to be supported by scaffold poles and was considered to be unsafe.

The meeting agreed to both the demolition of the Market Cross and the erection of a new gaol at the top of the High Street adjacent to the Workhouse. Demolition of the Market Cross also had the advantage that it would make more space available for the weekly horse and cattle market. The stocks were later moved to the junction of Castle Street and Museum Street.

Adjoining the Market Square in the north east corner was the house of John Emson (now the Midland Bank). Emson (later to be a Mayor) was concerned at the dangers and inconvenience to both him and his neighbours and tenants caused by the market. This complaint led to the Council considering an alternative site to the Market Square for the cattle market. In 1831, the Council decided to acquire the Eight Bells Inn in Hill Street, opposite its junction with Market Street and demolished the building to provide a new market for the horses and cattle and to prevent them roaming in the Market Square. The site cost £1,300, £625 of which was raised by subscription, the remainder coming by loan. An archway to record this event can still be seen today, incorporated in the redevelopment of this area in the 1980's.

Later during the 19th century a new site was purchased for the sale of cattle. This site, which was to remain the cattle market site until its closure in 1983, was the site of the old Bell Inn in Market Street, opposite the Town Hall.

The Market Square also contained the malt mill purchased by the town in 1618. In 1834 the Council decided to sell it to John Emson. It stood on the north side of the square, and Emson used it for warehousing and stables. Later it became Emson Tanners offices and today if forms part of Emson Close and the former Gayhomes shop.

On the west side of the Market Square stood a magnificent timber framed building. It was originally used as a medieval wool hall and later as a series of shops, which may have contained residences. Old prints of the building show differing uses. Sadly, perhaps, it was pulled down in 1844 to be replaced by the Corn Exchange. This building was designed by Robert Tress in an Italianate style, the work being commissioned in 1847 and the building opening in 1850.

According to Rowntree (45) the market place would have presented a

The building which used to stand on the site of the Corn Exchange and was demolished in 1844.

rural aspect. Several houses had gardens facing onto the square, as well as gardens around the malt mill and adjoining the building replaced by the Corn Exchange.

The other building erected from the public subscription in 1818, however, the new gaol, proved an unsatisfactory location. The Courts were held in the Town Hall, and the transporting of prisoners from the gaol in the High Street was inconvenient. In August 1836, following a visit from a representative of the Secretary of State, the Council were informed that they would only be allowed to retain the Quarter Sessions if a more convenient lock-up could be provided. The only suitable site was a building at the rear of the Town Hall. This house was owned by Mr. Henry Butterfield, who agreed to sell it to the Council. Tenders were invited for the work of converting the house to a lock up, and that of Mr. William Ward, amounting to £230, was accepted. It was decided to join the property to the Town Hall by enclosing the part of the lane between the two properties. This involved stopping up the lane and an order for this was granted at the Quarter Sessions at Chelmsford on the grounds that the lane was 'entirely useless to the public and a nuisance to the owners and occupiers of property near'. (Other owners later followed suit, but the route of this small lane can still be seen adjacent to the backdoor of 1, Market Place.)

However work had hardly began, when, legal difficulties were encountered in obtaining the stopping up order. It was therefore decided to investigate the possibility of acquiring another adjacent property, and it was realised that this was a more feasible scheme. The new lock up adjoining the Town Hall was eventually completed in 1841.

The Parish Church

Significant alterations were made to the Parish Church during the 19th century, particularly during the period between 1820 and 1840. In 1822 Thomas Frye, a Churchwarden, wrote to John Vincent a famous organ builder, concerning the possibility of building a new church organ. Vincent submitted a quote of £497, although advice taken by the churchwardens suggested that this should not be accepted as it was not believed that the work could be carried out that cheaply. Despite this the churchwardens decided to proceed.

A public subscription was called and succeeded in raising just over £500, the major contribution being that of £100 from Lord Braybrooke. However the advice proved correct and Vincent submitted a bill for £800. A second subscription only raised the total to £567. Whether Vincent received the balance is unknown. One item of interest concerning the organ, was that John Thomas Frye, the son of Thomas Frye, the churchwarden who started the appeal was to become the church organist for over 60 years, first performing in the church at the age of 12 in 1824, and not retiring until 1884. On his retirement it was decided to rebuild the organ at a cost of £1,147. The work was completed in 1885. Further work was subsequently carried out on the organ in 1911, 1948, and 1971.

St Mary's Parish Church in 1784.

At the same time that the organ was being installed, a clock was installed in the church tower. The clock, which cost £240 was provided by Messrs. Thwaites and Reed.

But the major alteration to the Church was the building of the Church spire. By 1831, the tower was in a dangerous condition. Where the spire now stands there was a lead covered timber lantern and it was decided that in the rebuilding this should be replaced. The architect selected to design the spire was Thomas Rickman, one of the countries leading experts on Gothic architecture. Rickman had in fact served his apprenticeship, as a grocer, in Walden with Richard Day. However on completion of his apprenticeship, he had joined his fathers firm of architects. A fund was established for the erection of the spire, two of the largest contributors being Lord Braybrooke and the Bishop of London.

Work was also carried out at this time on the churchyard. In 1820, railings were installed around the churchyard, along with 29 oak posts. In 1823, entrance gates were added to the south side. But more extensive work was needed on the east side of the churchyard. Here stood a house occupied by Thomas Bunting. It was located approximately where the present entrance to the churchyard from Museum Street is now. As the graveyard to the north, west and south sides of the church was now full, the Churchwardens were anxious to acquire the house and its gardens. An appeal raised £335 and the house and garden were purchased from Lord Braybrooke, the landlord. The proposal was to demolish the house, level the ground, and remove the wall separating the garden from the churchyard. A new wall was built along what is now the boundary with Museum Street.

Bunting's house – now the junction of the churchyard and Museum Street.

Schools

Although the 19th century was to see education made statutory, schools already existed in Walden. The Grammar School had been founded in 1525, and in 1881 moved into new buildings in Ashdon Road.In 1715 the Saffron Walden Charity School started after individuals provided sub-scriptions and by the 1830's 12 boys and 12 girls were being educated at this school. This was absorbed into the National School which was founded in Castle Street in 1815 and initially charged a penny a week to educate poorer children. An infants department was later opened in Museum Street where the building still exists today. In 1891 following a Government grant, the National School became free to all residents and was renamed Castle Street School, eventually becoming St Marys C of E School by which name it is known today.

In 1838, the British and Foreign School Society opened schools for both boys and girls. The boys' school was in East Street and the girls' school along with an infants department in South Road. Both buildings still exist; the boys' school having recently been converted into offices, and the girls' school being incorporated into the College. Saffron Walden College was also started by the British and Foreign Schools Society on land donated by George Stacey Gibson in 1884. To complete the education picture the Friends' School was opened in 1879 following its move from Croydon.(45)

The town library (the Literary and Scientific Institute)

The Literary and Scientific Institute started in 1832, and was founded by three men, John Player, Jabez Gibson and his brother Francis Gibson.

Originally there was some opposition to the Institute as universal education was not always regarded as a good thing, but encouragement from Lord Braybrooke helped to get the Institute off the ground. At first

The town's Literary and Scientific Institute in King Street.

meetings, in the form of serious lectures, were held in a room lent by Jabez Gibson, but as the Institute expanded they started buying books and it soon became obvious that a new meeting place and a more permanent library would become required. With the help of George Stacey Gibson, in the middle of the 19th Century, the Institute acquired the building adjoining the Corn Exchange in King Street, which still houses the collection today.

George Stacey Gibson was later to present his own collection of Natural History books to the Library and to help to make the building the centre of Walden's cultural life during the 19th century. It was fitting that when, in 1971, the Borough Council offered the Corn Exchange for sale, an agreement was reached with the County Council which enabled the Literary and Scientific Institute to be merged with the modern County Library. (32)

The museum

The early history of the museum is best described from this short article in the Saffron Walden Almanac of 1893:-

> 'This institution which is supported by voluntary subscriptions and a small endowment by the late Mr. G. S. Gibson, is an offshoot of a Mental Improvement Society, established in the town in the year 1832; among the members of which were several zealous supporters of science, foremost among them being Jabez Gibson, Esq. These gentlemen formed themselves into a trust and took the museum under their especial care, which soon out-grew its assigned limits, viz. a cottage in the centre of the town, when by the advice of Lord Braybrooke it was removed to its present site, at first occupying a portion only of the building, the remaining part being used for municipal gatherings etc. Ultimately more accommodation was required for the purpose of an Agricultural Society when the large room was added to the building, and for a long time it went under the name of the 'Agricultural Hall'. In this building the elite of the neighbourhood periodically met, at the time of their shows, held under the patronage and presidency of Lord Braybrooke. After a time this Society ramified over the County, hence originated the 'Essex Agricultural Society'. During this period the collection was housed in the upper part of this building, and the lower part continued to be occupied and took the place of a Town Hall until 1879 . . . (George Stacey Gibson) . . . with the assistance of many of the inhabitants of the town added considerably to the collection, and undertook its distribution over the whole of the building.'

The museum's early collection had a close link with an exile of the town, Robert Dunn. Robert had a son, John, who became known as the White Zulu Chief. From 1895, when John Dunn's death was reported in the Pall Mall Gazette, and until recently it was thought he had been born in Saffron Walden. However research carried out by Alastair Walters, Mayor of Saffron Walden in 1987, shows that this was incorrect.

The Saffron Walden Agricultural Hall, about 1900. Now used as the town's Museum.

Robert Dunn was born in Ware in 1795, but spent most of his formative years in Walden. In 1820 he moved to Algoa Bay in South Africa, where he married and had five children, one of them being John. Robert's brother was Hannibal Dunn, Mayor of the town in 1843, and at Hannibal's request, and spurred on by Jabez Gibson, Robert, who traded in ivory, sent many stuffed animals to Walden Museum. Robert was trampled to death by an elephant in 1847

John went on to befriend Cetshwayo, the last great King of the Zulus, who gave him a large track of land with the full rights of a chieftain. John Dunn died in 1895 at the age of 61 and left 49 recorded wives and 117 children!

The incorrect statement made in the past that John, the White Zulu Chief was born in Walden, almost certainly occurred because his Uncle, Hannibal, also had a son called John, who was born in Walden.

During the first half of the 19th century Central Government legislation began to have a significant effect on many institutions in Walden. Enclosure awards, Highway Acts, the Workhouse, Police and even the structure of Local Government were all affected. It is worth looking at all of these to see their effect on the town.

Various stuffed animals on display in the Museum in the 1900s.

The Saffron Walden Enclosure Act, 1812

In 1812 Saffron Walden received its own enclosure act. During the 16th, 17th and 18th centuries fields were usually farmed on a strip system. Each farmer would have a number of strips of land. The purpose of this was to ensure that each farmer received a fair share of both good and bad land. However this practice was very wasteful of land as clear divisions between strips had to be maintained, and this and the new improved farming methods being introduced by the agricultural revolution meant a new system of allocating land in enclosed fields was necessary. Enclosure was the name given to this practice and from about 1750 numerous private local enclosure acts were passed by Parliament. In 1801 a General Enclosure Act was passed establishing a framework for local acts, and on 9th June 1812 an "Act for Inclosing Lands in Saffron Walden, in the County of Essex" received the Royal Assent.

The act appointed Martin Nockolds of Tring in Hertfordshire, and Anthony Jackson of Barkway in Hertfordshire to act as Commissioners. It was their duty to visit the town, hear all claims for both land and rights in the land, and re-allocate the fields according to those claims. John King of Saffron Walden was appointed the surveyor, and it was his responsibility to ensure the fields were accurately surveyed. The act specifically excluded the Common from the enclosure. The act also gave the Commissioners powers to divert roads and award herbage (the right to pasture); and to make new drains. Special provision was made for the Lord of the Manor, Lord Braybrooke, to ensure that he received at least one twentieth of the waste lands. Once the decisions had been made the Commissioners made the award which became law on 30th June 1823. A copy of the award and another survey carried out by John King in 1825, still survive in the Town Council archives.

Opening page of the Saffron Walden Enclosure Act 1812.

The Fly, the Walden to London coach entering the town, 1832.

Transport, roads and the workhouse

The reforming legislation of this time also placed obligations on the parish to provide adequate roads as well as improving the poor law system designed, ostensibly, to provide shelter and accommodation for those falling on hard times. In fact the two were often combined, for the threat of the workhouse was often enough to ensure a cheap supply of labour for the roads.

The road system in Walden at the start of the 19th century was fairly embryonic, and etchings of the time show that the High Street in particular was well worn because of continual use and little substantial maintenance. By the 1820's there was considerable unemployment in the area and the Parish looked around for jobs to be done. They decided to reduce the steep hill into Walden from Sparrows End Hill and as a result the cutting between Gallows Hill and Beeches Close was made. Other work was also undertaken on Little Walden Road and the High Street. Gallows Hill had proved a particular difficulty for 'The Fly' the daily coach from the George and Blue Boar Inns in Holborn to the Red Lion in Cambridge which provided Walden with its solitary form of public transport.(32)

Lord Braybrooke was very concerned at the high level of unemployment, and had recently become aware of a number of 'Cottage allotments' being provided by other Poor Law authorities. He had visited Waterbeach in Cambridgeshire and seen the system in action and felt that the provision of such allotments had a number of advantages. In conjunction with other notables of the town he called a public meeting on Thursday 17th December, 1829 'for the purpose of taking into consideration the State of the Parish, arising from the great number of labourers then out of employ, and of determining upon them the expediency of engaging them in spade-husbandry'. (44)

The meeting, which was chaired by Lord Braybrooke passed the following resolutions:-

'1. That in consequence of the great increase in the number of labourers belonging to this parish who are destitute of work (the number at present in the roads being more than one hundred and thirty, or nearly double the number so occupied twelve months since), it is expedient to adopt all practicable means of giving them employment.

2. That after apportioning an adequate number to complete improvements in the roads, and to keep the highways in the best possible order, it is very desirable that the remaining labourers should be so employed as to give some return for the increasing expenditure on their account.

3. That a system of spade-husbandry has been introduced into some parishes, . . . and . . . it . . . appears . . . the labourer . . . would be enabled to earn, by persevering labour, an adequate sum for the support of his family, instead of wasting his energies upon unprofitable work, and of engaging demoralizing associations with the men of idle habits who are of necessity sent for occupation into the public roads.

4. That the men to be selected for spade-husbandry ought to be those who are competent to manual labour of this description, who have the best character for industry . . . and who have the largest families to maintain.' (44)

Other resolutions established a management committee and permitted the parish to hire up to 20 acres of land for allotments. The aims were certainly plausible, although not entirely altruistic, for the cost of the poor fell directly on the parish, and in turn on the largest landowners. The moralizing may well have had as much to do with this, as the desire to prevent the labourer wasting his time 'upon unprofitable work'!

The committee were able to report the following year that the project had been very successful. Using their powers under an 1819 Act of Parliament, a public notice was issued inviting applications from people who might wish to have their land dug in lieu of ploughing, and also advertising that the committee were willing to hire 20 acres of land. Sixteen landowners together offered 52 acres which were then dug by the parochial labourers. This was so successful, that not only was the labourer able to earn more than on the roads, but the parish also made a profit from that which it charged the landowner! Additionally the committee gave itself power to hire land. The land which was hired for this purpose was a field of four and a half acres, owned by Messers. Gibson, in Little Walden Road. This was hired at £2 per acre. A number of regulations were drawn up, and applications for plots were then invited. Eighty five people applied, but there were only 22 allotments, so preference was given to those living nearest, the largest portions being given to those poor men who had the largest families. Other fields were later hired from Lord Braybrooke, one between Audley End Park and the town, and another called Parkwall Field. Another 38 allotments were provided on these fields. Finally the Gibsons offered another field, Raily Field and 11 more allotments were provided here. The report showed that all rents had been paid in time, and that the fields had proved very productive. Prizes were awarded by the Horticultural Society, and the committee were able to report:-

'With respect to the apparently improved habits of the poorer classes, and the decrease of idlers in the streets of Walden during the last year, the Committee confidently appeal to the testimony of many of the inhabitants; and they learn from the same source, that the town has been, throughout the summer, supplied with vegetables from the allotments, in greater variety, and at a reduction of one half in price as compared in former years.' (44)

Of course the alternative to work on the roads or the field at a time of high unemployment was the workhouse. For many years the workhouse in Walden was situated at the top of the High Street opposite what is now the War Memorial. A hated institution, nonetheless it did at least offer food and shelter to the poor and needy.

However shortly before Christmas Day, 1835 a serious fire broke out. Initially it threatened to spread to the adjoining town gaol and nearby houses, 'but through the exertions of a large portion of the respectable inhabitants, it was, in about an hour and a half, got under after destroying the buildings in which it originated.' The 'lower classes' apparently were meanwhile enjoying the sight of this despised building burning and there were reports of shouts of 'Let it burn, it cannot be at a better place', 'No Poor Laws' and 'Put it out yourselves'. A £100 reward was offered by County Fire Office, the insurers, who believed it to have been arson, but there is no record as to whether this was paid out or the perpetrators caught. (26)

In 1834 Parliament passed the Poor Law Amendment Act which regularised the position of the poor law and the workhouse. This act was much harsher than the previous systems of poor relief tending to regard pauperism as a moral failing. Whereas the so called Speenhamland system of relief had made allowances to workers earning below a subsistence level the new law provided no relief for the able bodied poor except the workhouse. To meet the requirements of the act, a Saffron Walden Union was formed comprising of 24 local parishes under a Board of Guardians. Their role was to administer the Poor Relief within their union according to laid down rules. The first meeting of the Guardians took place at the Rose and Crown on 13th April, 1835. A requirement of the act was the provision of a suitable workhouse and so the first problem the Guardians had to face was the erection of a new building. Land was

The 1835 workhouse – now Radwinter Road Hospital.

acquired on a lease from Lord Braybrooke, in Radwinter Road, plans were drawn up with money lent by Wyatt George Gibson and the new workhouse was built during 1835-1836. The buildings now form part of the Radwinter Road Hospital. The workhouse was three storeys high and built on a cruciform plan. Rooms and exercise yards were split in accordance with the categories into which the inmates had to be divided. The building was later altered in 1841 and 1848, by which time it held about 400 inmates. The workhouse operated under a very strict regime. No visitors were allowed or excursions out without permission; attendance at a church service was compulsory on Sundays; uniform had to be worn; a spartan diet was provided, and work on such jobs as oakum picking, sack making and stone breaking was compulsory. Refusal to work led either to expulsion or confinement on bread and water. (30) The minutes of the Board of Guardians which reveal much of the detail of life in the workhouse are available at the Essex Record Office.

In 1835, further new legislation, the Municipal Corporations Act, created major changes in the local government structure of the country. Following concern at increasing corruption in both central and local government reforms were undertaken to the structures of these institutions. Parliamentary representation was made much fairer with the passing of the Reform Act of 1832 which had swept away numerous 'Rotten' boroughs.

Parliament now turned its attention to local government. Most boroughs, like Walden relied on charters for their powers – in Walden's case, that of William and Mary of 1694. At this time, Walden Corporation consisted of from four to eight members plus the Town Clerk who was allowed to vote at meetings. The Corporation appeared to meet at irregular intervals whenever there was something to discuss, and at various locations, including the Town Hall, the Rose and Crown, and the almshouses.

Many corporations were liable to considerable manipulation and even corruption. Aldermen were appointed for life, and vacancies would be filled by co-option. This meant that boroughs would often become run by one or two powerful families. In addition membership was restricted only to adherents of the established church under an act of 1673. To prove membership of the Church any potential member of the Corporation had to produce a sacrament certificate, signed by the vicar, churchwarden and one other member of the congregation, and numerous examples of these survive in the Town Council archives. Unfortunately this meant that notable figures of the town, such as the Gibsons and John Player, were ineligible for the Council. This led to a movement towards reform.

The Whig government of the day established a commission to investigate the existing Borough Corporations, of which there were 178, including Saffron Walden. The commission were empowered to make local enquiries and it must have arrived in Walden in late 1833 or early 1834. A Corporation meeting was called on 10th January 1834, 'for the purpose of discussing the propriety of the Corporation submitting to the

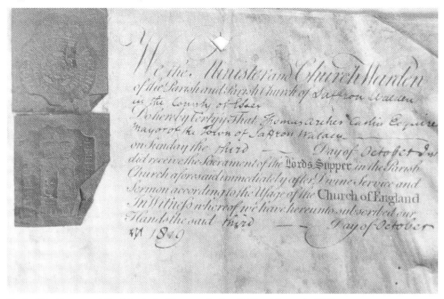

Part of the Sacrament Certificate for Thomas Archer Catlin, Mayor in 1819.

inquiry of the Municipal Corporation Committee'. Walden's answer to the commission was quite remarkable – it stated that it considered the commission illegal and unconstitutional. This was probably a political decision for the commission was established by a Whig parliament while Walden was Tory ruled. Unfortunatly the reasons for this statement were not given and one would like to ask on what basis the commission was considered illegal. However the corporation, having made such a controversial statement, tempered this by stating:-

'That at the same time associated with severential attachments to the King, unwilling to be deficient in proper respect towards functionaries acting in the Sovereign name and above all unconcious of having either in a corporate or magisterial capacity done any act calculated to prejudice the interests of the town or to bring discredit on themselves as a body, order the Town Clerk to give the fullest information for which the Commissioners may think fit to call.'

The commission reported back to Parliament in late 1834 and by June 1835, the Municipal Corporation Bill was before Parliament. On 17th June, Saffron Walden Corporation met and a letter was read from the Town Clerk of Berwick on Tweed, a borough in a similar position as Walden. Berwick wished to know if Walden, amongst other towns, would join their deputation to the House of Commons to oppose the bill. Bearing in mind the time it would have taken a deputation to travel from Berwick to London it perhaps gives some indication of the strength against the bill.

However despite these protests, mainly from the Tory controlled boroughs, the Commons, in Whig control since the Reform Act, passed the bill and it went on to the Lords. The commission had suggested that there was considerable corruption amongst the boroughs, and although there undoubtedly was some corruption, it certainly could not have been levied at Walden Corporation. On 5th August 1835, The Corporation met at the almshouses to consider a letter from the deputation now in London. The deputation urged Walden to petition the Tory con-trolled House of Lords. The Corporation had little hesitation in agreeing, for:-

'. . . having undergone the fullest examination by the Municipal Commission (there was) no instance of any violation of the trusts committed to their charge.'

But their actions failed, and on the 11th September 1835 the bill became law. Saffron Walden Corporation was wound up, and Saffron Walden Borough Council created, a body which was to continue until 1974. The act removed all religious disqualifications, extended the franchise to ratepaying householders, and placed Council meetings on a regular basis. Walden Council was to consist of four Alderman and twelve Councillors. At the elections held later in 1835 nine of the sixteen members returned were non conformists, and one of them, John Player was unanimously chosen as Mayor.

The new Council decided to petition the King, William IV to keep the towns Quarter Sessions and on 3rd June, 1836 the town received Letters Patent from the Crown, granting the Mayor, Aldermen and Burgesses the right to hold the Court of Quarter Sessions. Just one year later, William IV died, and Queen Victoria took the throne. The new Queen was proclaimed in Walden on 26th June, 1837. The Guild of Holy Trinity Accounts Book, 1652-1835 (28) has a record of the official proclamation. A procession was lined up outside the Town Hall comprising of trumpeters on horseback, followed by the Chief Constable also on horseback; Constables on foot; Union Jacks; the band; the Beadle; and then, the Town Clerk, the Vicar, the Mace Bearer, the Mayor, magistrates, Aldermen, Councillors, the Treasurer, the Auditors and the assessors, all on horseback, and finally the 'Burgesses and Inhabitants on Horseback four abreast'.

The procession went from the Town Hall through Hill Street to Gold Street, High Street, Castle Street, Church Street, High Street and back to King Street and the Town Hall. The proclamation was made in various locations:- first at the Town Hall; then on 'Workhouse Hill' (i.e. the southern end of the High Street near the present day war memorial); then on 'Brewhouse Hill' (i.e. adjacent to the present day Raynhams in the High Street); then in the middle of Castle Street; then on 'Sun-Hill'; and finally at the corner of King Street and High Street. (28)

Following the funeral of the past King, when the market was held on the Friday to avoid clashing with the date of the funeral, the Council sent the following loyal address to the new Queen:-

'To the Queen's most excellent Majesty;
Most Gracious Sovereign,
We your majesty's dutiful and loyal subjects, the Mayor, Aldermen and Burgesses of the Borough of Saffron Walden beg leave to address your Royal Person with expressions of condolence on the bereavement which the Nation has sustained in the Decease of your Royal Predecessor whose Virtues are gracefully remembered and whose main object we must ever feel was to promote the welfare and and happiness of all and every part of his dominions.

We at the same time presume to offer our congratulations upon your Majesty's ascending the British Throne with the warmest expression of our loyalty to your Majesty as well as sincere attachment to the Constitution of this highly favoured Country.

May it please that Divine providence which enabled our deceased and beloved Monarch to preserve peace during his reign and rendered his Merciful and benign rule prosperous and revered to grant to your Majesty long life, health and Happiness and that high satisfaction which cannot fail to be derived by a noble and generous mind while living in the affection of a free and united people.'

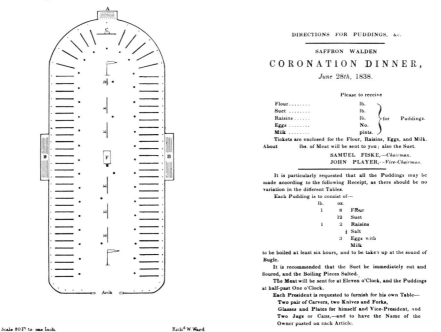

A plan of the tables used on the common with directions for the puddings to be used at the 1838 coronation celebrations.

Walden celebrated in the coronation in style. A festival was held on the Common on the 28th June, 1838, the day of the coronation. A report in the Walden Weekly of 25th June, 1897, gives an account of the celebrations as recalled by a resident at the time, Mr. William Lagden:-

'By the 11th June, the estimated amount was raised and a further guarantee assured. It was resolved to have dinner on the Common and here a space was set apart, the length of ground occupied for the dinner being 490 feet, exclusive of booths, and 198 feet. There was a marquee and galleries for ladies, a stewards table, and four tables for ringers, band, tapsters assistants and orchestra. There were also 70 tables each 33 feet long and these were arranged in the form of a horseshoe. Nearly 4,000 sat down to dinner, the meal costing £334 11s. and 10d. The dinners were sent to about 100 infirm people. The articles used included 250 stones and 2lbs of meat, 35 stone and 4lbs. of suet, 16 bushels of flour, 695 lbs of raisins, 1,808 eggs, 959 yards of table cloths, 66 yards 3 inches of pudding cloth, a bag of salt, 3,800 loaves and rolls, 1163 gallons, one quart of beer, 18lbs of tobacco, and six and a quarter gross of pipes. The cooking was undertaken by 74 ladies to whom the articles were sent. It was a beautiful day and the arrangements were carried out with success. Thousands of persons visited the Common to watch the proceedings. There was an abundance of food left and this was distributed in the town the next morning.'

It must have been some party for the towns population was then only about 4,500!

When the Queen married Prince Albert on 10th February, 1840, the Mayor and Council 'With many of the Respectable Inhabitants' dined at the Rose and Crown 'In a most harmonious manner'. Following this the Council again made a loyal address and on this occasion the Mayor, Samuel Fiske, along with Alderman Player and Councillor Thurgood were permitted to present the address personally to the Queen. According to the Guild Accounts Book (28) they 'were most graciously received and had each the honor (sic) of kissing Her Majesty's hand'.

Similar loyal addresses were made on the occasion of the birth of the Princess Royal in 1840, the birth of the Prince of Wales in 1841, and the Queen's 'Providential escape from the hand of the Assassin' in 1842.

The address made to the Queen at the time of the birth of the Prince of Wales is particularly interesting as it was again presented personally to the Queen and presents a fascinating insight into Court life of this time. The Mayor of the time, John Emson had obtained permission to attend at the Palace with Councillors Thomas Spurgin and Charles Baron, and he recorded in the Guild Accounts Book (28) the events of the day:-

'Being set down at the Palace at about a quarter past one on the 13th of April, 1842 we proceeded through the Entrance Halls to the Grand Staircase, passing Groups of Military Officers, amongst whom we noticed the Marquess of Salisbury, Quintin Dick Esquire, M.P. and others unknown to our party. A second series of rooms lined with

Yeoman of the Guard were passed till the great waiting room was reached where we waited some little time seeing in succession arrive a great number of officers, Clergymen and others in great variety of Costume forming a splendid scene. Soon after two o'clock a general movement announced the ceremony of presentation had begun and in a short time we found ourselves passing along into a second room from which we could see the Throne room and in a few minutes more we were ushered into the presence of Her Majesty who honoured the party by presenting her hand to receive the customary salute. This finished, the party retired in due order, to give way to numbers behind them, pleased with the grandeur of the scene we had left and the kind manner of the Queen herself. Professor Whewell, the Lord Chief Justice of Scotland and the Duke of Wellington were almost the only other persons pointed out to us. The day closed by most of us partaking of the Hospitality of the Recorder of this Borough, N. Knox Esquire in the shape of a handsome dinner provided on the occasion by him.'

A similar loyal address was also made personally to Prince Albert.

Two important Walden institutions were founded in 1838, the Boys' British School and the Saffron Walden Provident and Friendly Institution. The creation of the Boys British School followed a meeting held in the Town Hall on the 26th July 1838 attended by John Player, Nathaniel Catlin, C.B.Wilkins, Wyatt George Gibson, Rev. Luke Foster, George Youngman, Thomas Spurgin, William Burrows, James Starling, William Chater, John S. Robson, George Stacey Gibson and Francis Gibson. Those present felt that the town needed better educational facilities than presently existed, and in particular, better education for the poorer classes. As a result they passed the following resolution:-

'That whilst this meeting is deeply sensible of the value of the laudable exertions of those gentlemen who have hitherto devoted their time to the cause of education in conducting the various schools now in operation in the town, it is nevertheless of opinion that additional provision for the instruction of the poorer classes is highly desirable and that it is expedient to establish a school on the British system.'

This referred to the British and Foreign School Society who were encouraging the formation of schools throughout the country. The school was to be open to children of parents of all religious denominations, and the school age was fixed at 7 (later reduced to 6) to 14. Parents had to pay 2d a week for each boy. The school was immediately given a building in East Street by the Gibsons, and William Jenkins was appointed the first headmaster at a salary of £60 per year. He had previously ran a small private school at the bottom of Gold Street. The school proved extremely popular and by the end of its first year it had 106 pupils.

The School carried before it an excellent reputation and when inspected in 1867 by Matthew Arnold he said of it:-

'. . . the boys in this school, much more than in most schools I inspect, appear to belong to what is really meant by the working class. The school is really full . . . and the discipline is excellent. Nearly the whole average attendance are presented for examination, 36 per cent of them in paper work. The papers are worked in fair style, but there is still room for improvement in this particular. The rate of failure has again fallen, and is now 12½ percent.'

The Boys' British together with Castle Street School continued throughout the 19th and early 20th century to be the major source of education for the boys of the town.

The Saffron Walden Provident and Friendly Institution was formed in February 1838 at a public meeting in the Town Hall. Following a proposal by John Player it was agreed that:-

'it is expedient and would be highly beneficial to establish for this town and its vicinity, and upon the most approved principles, a Provident and Friendly Institution to embrace the following objects, namely the relief and maintenance of members, their wives and children, in sickness and advanced age.'

Following an appeal a subscription list raised £121 and Wyatt George Gibson was appointed treasurer. By 1841 there were total funds of £231, and by 1846, membership stood at 60 honorary members and 273 ordinary members.

In 1850 insurance against sickness was extended to the age of 65. All meetings of the Society were held in the Town Hall, and in its early days the Society had several members of the medical profession acting in a consultancy capacity. The Provident and Friendly Institution acted as a form of insurance, but savers were offered another way of investing money, that of the Building Society. Such institutions were springing up throughout the country during the middle of the 19th Century, and Walden was to be no exception. In 1847 a Building Society was formed in the town. Often these societies only existed until their aims of developing a particular area of land were achieved. It is not known what happened to the Society formed in 1847, but two years later, the Saffron Walden Second Building Society was formed, initially operating from a solicitors office in Lime Tree Passage. In 1857 it took the grandiose name of the Saffron Walden Second Benefit Building and Investment Society on the Permanent Plan, and continued to grow rapidly. By 1900, what is now, the Saffron Walden Herts and Essex Building Society had assets of £37,000 and today these have increased to a figure in excess of £170 million.

The necessity for a police force in the town was becoming evident in the early 19th century. Probably the nearest Walden had to a police force, before the 1830's was the 'Saffron Walden Association for the Detection and Prosecution of Persons Guilty of Felonies and Misdemeanours within the same Parish.' According to its rule book, the aim of the association was:-

'. . . the speedy apprehension and effectual prosecution of felons and thieves of every denomination, and of other persons committing offences on the person or properties of members.'

The association must have been limited to the wealthy, for membership entailed an annual subscription of £1, a very large sum in those times, and a dinner at the Rose and Crown followed each meeting of the society.

A scale of rewards were offered as follows:-

'Setting fire to any house, stable, stack or other property, £10
Burglary or housebreaking, £10
Stealing, killing, maiming any horse, cattle, sheep, swine etc. £5
Stealing in a dwelling house, warehouse, shop, or for embezzlement, £3
Stealing or injuring fruit, vegetables, trees in any orchard or garden, £2.'

For minor offences, such as receiving stolen goods, false pretences, and damaging property, the reward was £1, but there was also a rule,'that no allowance from the funds shall be allowed for prosecutions under the Game Laws'.

Whether the association was effective is not known, although in 1827 two men were sentenced to hang at Chelmsford Prison for highway robbery at Walden. (32)

Exactly when a Police Force came to Walden is unknown. Sir Robert Peel succeeded in introducing legislation for an organised Police Force in 1829, but the earliest record of a force in Walden was in 1848.

In 1849 the town's Chief Constable, William Campling was murdered almost certainly by Benjamin Pettit, although at Pettit's trial he was found not guilty. According to the prosecution witnesses Pettit had spent most of the day, the 31st October until about 11.00 p.m. drinking at the Waggon and Horses beer shop in Castle Street. However he disappeared for about an hour from 9.00p.m. when he had apparently taken one of the landlords guns, which were kept for shooting rats. It was then alleged that he went down the back of the Waggon and Horses to the Slade which he followed into Bridge Street, where Campling lived.

At about 10.10 p.m. Campling left the Eight Bells, to go to his house across the road, about forty yards away. As he left the pub he entered into conversation with a Mr. William Brand, a local baliff from North End at Littlebury who walked with him to his door. As Campling entered his house, he was shot in his legs. Campling suspected he had been shot by Pettit, as he had threatened him in the past, and he instructed his officers to look for Pettit. Meanwhile Pettit had apparently returned back to the Waggon and Horses in Castle Street by way of the Slade, where footprints were later found. He was alleged to have returned the gun undetected and then strolled innocently along Castle Street, Market Hill, King Street and what is now Park Lane. Here he was arrested by a Constable and taken to the Mayor's house.

Campling died from his wounds on the 9th November, and the Watch Committee appointed Superintendent Clarke of Newport to investigate the murder. He appears to have failed in his task having failed to find any witnesses so the Watch Committee contacted the Metropolitan Police. They sent an Inspector Lund to investigate, and on no more than hearsay, he arrested Pettit. At Pettit's trial at the Quarter Sessions in Chelmsford, the defence alleged that the evidence was all circumstantial, and that no one in Saffron Walden had behaved fairly to him. It was a blessing, said the Defence that he was not tried in Walden. The jury found him not guilty. (58)

Walden's police force at this time was still independent, and consisted of a Chief Constable, two assistants and about five Constables. There was also a parish Beadle. (23)

Following Campling's death Sergeant Benjamin Judd was appointed Head Constable in 1852. His salary was fixed at 25s. per week, and he was allowed the occupancy of the police cottage at the back of the town hall in Butcher Row. Judd resigned in 1856, and a circular was sent to various authorities advertising the vacancy. (58) The post was advertised as:-

'Cash Salary £65, Residence free, a new suit and two pairs of boots, a new Cape and Great Coat every two years.'

The replies were not helpful. The Metropolitan Police advised that 'no man can be found who is willing to leave this service to fill the situation of Head Constable at Saffron Walden'. The City of London Police said 'It is not an easy matter to meet your requirements, a good man is worth more wages; an indifferent man is of no value'. The Cambridge Chief Constable could offer nobody whom he could recommend and be willing to accept the pay offered.

The situation seemed to go from bad to worse. In a second letter, the City of London Police suggested that a Samuel Heywood would be a suitable person, but his reference was hardly a glowing testimonial – it appeared that he had five charges against him on his record including two of irregularities and one of neglect of duty! Perhaps in a sense of desperation the Watch Committee made further inquiries, but eventually turned down his application. A letter was then sent to the Town Clerk of Colchester, who was able to recommend Oliver Kerbey. Even his testimonial was somewhat dubious – the Colchester Town Clerk said of him 'He was originally in the army as a Private, became a Sergeant, but for some irregularity of no very heinous nature he got degraded to the ranks again'. (45)

Despite this he was appointed Chief Constable in August 1856. However perhaps more attention should have been paid to his record, for within a month of taking office, he was sacked for being drunk on duty. His replacement was Inspector Harvey of the Cambridgeshire Constabulary, who was appointed in Oct. 1856 at a salary of 28s. per week as well as occupancy of the police house. However, he also quickly resigned.(58)

These unfortunate problems allied to pressures from property owners to amalgamate the police force with the County's led to the Council inviting Captain McHardy, the Chief Constable of Essex to a meeting to discuss amalgamation with the County Police force. On 1st November, 1857 the forces were merged and the area Superintendent, John Clarke of Newport, posted an Inspector and four Constables to cover the town. The Police Station remained in the increasingly inadequate accommodation at the rear of the Town Hall until 1884 when a new Police Station was built in East Street. The Police Station has remained there to the present day.(58)

East Street Police Station shortly after its completion.

Chapter 10
19th Century Walden – 1851-1885

Two good published sources exist which give an idea of what Saffron Walden was like in the 1850's

The first is a report in the Saffron Walden Weekly News of June, 1906 in which J.W.Burningham an old resident of the town wrote an article on his reminiscences of the town, fifty years previously:-

'. . . The paths were mostly paved with pebble stones and there were many more old houses in some of the streets than as now. . . . In the Market Place, now occupied by Messers Barclays Bank was a china shop up three steps held by the late Mrs Knowldeu. In Market Street the present saleyard was in ruins with an old house adjoining, down two steps with an old fashioned bow window in front. New roads and buildings have sprung up since in South Road, West Road, Mount Pleasant Road, and lately Victoria Avenue. At Freshwell House, Bridge End, was a large Tanyard. . . . On May Day each year our 'City Folk' in Castle Street as they were then called held their gala 'Piggidy Gutter'. The tribes gathered in the evening headed by a merry old soul 'Royal Moll' and danced around the town hand in hand, about 200 in number. When Moll saw a chance to sit around a few persons she would lead on and hem them in not letting them go until they had paid toll. The leader always dressed in colours and flowers and the townspeople turned out to see the fun.'

The second source is the 1851 census returns. From these we know that the population of the town was 5,393, and that the town appears to have been virtually self sufficient. A detailed analysis of the census has been written (35), and from this we can see that the town had its wealthier area (mainly the High Street and areas to the west of the town) witnessed by the number of live-in servants; and it also had its poorer areas, such as Castle Street, Gold Street and East Street, where it was not unusual to find as many as ten people in one house. As an example of the overcrowding, the population of just one street, Castle Street, was 955.

Occupations at that time included a 'buss driver', surgeons, an officer of the Inland Revenue, tailors, carpenters, wheel wrights, dressmakers, lawyers, and fishermen as well as servants and agricultural labourers. There only appears to have been one general practitioner in the town, although there were a number of surgeons, apothecaries, and chemists. In addition there were of course clergy, blacksmiths, carpenters and shoemakers.

The Gibsons
The history of Saffron Walden in the second half of the 19th century was dominated by the munificence of the Gibson family. Not only did they

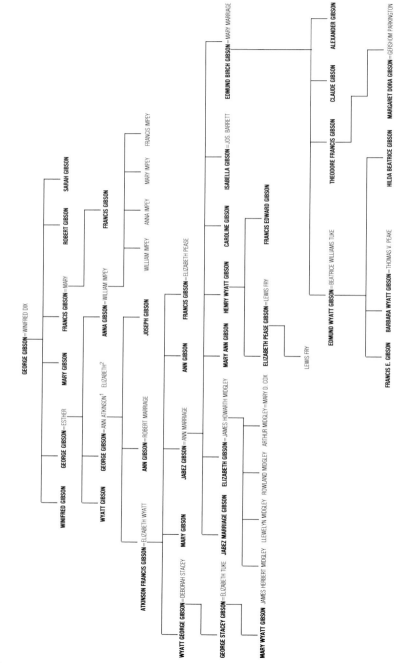

THE GIBSON FAMILY TREE

donate numerous properties to the town, but they also served the town in various civic capacities.

The family first came to the town in 1763, when George a miller and his wife Ann moved from Maldon to open a shop in the Market Square. Their business was very successful, but it was through the marriage of their son, Atkinson Francis to Elizabeth Wyatt, in 1799, that the Gibson family became involved in brewing. Elizabeth's family owned a brewery on what is now the site of Raynhams Garage, and it was through this brewery and its subsequent history that the Gibsons were to make their money.

On their marriage, Atkinson and Elizabeth moved into no. 7 High Street, where they had four children, Wyatt George, (1790-1862), Jabez, (1794-1838) Francis (1805-1858) and Mary (1791-1839). Wyatt George and Jabez went to a private boarding school at Reading, and ultimately all three boys went into their fathers brewing business on leaving school. No doubt the Gibsons were content to continue in the brewing business but local banking events were to influence their careers.

Banking in the early part of the 19th century in Walden was the sole preserve of Messrs. Searle and Co. When Searles decided to enter into competition with the Gibsons by starting malting in kilns in King Street, the Gibsons felt it only fair that they should retaliate by entering banking! In 1824 they opened the Saffron Walden and North Essex Bank. In 1825, a panic in the financial markets led to the closure of Searles, and with just a year's experience in the field the Gibsons were left with the towns only bank. The bank was however remarkably successful so that the Gibsons eventually left brewing and concentrated on the bank.

The three brothers were all to marry. Wyatt George married Deborah Stacey and moved into what is now 4, High Street. Jabez Gibson, on his marriage moved into no. 5, Hill Street (later to become the Borough Council offices,) and Francis moved to The Close, on the corner of High Street and Castle Street. The Close, itself has an interesting history. It was probably built in the 15th century, and had a large extension added in 1554. The extension was situated in what is now the gardens of the present house. As was the practice at the time, Francis had the extension, a timber framed building, encased in brick in 1854. The extension was later pulled down and re-erected, without the brick casing in West Grinstead in Sussex. The Close was later taken over by the Catholic Church in the early 20th century and used for a short period as a Church until the new Catholic Church was built in Castle Street in 1906.

It was said of the Gibsons (32) 'Their business instincts impelled them to make money; their faith compelled them to give it away' and it was this generation of Gibsons' who began to implement this philosophy by providing the town with generous gifts.

Wyatt George was the first to make a major gift to the town when he gave £5,000 for the Hospital. Jabez followed suit by boring the first artesian well in the town, at his own expense. He later gave the site of the well, on the north side of Hill Street opposite the present fire station, to the town. Both Wyatt George and Jabez served on the Council, both being elected at the first elections for the new Borough Council after the Municipal Corporations Act in 1835. They were both immediately made Aldermen on 31st December 1835.

Francis, though not a great businessman was able through the family wealth to indulge in his love of landscape gardening. As he did not consider his own garden at The Close of sufficient size for his plans, he acquired land at the rear of cottages in Castle Street for his scheme and there, laid out what is now Bridge End Gardens. The Gardens passed to the Fry family through the marriage of Francis daughter, and in line with the Gibson tradition they leased the gardens at a peppercorn rent to the Borough Council, an arrangement carried on by Uttlesford District Council to this day. Francis was also an artist and created the small art gallery in Castle Street, still in existence today as the Fry Art Gallery. Like his brothers Francis also served on the Council being elected on 14th March, 1838 and serving until his death twenty years later.

Over the years the Gibsons owned a considerable amount of land in the town, particularly on the west side of the High Street. Wyatt George's son, George Stacey Gibson (1818-1883) was prepared to give away much of this for good causes. He was a practising Quaker and was closely involved with that movement. When the Quakers sought a new home, he gave the site of the Friends' Meeting House to them. He also gave land for

George Stacey Gibson (1818-1883).

the Friends' School which was an important reason in their decision to relocate the school in Saffron Walden following an out break of typhoid in the school at Croydon. George Stacey also presented the town with the fountain in the Market Square in 1863; gave the land and £10,000 for the Training College (now the Bell College); gave land for the western end of the almshouses in 1881 and in his will left substantial grants to the Museum, the Library the almshouses and local schools. But perhaps his major contribution to the town, was the generous gift of the Town Hall in 1879.

George Stacey lived, first in the house on the corner of Abbey Lane and the High Street, (later to become the Abbey Temperance Hotel) and later at Hill House, where his garden comprised of what is now the Gibson estate. He was a botanist of some note, publishing 'Flora in Essex' in 1862, which remained the standard work on the subject until 1974. George Stacey was also a historian of some note and assisted in the creation of the Museum. In 1878 he was responsible for the excavation of land adjoining the battle ditches, in the garden of Hill House, where an Anglo Saxon burial ground was discovered. Some 200 skeletons were uncovered, complete with various ornaments and implements, several of which were sent to the British Museum. George Stacey also served on the Borough Council being first elected on 4th January, 1859, becoming an Alderman on 6th February, 1864 and being elected Mayor in 1875 and 1876. He remained on the Council until his death in 1883.

Jabez died at the early age of 44, but left a son, Edmund Birch Gibson, (1837-1911). Edmund lived first at Elm Grove where his garden joined that of his fathers' by a tunnel which can still be seen today in Jubilee Gardens. He later moved to a farm at Little Walden, and whilst there built the church so that evening services could be held there. In 1903 he gave the town the plane trees lining the High Street. Edmund was also a Borough Councillor being elected in November, 1867, becoming an Alderman in 1883, and serving the town as Mayor in 1883 and 1884. He died in 1911.

Mary Wyatt Gibson (1855-1931) was the only daughter of George Stacey Gibson and his wife Elizabeth Tuke. She gave the town the site for the swimming baths in Hill Street in 1910.

The family as a whole were involved in other major projects in the town. They were responsible for the founding of the Boys' School (in East Street) in 1838, and the Girls' School (situated in Debden Road) in 1844. They were also involved with the Literary and Scientific Institute, the Library and the Museum. They were also responsible for the first paving of the streets in Walden, the first allotments, when they gave land in Little Walden Road, and for encouraging the railway to open a branch line to the town in 1866. The family were also, as would be expected, generous to their employees and provided the Gibson free dwellings as retirement homes for their former workers. Further details of many of these gifts can be found later in the text.

The High Street showing Hill House (on the left), home of George Stacey Gibson.

Many Walden organisations began in the 1860's including the Horticultural Society, the Working Mens Institute in Gold Street and the Church of England Young Mens Society. Following various crisis in the countries relationship with France, Volunteer Corps began to be created throughout the Country. Such a body was created in the town in 1860, being gazetted on 23rd October 1860 as 17 Company, Saffron Walden, of the Essex Volunteer Rifle Corps. The first Captain being the Hon. Charles C. Neville. Later, for administrative reasons, this became part of the Cambridgeshire Battalion, although remaining essentially a Walden based Company. In the 1870's the Essex Volunteer Companies were reorganised and 17 Company, Saffron Walden, became part of the 2nd Battalion of the Essex Regiment.

Sport also began to become more organised in the town. In 1859 the Saffron Walden Cricket Club was formally established with Joseph Lecand Taylor as President. A number of ad hoc cricket matches had been played on the Common since at least 1812 including a remarkable match against Bishops Stortford on 11th July 1837. In this game Walden scored 474 with Alfred Adams scoring 279. Rowntree (46) records details of some massive hitting in those days. A Boys' British school master, Philip Cornell is alleged to have hit a ball from the Common into the Rose and Crown yard (now Boots car park)!

In 1872 the town's Football Club was formed, and like the Cricket Club played regularly on the Common. However this presented problems, because of the public exercising their rights to walk across the pitch, even when games were in play! So the Club looked around for a pitch of its own, and in 1890 decided to move to its present ground at Catons Lane.

During the second half of the 19th century, the Essex Show was held in Saffron Walden on a number of occassions – 1860, 1870 and 1884. A 1906 report in the Walden Weekly said of the 1860 show:-

'The year 1860, was a most unfortunate one for many. It was very wet and rained almost every day for the whole year. On 12th June Essex Agricultural Society had their show in the deer park, a one day show then and a most unfavourable day it was. It began to rain at about 4 a.m., and kept on a steady downpour until after 4 p.m. A great number attended the show, and ladies that day wore hoops and crinolines, and the sight towards the latter end of the day was never to be forgotten. The ladies were terribly bedrabbled with rain and mud, and the gentlemen were badly spattered with mud over their ankles and half way up their legs.'

During the 1860's and 1870's Saffron Walden was to see a considerable expansion in new facilities as major new services were either modernised or introduced to the town. These included the hospital, the railway, the fire brigade, gas and water services, as well as buildings such as the Town Hall and the Church. The Parish Church provides a good example of what facilities were like before these improvements began to be made. Further restoration work was carried out on St. Marys during the 1860's, and in an article in the Saffron Walden Weekly News of 29th June 1906, J. Burningham describes the church before the restoration work was carried out:-

'. . . the church was a cold uncomfortable place of worship – no warming apparatus, high pews, slanting pew galleries, north and south aisles up to the window sills and a small gallery at the west end. Lord Braybrookes pew was in the middle of the chancel arch and popularly named 'The Opera Box'. The pulpit, a three decker stood half way down the nave on the left, with a sounding board on it. . . . Half the congregation face east, the other half west. In front of the pulpit stood a large square pew for the corporation, the Mayors chair being raised a little and facing the pulpit.'

During the restoration work, the services of the Church were held in the Agricultural Hall (now the Museum). The high pews were replaced, first with chairs and then in about 1885 with oak pews. These were paid for either privately, by families, or by subscription. During the restoration both the tower arch and the great east window, over the altar were opened up and stained glass inserted. The restoration works were finished in time for the celebrations of Queen Victoria's Silver Jubilee in 1862, and a special Church service was held to commemorate this. The town was decked out in flags and bunting for this occasion and a number of large archways were constructed in London Road and the High Street and suitably decorated.

One of the archways erected in the High Street in 1862.

126

The drinking fountain presented to the town in 1863.

1862 was in fact quite a significant year in the towns history. During that year the Fountain in the Market Square, was on display in the Imperial Exhibition. George Stacey Gibson was to purchase it and present it to the town the following year. But more importantly, it was the year in which the hospital was to be founded. At this time care of the elderly and infirm was very much a hit and miss affair in Britain. Generally their welfare was taken care of by the local Board of Guardians. This was the case in Walden, and for many years the Chairman of the Board was Wyatt George Gibson. His long experience in this post left a very strong impression that 'life was constantly being wasted and that undue sufferings were occurring for want of proper nursing.' So, when he died in 1862, he left the sum of £5000 for the creation of a hospital in the town. A public meeting was called and a committee established to act as trustees. Lord Braybrooke was approached to see if he would donate a parcel of land at the top of the Common. This he declined but instead offered a two acre site in London Road, which was duly accepted by the committee. It was decided to invite architects to submit plans for a building to the value of about £3,000. Tenders were submitted under a number of pseudonyms, and the successful architect was William Beck. The plans were modified as they were considered 'too extensive and elaborate' and tenders were invited. The tenders ranged in price from £4896 to £5704.8s.1d and after further negotiation with Messrs. Bell and Sons, the lowest tenderer, a revised figure of £4,206 was agreed.

The building work commenced in 1863, and in December 1864, the workmen were provided with a 'Raising Feast' by Mr. James Day. Work completed early in 1866, and in May of that year, George Stacey Gibson was authorised to appoint Sarah Ann Cogle as the hospitals first Matron at a salary of £40 per annum. The building was described as being 'substantial and commodious' and was capable of accommodating between twenty-five to thirty patients. The final cost was £5,504.12s.2d plus an additional £600 for furnishings and another £100 (provided by George Stacey Gibson) for the dispensary. In addition to Wyatt George Gibson's £5,000, his sister-in-law provided another £500 and the remainder was raised by subscriptions. An appeal letter circulated at the time makes interesting reading showing the views towards health and hygiene at that time:-

'. . . The utility of such an Institution must be apparent to every one, affording as it does, one of the best means of assisting the poor when suffering from illness, as well as enabling the employer of labour, at a trifling cost, to ensure good nursing and medical aid for the labourer in time of sickness, It may also frequently render important service in preventing the spread of dangerous and often fatal diseases, by the early removal of infectious cases from the dwellings of the poor, so unsuited for their proper treatment. Good fresh air and careful nursing, are two most important elements in promoting the recovery of patients, and for obtaining these, this hospital will afford especial facilities.'

Walden was very much a leader in the field of hospital provision at this time – the pamphlet continues:-

'It is not intended, in any way, to interfere with kindred establishments; but as there is nothing of the kind, to the North, nearer than Cambridge; to the South, than Hertford; or to the East, than Bury or Colchester, it is believed, that to many places between these towns, this Hospital, situated as it is, so near to the railway will prove a great boon.'

The hospital was very successful in its early days. In the annual report of 1874 it stated that the hospital had been a great use in checking a serious outbreak of fever, by the free admission of patients from North End and Littlebury. Eighteen patients had been admitted but only three had died. Later additions were to improve the facilities – in 1877 two bathrooms were fitted for the patients (!) and in 1893 an operating theatre was provided. The addition at such a later date of facilities which today seem the very essentials of a hospital give an indication of the tremendous advances in the ensuing years.

Another major facility to arrive in Walden in the 1860's was the railway. Although Walden was served by the London to Cambridge 'Flyer' – a regular stage coach run from the George and Blue Boar Inns at Holborn to the Red Lion at Cambridge – major roads and canal navigations completely bypassed Walden. An attempt had been made to extend the

Saffron Walden General Hospital shortly after its opening in 1866.

Stort by canal from Bishops Stortford to Cambridge in the late 18th century, but this had failed when Lord Howard objected to it passing through his lands at Audley End. Such intransigence was not seen elsewhere and as a result Walden's malting industry declined whilst that of Bishops Stortford, situated at the head of the navigation increased substantially.

The main road, the turnpike to Cambridge, bypassed Walden to the west, and within the town many of the roads were in very poor condition and unable to stand heavy traffic. All of this meant that as railways began to spread across the country, residents of the town and particularly traders were keen to see the railway come to Walden. As early as 1835 the area was surveyed when a route was proposed from London to Dunmow, Walden, Cambridge and ultimately York. The Great Northern Railway Bill incorporating this route was presented to Parliament in 1836, but fell at its second reading. A second bill presented to Parliament at the same time, which was eventually passed, laid the route of the Liverpool Street to Cambridge line, which like the main turnpike ran two miles to the west of the town. It will be noted that this line does not follow the natural line of the Cam Valley, but swerves to the west to avoid Audley End. Had it followed the Cam it would have gone past the front of the Mansion.

The railway company were in fact keen to bring the line through Walden. Two sites were suggested for a station, either the Common, or near the east gates of the park at the entrance of Abbey Lane. Allegedly, Lord Braybrooke, felt it undesirable to cut the park off from the town and so favoured using the Common as the station. This apparently found favour with the townsfolk, but thereafter arrangements were made with the railway company to build the station at Wendens Ambo. (2)

An interesting sideline to this is the grandiose tunnel entrances, on the cuttings below Audley End, which can still be seen today. Lord Braybrooke insisted these should be built where the tunnels ran through his land.

Because the mainline did not run through the town and there was no canal to assist trade, many people in the town were keen to see a branch line built as quickly as possible. A meeting was held in the Town Hall in 1845 to discuss the possibility of a branch line which would link Bedford to Maldon. Another scheme mooted in 1848 extending a line from Maldon, Witham, and Braintree was also considered but both schemes failed to find backers.

Meanwhile the town continued to suffer the effect of its isolation from easy transport, with the towns population actually dropping in the ten years between 1851 and 1861. A series of meetings were held in the town to promote the benefits of a railway, and this time succeeded in having the support of major landowners. The Gibson family became involved in the discussions and a temporary committee was appointed with W.B. Freeland a local solicitor as its secretary. An approach was made to the board of Eastern Counties railway who, however, were not prepared to be involved in its construction. (36)

Financial support for the project was promised locally, and with the consent of the Eastern Counties Railway already obtained the necessary act of Parliament was passed. Called 'An Act to authorize the Construction of a Railway from the Eastern Counties Railway to Saffron Walden in Essex', it received the Royal Assent on 22nd July, 1861. The act permitted the construction of a line from a junction with the main London to Cambridge line to a field belonging to the Trustees of Erswell's Charity in Debden Road. (36)

The new company, the Saffron Walden Railway Company was set up with Wyatt George Gibson as its Chairman, George Stacey Gibson as its Vice Chairman and Messers John Stephenson Robson, James Stanley, and Joshua Clarke as its Directors, and held its first meeting in the Town Hall on 21st October 1861.

Despite problems with raising sufficient capital, and complications with the eastwards extension to Bartlow, work was eventually able to proceed and on Monday 18th May, 1863 the first sod was cut by George Stacey Gibson in a field half way between Audley End and Saffron Walden. On the 22nd June 1863, the Saffron Walden Extension Act received the Royal Assent and this formally authorised the line to be built from Audley End right through to Bartlow.

Financial difficulties continued to plague the project, and numerous negotiations with the Great Eastern Railway were necessary, but the work was able to continue. By 1864, the Cam Valley had been crossed, and the embankment along the Fulfen Valley (and still visible along the Audley End Road) erected. By now well over 300,000 cubic feet of earth had been moved. The line was more or less completed by the late summer of 1865, the station being erected in Station Street. However on inspection

View of Station Road from the Friends' School c.1880.

131

by the Board of Trade, a number of faults were found and these were quickly corrected. It was agreed to open the line on Thursday 23rd November 1865. Large crowds gathered to witness the opening and were entertained by the Town Band. At 7.20am, the first train driven by John Duce, left Saffron Walden station, with three coaches and a luggage van with over 50 people.

The line had initial teething problems and part of the track had to be relaid. To start with the line was not particulaly well used although events such as the Essex Agricultural Show, which was held in the town in 1860, 1870 and again in 1884, did help to increase its use. In 1876, a fire broke out at the station, and a pig and its sty were destroyed. This resulted in admonition for the station foreman, who was keeping the pig contrary to regulations!

In 1877 the line was taken over by the Great Eastern Railway Company by virtue of the GER Act of 12th July 1877. During the 1880's various outbuildings were erected, including cattle pens, an office for the station master and a signal box. By the end of the century, goods traffic, in particular had increased considerably. (36)

Other major facilities began to be modernised. A fire brigade of sorts existed during the early part of the 19th Century, for records exist to show that a meeting of the Parish Officers and Fire Office Agents took place at the Rose and Crown on January 4th 1831. It appears then, that a 'new large engine' was purchased at this time, paid for by various insurance companies. However the Saffron Walden Voluntary Fire Brigade was only formed on 1st May, 1865, with 16 volunteers. The Saffron Walden Almanac of 1866 gave the following description:-

'(The brigade) . . . has two powerful engines, one being the old one belonging to the town which has been thoroughly repaired, and the other one being an entirely new one by Merryweather and Son. (There is also) . . . a hose reel with 500 feet of canvass hose and 400 feet of leather hose and a set of fire escape ladders which will reach to a height of 42 feet. The members are each supplied with a waterproof tunic, helmet and high knee boots.'

The brigade attended a large number of fires in the 19th century, probably the worst being in 1887 when fire gutted the Copt Hall Buildings in Ashdon Road, leaving 17 families homeless.

In other cases certain essential services would be supplied by a private company, and then later acquired by the Council. The waterworks were a good example of this. New waterworks were constructed in 1862 by a private company, on the site of an artesian well in Hill Street. The well was originally bored at the expense of Jabez Gibson. He had been concerned that the surface wells whilst sufficient normally, were inadequate during periods of drought. In 1836, following two dry seasons, Gibson had engaged the services of Samuel Purkis of Little Baddow to provide a bore hole. Work started in October 1836, and drilling continued to a depth of 1,004 feet 4 inches. The results of the bore showed that the ground below Hill Street comprised of Alluvial Gravel, Upper Chalk, a 10 foot bed of Inferior Oolite, and further chalk. At 275 feet a very fine spring of water was discovered in a bed of sand 7 feet in thickness. The spring was quiet abundant, yielding about 80 gallons of water per minute, but did not come above the surface, so boring continued to over 1,000 feet, but no further supply was found. The spring was therefore tapped at 275 feet.(25)

Subsequently the Corporation bought the works in 1878 and at the same time Edmund Birch Gibson, (the son of Jabez) agreed to present the well to the Council.

In 1887 a sub committee was set up by the Council to look into ways of providing softer water for the town. Because the town's water comes from a chalk base considerable problems occurred. Following the sub committee's investigations, the 'Atkins' system of water softening was installed at a cost of £2,500. It was operational by 1890. The well continued to supply the town with its public water supply until in 1899 it was found that, as the bore was unlined surface water was percolating and a new well had to be provided.

A gas supply first came to the town in 1836, when the gas works in Thaxted Road (now Jossaumes) were opened by a private company. John Player, later to be a freeman of the town was one of the seven directors, and Jabez Gibson, one of the trustees. The capital used to launch the company amounted to £4,500 divided into 225 shares at £20 each.

Saffron Walden Gas Works, 1836.

133

The company was purchased by the Corporation in 1879 on a 30 year loan, for the sum of £10,600. The 1898 Saffron Walden Almanac was able to proclaim that since the Council acquired the works the cost for a thousand cubic feet of gas had fallen from 5s 10d to 3s 6½d. and consumption had increased from 839,300 cubic feet in 1835 to 7,183,000 in 1879.

Other works took place in the Market Square in the 1860's and 1870's. As mentioned, in June 1863, George Stacey Gibson presented the town with the Drinking Fountain in the Market Square. The fountain had been on display at the Imperial Exhibition of 1862 and was designed by John Bentley who was also involved in designing Westminster R.C. Cathedral. Bentley had built it to commemorate the marriage of Edward, Prince of Wales (later King Edward VII) and Princess Alexandra of Denmark. Then, in 1874, the building, which today is Barclays Bank was erected for the Gibson Bank. It was designed by Eden Nesfield a noted local architect.

But the major change to the Market Square at this time was the modernisation of the Town Hall. The town was becoming more and more important as the major town for a large rural area. The Saffron Walden Poor Law Union centred on Walden consisted of 24 local parishes and the town also served as the County Court district serving 35 parishes. The Town Hall continued to house the police station at the rear although this eventually became too crowded because of lack of space and by 1871 the condition of the building was giving the Council some concern. It was obviously of inadequate size and its inability to meet its various purposes was causing problems. The Town Hall was surveyed by a local architect, with a view to remodelling the interior. At the same time the Police Authority were approached to see if they were prepared to move the main police station from Newport to Saffron Walden, if proper accommodation could be found. However the matter was dropped when legal difficulties were encountered with the Crown over the rent to be paid for the Magistrates Court in the Town Hall.

The matter could not be left for long, and in 1875, a committee was appointed to investigate the possibility of improving the Town Hall. In May, 1877, the Council acquired a house at the back of the Town Hall and the police were moved into this, although still retaining a room in the hall.

By October 1877, the committee was able to report back to the Council. Plans drawn up by Mr. Edward Burgess, an architect had proved satisfactory. The Council approved the plans although the financing of the work would have proved difficult. But once again the Gibson family were to come to the rescue. A letter was read by the Town Clerk:-

'To the Town Council of the Borough of Saffron Walden.

Gentleman,
The long residence of my family in this town and the close connection they have had with its public institutions, especially during the last fifty years, has led me to desire to leave some lasting evidence of their and

Opening of the Town Hall 1879.

my own interest in its own welfare and prosperity. It has long been a desideratum to have a Central Hall for Lectures and Public Meetings of various descriptions together with suitable accommodation for the Corporation and other public bodies; this the present Town Hall does not supply, but it is thought that the plans now submitted to the consideration of the Council will meet these requirements, as far as the space at disposal will admit, and that the proposed Building will add a pleasing architectural feature to the present Market Place. The cost of the building is roughly estimated by the Architect at £3,500, and I feel that it would be a satisfaction to myself and a fitting conclusion to my two years term of office as Mayor to place the sum of £4,000 at the disposal of the Corporation, to carry out these Plans, so that the Town may be provided with a building creditable to itself and calculated to promote the convenience and pleasure of the inhabitants.

I remain yours very respectfully, G.S.Gibson, Mayor.'

Work began in 1878, the Council moving out of the hall and meeting in the interim in the Agricultural Hall (now the Museum). However problems occurred over the builders. Gibson was keen that the hall should be built by the firm of Joseph Bell. But as Bell had just taken over as Mayor from Gibson, this was not legally possible. So to overcome this problem, the Council, in February gave Gibson permission to build the hall himself instead of paying the £4,000 he had offered to the Council. To prevent any legal difficulties, the Council agreed to give the Town Hall and other buildings to Gibson! The work was completed in 1879, and the hall was formally opened on 1st October 1879.

Women folding crêpe in Gold Street during the mid 19th century.

The police still used a room in the hall, after the opening of the new Town Hall, probably that above 1, Market Place. The County Council, as the Police Authority, wished to erect a purpose-built police station. Plans were drawn up in 1882 with a view to the Town and County Councils erecting a jointly financed building, but these plans proved too costly. Eventually in 1886 a new Police Station was built in East Street on former charity land. This station is still in use today.

The Grammar School was another institution that expanded in the second half of the 19th century. The school had been based for many years in the building next to the Friends Meeting House, but the accommodation was inadequate and too small. Through the generosity of Lord Braybrooke, who gave the land, and George Stacey Gibson, who gave £1,000 the school was able to erect a building in Ashdon Road, where it was to remain until its closure in 1940. Today the building is used as the Dame Johanne Bradbury School. (48)

Industry

There was a considerable variety of work being carried out in the town and this suggests it was reasonably prosperous. We know from the 1851 census, for example that there were 42 people employed in the straw-plait industry; and that, between 1815 and 1823 there was a tanners; that spinning of worsted yarn took place; Norwich crêpe' was being weaved and there was also a gun making business owned by a Mr. F.R. Furlong. Wool as a major item of industry had largely died out in the area as farmers moved over to arable farming. This is probably best reflected in the building of the Corn Exchange on the site of the old Woolstaplers Hall. This also had a 'knock on' effect and weaving gradually declined in importance. By 1851 the worsted trade was also virtually non existent in the town.

The manufacture of silk crêpe by a company with the name of Grout, Baylis & Co. had started in Walden, in a house opposite the Eight Bells in Bridge Street. This relied heavily on people working from home, and as a result has left its legacy to the town to this day – Mount Pleasant Cottages and the row of brick and flint cottages in East Street were houses specifically built for loom workers. Each house would have a small room to contain the loom. The company closed in 1836.(32)

Other important industries in the town during the 19th century included the traditional agricultural related industries, such as malting and brewing, manufacturing of agricultural implements, and printing, with Henry Hart being a leading printing firm.

Malting was particularly a growth industry – in 1851 there were 41 maltsters in the town, mainly in three areas, Bridge Street/Castle Street; Gold Street; and Rosse Lane (now Debden Road). There were twenty nine grocers in the town, along with three fish shops and two fruiterers. The town also had fifty five tailors, sixty five dressmakers and sixty two boot and shoe makers in 1851. Blacksmiths, tanners, coachmakers, button and sack making also offered employment at this time. (35)

Nursery gardening was also a successful venture in Walden. Perhaps the most famous nurseries were those of Mr William Chater, whose speciality was the hollyhock. Early in the 19th century a Mr. Charles Baron, a shoemaker had carried out experiments with the hollyhock, and had succeeded, by hybridization, in creating a large number of semi-double flowers of different shades. His work was continued by Mr. William Chater, who at that time ran a general nursery business. In 1847, Chater produced his first catalogue which was reissued each year with new forms and shades. But in 1873, disaster struck. A hollyhock disease, caused by a fungus, (Pucciania malvacearum) swept through his nurseries and totally destroyed many of his best stock. However Chater persevered and managed through careful husbandry to restore much of his stock. On his death in 1885, Messrs. Webb and Brand took over his business and by the turn of the century they were probably the largest growers of hollyhocks in the world.

The 19th century was also important for brewing and malting. Brewing had flourished in the town since at least Elizabethan times and was still an important industry until the inter war years. Malting started in about 1725 but was declining by the first world war, when output from the town's maltings was down to about 23,000 quarters.

The North Essex Portland Cement Works were started in 1877 in Thaxted Road as a patent brick works and later was reorganised as Dix, Green and Co. to produce bricks manufactured from chalk and clay. By the end of the century it employed about 40 men. The chalk was dug in Walden and the clay was obtained from works about a mile to the east of the town, near Cole End Lane. The clay was brought to the Thaxted Road works by means of a narrow gauge tram road, where it was mixed with the chalk and ultimately produced Portland Cement. It also produced a whiting agent as a by-product. At the turn of the century, the company was forced to merge with a combine of cement producers. Before the first world war it had a major contract producing cement for the town's new sewage works, but after the war it hit a slump and was forced to close. It was reopened in the 1930's with the decision to build the aerodrome at Debden, when the works were again used to provide the cement for the new airfield.

Chapter 11
19th Century Walden – 1885-1900

Until 1885 Saffron Walden did not have a Member of Parliament solely for this area; instead it was represented by 'two Knights of the Shire'. Then, in 1885, the Redistribution of Seats Act was passed. As a result of this a Royal Commission divided the Country into a number of seats, and the North Division of Essex was named the Saffron Walden Division. A Saffron Walden constituency has remained ever since albeit with minor variations to its boundaries.

In November 1885, a General Election was held. Herbert Gardner, a Liberal, was returned as the first member for the Saffron Walden area. He polled 4,775 votes to that of 3,006 of his Conservative opponent, the Hon . C.H.Strutt. Gardner had been educated at Harrow and Trinity College, Cambridge and lived at Debden Hall. In addition he had a residence in London.

Gardner was successfully returned in 1886, when he received 4,059 votes against 3,319 votes for the Conservative, G.W.Brewis. In 1892 there were two elections:- in the first he received 4,564 votes against the Conservatives' P.V.Smith who obtained 2,683 votes and in the second election he was returned unopposed. He remained the member until 1895. (57)

The Queen's Golden Jubilee was celebrated in 1887. The usual celebrations were held in Walden and succeeded in raising £585. A special Church Service was held in the Parish Church on 20th June, and the following day, the Mayor attended a celebration service at Westminster Abbey. Following the service in Walden, the Council unveiled the drinking fountain on the top of the Common, and 169 trees, mainly limes, were planted on the south side of the Common. Sports events were held on the Common and a large crowd watched the events. (48)

Later in 1887 a terrible fire swept through Copt Hall Buildings, to the north of Ashdon Road. These buildings comprised of 20 cottages, originally built in 1822 to house local silk weavers. As they were of back to back construction and divided only by a 4½inch wall once the fire started it rapidly burnt. Seventeen families were made homeless.

In 1889 The Cambridge News decided to start a local paper in Saffron Walden. The first edition of the Saffron Walden Weekly News was published on 1st June 1889 with the following editorial outlining its policy:-

'Our correspondence columns are open to all for the discussion of local questions. We ask the public to make use of them. The only exception we make is regards the subjects to be debated. We refer to politics and religion. We report fairly and impartially all political meetings to which our representative is invited, but the correspondence columns is not the place for religious or political controversy . . . . We have rigidly excluded reports of divorce courts and other objectionable matters. There may be times when we shall have to speak out upon disagreeable subjects . . . but for those who seek prurient details of proceedings in courts of justice, we make no appeal.'

The years since have suggested that policy was certainly not rigorously adhered to!

The first year of the Walden Weekly gives a good opportunity to see a typical year in the life of the town at the end of the last century.

There was obviously a tremendous community spirit in Walden at this time, numerous clubs being formed including the Saffron Walden Cycling Club. Athletics were particularly popular. A report in the paper on 10th August 1889, gives details of an athletics meeting held in a meadow owned by Mr. W.M.Tuke. Despite a heavy downpour over 1,000 spectators were present, and this at a time when Walden's population was barely 5,000.

Outdoor events were always popular. During the 19th century there were two annual fairs, one held on the Saturday before Mid-Lent Sunday, and the other on the first Saturday in November The following is a report of the November 1889 horse and pleasure fair:-

'The November horse and pleasure fair was held on the Common on Saturday and was the centre of attraction throughout the day, the fine weather attracting a number of visitors from the surrounding neighbourhood. With regard to the horsefair, there appears to be a lack of interest as compared with former years. There were a number of animals of all grades from cart mares to ponies, the latter including several consignments of 'real Irish and Russian blood'. There were also a few hunters on sale (lightweight of course) but with all the trotting and whipping up no one appeared to speculate very extensively. . . . Thurston of Cambridge was there with his great show of flying horses, american trapeze etc., together with a fine new organ which was a source of attraction completely putting one or two others in the shade. Shooting galleries were numerous; there was a grand circus as well as peep shows, cocoa-nut alleys and 14 young ladies of the 'Aunt Sally' persuasion. Numerous stalls were arranged with the paraphernalia of tempting commodities to lure the younger fraternity whose purse strings were well pulled to appease their cravings for the luxuries. Undoubtedly good business was done by the caterers who had a fine time of it from one till ten o'clock.'

During 1889 suggestions were made concerning the formation of a number of new roads in the town. It was felt there was the need for a new road to run from the railway bridge in South Road. This resulted in the building of Victoria Avenue. Other suggested road improvements, however failed to see the light of day including suggestions to widen King Street, and to extend the top of Gold Street to join Station Road.

The Rev. R. Pelly, the town's Vicar caused a stir during the year when he remarked from the pulpit that he had seen more drunkenness on market days in Saffron Walden than during all the time he was at his previous parish in Stretford. A reply in the newspaper's letter columns said:-

'This is a very extraordinary thing, indeed almost incredible assertion. It may be that Mr.Pelly is induced by the clearer air to walk outside more, or possibly the working men of Stretford have a greater variety of amusements. There is another conjecture; the working men of Stretford may be greater adept at concealing drunkenness, for thoughts on this subject say that some men carry a load better than others.'

Two major events occurred in Walden in 1889, the opening of a new Post Office in King Street, and the arrival of the telephone in the town. Both were covered in detail by the press, and it is worth recording in full the report on the Post Office as it also contains a history of the Post Office and its various locations within the town throughout the 19th century.

The town had always been proud of the fact that it was one of the original towns to support the introduction of the postal system. At a Council meeting held on the 6th May 1839, it had agreed to petition parliament in support of a uniform postal rate, as proposed by Rowland Hill. Until then post had been paid according to the distance it had to travel. The following article appeared in the Saffron Walden Weekly News of 21st September, 1889, complete with an illustration of the new building which comprised of the Post Office, three shops to the west and one to the east. (These buildings all still exist as nos.8 to 16 King Street).

'Our readers will no doubt like to know a little of the history of the post office in the town during the past forty years. Previous to 1848 business was transacted at an office which stood on a site near the present Corn Exchange, the postmaster then being Mr. Francis Turner who succeeded a Miss Spicer, postmistress. About 1848 the then existing Post Office was demolished, the ground being required for the erection of the present Corn Exchange and Literary Institute. During this time, the business was temporarily carried on in Gold Street. The new public buildings being completed, provision was made at the new institute for a Post Office. Here business was transacted until 1876 when it was found, owing to an increase in postal work, that more commodious premises would be required. At the time Messers Gibsons were moving their banking business from Sun-Hill [i.e. Market Hill] to the present splendid buildings in Market Place, and the Post Office authorities were successful in securing the Sun-Hill premises from which time to the present day postal transactions have been successfully carried on with the exception that there is insufficient room for growing postal demands which explains the erection of the present building. Mr. Turner resigned the Postmastership in 1866, when he was succeeded by Mr. Spicer, who held the office until March of the present year when

Saffron Walden Church c.1880.

the present postmaster, Mr Pirie, from the Secretary's office General Office, London, where he had over 19 years' experience, was appointed.

Growth of the work since 1866 may be gleaned from the few following facts. In that year there was only one letter carrier, a woman named Mrs. Mercy Smith. She was allowed to sort her letters in the office, but mostly did so in a niche in the wall nearby or repaired to a favourite tombstone in the Churchyard where she would arrange them in her little fleet basket. She was succeeded in 1872 by the present courteous and honest John Brand. The postmaster could then do all the office work easily. There were only two deliveries and two dispatches. Now things have entirely changed, and there are, besides the postmaster, four clerks, three town postmen and five rural postmen, two of whom are mounted. There are 13 sub offices under the supervision of a head office which embrace an area of 36 miles. There are 4 dispatches daily for letters and parcels for which the wallboxes are cleared at 11.30am, 1.30, 7.40 and 10.00pm. Also 3 deliveries at 6am, 10.45am and 4.15pm.'

The coming of the telephone was partly due to the foresight of the Mayor of the day, Mr. J.J. Robson. Again the editoral column of the Walden Weekly provides an insight to the circumstances surrounding the introduction of the telephone system:-

'. . . Walden has for long been stigmatised as a kind of 'sleepy hollow' . . . we live in vigorous business days . . . Saffron Walden is evidently feeling the pulsation of the nation's commercial heart and is awakening as a man from a somewhat long sleep. In fact it is perhaps not drawing the long bow to say that it bids fair to enter upon a new era. Although avoided by the Great Eastern's main line to London, Walden, at the suggestion of the Mayor, is about to avail itself of one of the latest aids to commercial activity, the telephone; for what more necessary in business than speedy communication with a manufacturing centre. It appears that direct telephonic and telegraphic communication is being laid between Newmarket and London via Audley End and the Mayor with the foresight which does him credit, and which argues well for his usefulness in his year of office and indicates his interest in the welfare of the town, makes the suggestion that as the wires originally arranged would pass within a mile of Walden . . . (that it should be possible to make) . . . telephonic communication between Walden and London a practical matter.'

The commercial life of the town at this time very much centred on the various markets. So a suggestion in 1892 that the market day be altered from Saturday to Tuesday caused considerable interest. The Saturday market, particularly the corn and cattle side had shown a drop in trade, so a meeting was held in the Town Hall on 19th Feb 1892 to discuss the suggested change. A proposal 'that the Corn and Cattle market day be changed to Tuesday, the Saturday market with these exceptions be continued as heretofore' was debated. Mr. A.A.Ripon, claiming to speak on behalf of 76 tradesmen who had signed a petition opposing the change argued strongly against any alteration. He was concerned that if the market day was changed to a Tuesday, Cambridge would become the centre of the stock trade. As the Cambridge market was held on a Monday it would take away any Tuesday trade in Walden. He was also concerned that if the 'labouring classes' came into town on a Tuesday they would have no need to come into town on a Saturday and this would be playing into the hands of the country tradesmen.

Despite this argument the public meeting supported the resolution and the matter went forward for debate at the Councils next meeting in March 1892. By this time the Mayor had examined the petition and informed the Council that of the 76 names on the petition, 58 were people who would not be at all affected by the day of the market. A market day committee was set up to investigate the possible change. After interviewing farmers corn buyers and tradesmen, they presented a report to the Council in April. They reported that the Saturday market was poorly attended; the majority of farmers and the majority of corn buyers currently attending would prefer a Tuesday; that several important traders not currently attending would attend on a Tuesday and that butchers in the neighbourhood found it virtually impossible to leave their shop for the market on a Saturday. These arguments swayed the Council who agreed to the change. A special luncheon was arranged at a cost of two shillings per ticket to inaugurate the first Tuesday market in Walden which took place on Tuesday 27th September, 1892.

King Street in the mid 19th century before the development of Nos 8-16 King Street.

144

The town came under the spotlight of ecclesiastical matters in 1894, when for the first time in 20 years the St. Alban's Annual Diocesan Conference was held in Walden. After Communion in the Parish Church, various high ranking officials of the Church, including the Bishop of Colchester went on to the Town Hall to discuss matters relating to the new Parish Councils Act, elementary education, defence of the Church, and Welsh disestablishment.

The same year, 1894, also saw an outbreak of diptheria in the town, ten cases being reported two of which proved to be fatal and interest being aroused by the 'scientific observation' that a coal seam had been found to run across N. Essex. The Walden Weekly's prediction 'that before many years coal will increasingly be an industry in this division of the County' did not come to fruition.

Details of one particular Walden curiousity, the bone wall were given in the Walden Weekly of 9th February 1894. Prior to the discovery of the use of bone as a fertilizer, farmers would be left with the strenuous job of burying dead cattle. According to the paper:-

'An ingenious individual of Walden, of former days had devised and carried out a scheme for disposing of a large quantity of these then useless bones, by building a wall with them. The place selected for this wall was at the top of High Street, then called 'Cucking Stool End' (for the reason that here was the pond beside of which was placed the machine for ducking turbulent and slanderous women), that part of it where the Debden-Road, then called Roos-Lane, leads from it. That curious wall, commenced where now stands the Duke of York inn, and by a gentle curve bent its way for about 200 yards on the left or east side of the road going towards Debden. The wall was about seven feet high, and composed entirely of the fore parts of the cranium of oxen, with the core or slug of their horns worked inwards towards the bank of earth against which they butted after being neatly interlocked into each other, thus forming a curious and conspicuous spectacle, exciting the notice of strangers coming into the town by way of London-Road. It was known far and wide as the 'bone wall of Walden'. This curious structure had in the early part of the century assumed the grey and hoary appearance that notified its antiquity, and being overshadowed with elm trees that grew on the bank behind it, added much to its picturesque attraction; but in later times the value of the material of which it was composed had increased, so that it became by removal less and less, until about the year 1820 it disappeared altogether.'

By 1894 the town had a thriving social life. A look at the Saffron Walden Almanac for that year shows a large number of societies and organisations in existence. The Horticultural Society, claiming to be the oldest society in England met in the Museum; the lecture rooms in Hill Street played host to the Total Abstinence Society as well as the Band of Hope; the YMCA met in a class room in the Grammar School, and the Amateur Music Society at the Boys British School. In addition there were the

Walden Fire Brigade v. Walden Police c.1895.

Cricket and Football clubs; the Clothing club and the Coal club which were forms of savings clubs, the Church of England Temperance Society; the 'I' company 3rd Cambridgeshire Volunteer Battalion of the Suffolk Regiment, and bodies such as the Mechanics Institute and the Literary and Scientific Institute.

With such a large number of organisations and society, it was probably to be expected that the town would rally to the aid of the poor and unemployed when they were in difficulty. The winter of 1894/95 turned out to be extremely cold with heavy falls of snow. In February 1895, over 38 degrees of frost were recorded in the town, and whilst it provided plenty of entertainment, with ice skating and tobogganing on the Common, it caused great misery to others.

Following the Magistrates session in February, Mr. E.B. Gibson suggested to his fellow magistrates that a soup kitchen should be established in the town. Sergeant Homan of the local police agreed to arrange to find all the necessary appliances and a ladies committee was formed and met the same day to collect funds for the project. The sum of £79 2s and 5d was quickly collected and the first distribution was able to take place on Monday 4th February, just 48 hours from when the idea was first mooted!

Over the next four weeks there were 13 distributions to the poor and needy. The food involved was 4,112 quarts of soup, 490 lbs of suet puddings, 400 lbs of beef steak puddings and 894 quartern loaves. Free dinners of soup and bread were given in the Corn Exchange to 3,570 children; and meals of soup, suet pudding or beef steak pudding and bread were given to 1,149 men. In addition, 1,628 quarts of soup were sold to those who could afford to pay, and beef tea was distributed around the town to those in bed with the influenza epidemic.

These figures (divided by the thirteen distributions) give some idea of the poverty in Walden at this time. But yet again the town to its credit seems to have responded in a charitable manner.

In the summer of 1895 a General Election was held. The town's sitting Member, Herbert Gardner had decided not to stand and was created the first Baron Burghclere. In an open letter to his constituents he said:-

'Private considerations, not to be neglected, have for some time past made it necessary that I should at an early date seek relief at your hands at the arduous duty of representing you at the House of Commons, the honour which Her Majesty the Queen has been graciously pleased to confer upon me whilst terminating our present relations, leads me free still to devote myself in some ways to your interests and to that Liberal cause whose triumph in the N. Essex division has been the greatest pride of my political career . . . (I) . . . humbly express a hope that political battles of the future may be fought with that mutual forebearance, and fair play which alone are worthy of the citizens of our great Country.'

As a successor, the Liberals chose Charles Gold to represent them. Gold had married a daughter of Sir Walter Gilbey, a wealthy family whom owned land and properties in the Bishop's Stortford and Elsenham areas. The Conservative candidate was C.W. Gray. At the Election Gold won the seat obtaining 3,806 votes to Gray's 3,381, a majority of 425. In his election address Gold gave support to Irish Home Rule and reform of the House of Lords – interestingly enough two topics still not settled today.

A disastrous fire occurred in September, 1895, when the steam mill works of Messrs. T & H. King in South Road were completely destroyed. The fire which started at 2.30 in the morning, rapidly took hold, and by 4.00 a.m. the roof had collapsed. All the machinery plant as well as the building was lost.

In 1896, the bank of Gibson Tuke and Gibson, founded by the Gibsons in 1824 amalgamated with 20 other private banks to become Barclay and Co.Ltd., later Barclays Bank. It was a remarkable tribute to the skills of the Gibson family, that a small bank started out of rivalry, by brewers should go on to become one of the leading banking companies of the world. To this day, the Walden branch of Barclays Bank bears the legend 'Gibson and Co.' on its doors.

The big event of 1897 was Queen Victoria's Diamond Jubilee. The town was liberally decorated for the event. On the front of the Town Hall there was a large gas crown with the initials 'V' and 'R' either side of it. There were numerous Union Jacks and bunting on the hall. The Corn Exchange had a series of gas jets along its King Street elevation, as well as flags, and a large sign saying 'God save the Queen' was erected over the entrance to

Gibson & Co. Bank, later Barclays Bank in about 1881.

the Rose and Crown. There were lines of flags across King Street and fairy lights on many buildings, and generally there was a profusion of flags, and 'God save the Queen' signs throughout. A handsome double 'triumphal arch' was erected at Bridge Street, spanning both the road and the pavement, and there were similar arches at the junction of King Street and the High Street and in the High Street. The arches themselves were heavily constructed of evergreen – that in the High Street bearing the motto 'She has wrought good for her people' on one side, and 'Victoria, Queen and Empress' on the other. Generally all of the High Street, King Street, the Market Square, Market Hill, Castle Street and Bridge Street were extensively decorated.

There was considerable discussion, by the Council, as to what the proceeds of the jubilee celebrations should be put towards. Suggestions included a swimmimg pool, new public gardens, a bandstand or further endowments for the almshouses and hospital. A letter published in the Walden Weekly of February, 1897 suggested that a block of houses suitable for mechanics (or labourers) should be built, as:-

> 'this would prove of double advantage. One by providing a class of much needed housing in Walden, and two, secure a home for our deserving aged townsfolk who are now kept out of the almshouses for want of funds owing to the agricultural depression.'

A public meeting was called in March to discuss the various suggestions. There was considerable debate over the various ideas with a number of people favouring a swimming bath. However the Mayor pointed out that the minimum cost of a swimming bath would be in the region of £1,000 and as the Golden Jubilee of 1887 had only raised £585, it was unlikely that such an amount would be forthcoming. Instead it was suggested that an approach be made to Lord Braybrooke to have part of the river apportioned off by the Home Farm, so that this could be used for bathing. This idea was later dropped as sewage was still being found in the river!

Eventually it was agreed to give further consideration to providing swimming baths, but the committee appointed by the public meeting had to report the idea as being impractical and it was finally decided that money raised from the Queen Victoria Diamond Jubilee Fund would be used to augment the hospital fund.

The town saw a sensational murder charge in June 1897. The accused were Emily Pask, a woman of 33, and her father, Joseph Pask aged 60 who was employed as a shepherd at Little Walden Park. Emily was not married and lived with her father and her 17 year old daughter and 13 year old son in a cottage on the park premises. The four of them slept in a single room just 10 feet by 7 feet. For undisclosed reasons, the police had had the cottage under observation and after inquries they made a search of the place. A small child was found dead in the washhouse. Dr. Bartlett was promptly called and he was to give evidence that the child had been born alive and had probably died of strangulation.

Both Joseph and Emily Pask were charged with wilful murder. At the Inquest in July, 1897, the Police gave further details of the history of the Pask family. In 1881 they had lived in Little Wratting, where Emily had a child which lived a month. Another child was the subject of an inquest in 1893, on this occasion the verdict being death by natural causes. The police added that in consequence of questions put to Joseph Pask, at the time, in respect of his relations with his daughter, he had been discharged from his employment.

The Inquest returned a verdict of wilful murder and the case was referred to the Essex Assizes at Chelmsford. According to the Walden Weekly, at the start of the trial the Judge told the jury:-

> 'the question as to who was the father of the child could not be asked now. The jury would find when the case for the Crown was over that the facts could hardly be disputed. But, what was the proper inference to be drawn from these facts as against the prisoners charged with the crime was of course a very different matter.'

Whether this suggestion of nepotism could be substantiated, we do not know, but following an admission by the Crown, that the child might have turned over and suffocated, the couple agreed to accept a charge of concealment, for which they were sentenced to 12 months imprisonment.

Another murder took place in the town in November 1898. On Sunday 31st October a tramp had been seen in town soliciting alms. Later he was admitted to the casual ward of the workhouse where he spent the night.

Bridge Street, c.1900.

The tramp, a Thomas King, aged about 30 was required to break 8 cwt. of granite in the morning, but initially refused. However on being told he would be brought before the magistrates he reluctantly started work. Then, for no apparent reason he suddenly left the yard and proceeded to an adjoining yard where the trampmaster, William Woolard, aged 64, was sweeping. King started to beat him with the hammer and after 2 or 3 blows Woolard fell to the ground. One of the gardeners, a man called Shelford, and the Union Messenger, Robert Barrett tried to pull King off but he managed to land two more massive blows. Then Blaxsell, the labour master, and Shelford managed to pull King away and detain him.

According to the report Woolard's head was battered beyond recognition – little surprising as the hammer weighed over 5¾ lbs with a 6 inch long head. Superintendent Pryke and Doctor Bartlett were called but could do nothing for the victim. King was arrested and committed to appear before Chelmsford Assizes.

Although some paving of the streets had taken place earlier, by 1898, the Council were becoming very concerned that large areas of the town were still unpaved. After considering a lengthy report, the Council agreed to pave the following areas:-

High Street: the west side
Bridge Street: the west side from Myddylton Place to Freshwell Street
East Street: south side as far as Audley Road
Station Street: the east side
Station Road: from opposite the railway station to Station Street
Church Street: the north side
Museum Street: as far as the Churchyard gates
Debden Road: from Station Road to Mount Pleasant Road
Market Street: west side from Hill Street to Market Row

The cost of this work was estimated to be between £948 and £1,358 and it was agreed to apply to the Local Government Board for loan sanction for £1,400.

A public inquiry had to be held into this request and a Local Government Board Inspector, Mr. G.W.Wilcox was appointed to conduct the proceedings which took place in the Town Hall on Friday 23rd September 1898.The inquiry was interesting not so much for the application for the loan, but because the Inspector had a wide ranging brief and was able to investigate related matters such as sewerage disposal. Thus the inquiry gives an interesting picture of the sanitary conditions of the time.

A number of local ratepayers attended including a local builder, Mr. Dix. He expressed his and other ratepayers view that what the town needed most was not made up streets, but proper sanitation. He stated that in Sewards End Road (now Radwinter Road) there were 47 houses as well as the Union building (the workhouse) and these had no drainage of any kind. There was an open ditch at the back of the houses but the

Radwinter Road at the turn of the century.

residences were not directly drained into the ditch. However the ditch inevitably received sewage and often overflowed - indeed the Sanitary authority had occasion to serve a notice on the Union to abate the nuisance this caused. In addition there had been a case of diptheria in the street. Both Ashdon Road, with 85 houses, and the Grammar School; and Thaxted Road with 55 houses had no sewer; and a child in Thaxted Road had recently died of diptheria. Mr. Dix estimated that up to 25% of the population had no sewer.

Edmund Birch Gibson, however, felt that the town was not in a bad sanitary condition, but quite the reverse. Cesspools existed in the unsewered parts of the town, in chalk and under constant supervision. The Inspector expressed concern at this statement because he felt that this could result in pollution of the watercourse, but Gibson refuted this and pointed out that the towns death rate was only 14.5 persons per 1,000. The sewage was treated chemically and the water level of 280 feet meant pollution did not occur. In the light of the Inspectors comments the Saffron Walden Weekly News of 30th September 1898 came out with a strong condemnation of the Councils attitude:-

'. . . The facts that were brought before the inspector made it abundantly clear that something must be done about sanitation and that speedily. There is no need to exaggerate the situation which is serious enough nor is there any need for alarm provided the matter is taken into hand at once. But is there any wonder that the Local Government Board Inspector should ascertain that some of the chief streets are entirely without drainage and that cesspools – dangerous always, but doubly dangerous when the soil is chalk – are in general use, that words of strong condemnation should have been employed.'

The subsequent report of the Inspector was considered at a Council meeting held on 14th January, 1899. The Local Government Board did indeed consider that the towns sewage disposal was inadequate and felt that the provision of large sewage works should be undertaken quickly. The Medical Officer of Health, Doctor Armistead pointed out that the risk of contamination to the water supply was very small as the existing well (that bored by Jabez Gibson in Hill Street in 1836), was lined with 4 or 5 inch iron tubes. Ideally it should have been lined with tin lined copper tubes. As it would mean the town would be without an adequate water supply if an attempt was made to reline the well it was therefore suggested that a new well be bored at a site approximately 70 feet away (probably in the grounds of the present fire station). It was agreed that the new well would be bored, initially to 74 feet and this section lined with 7 inch diameter stout tin lined tubes. An additional 200 feet would then be bored and this lined with 6 inch diameter tube. Once this was done it was felt that the water supply would be beyond contamination, since contaminated water only reached to levels of between 17 to 23 feet and should therefore answer the criticisms of the Local Government Board.

The work would cost about £500. The Council felt this was an adequate response and therefore deferred any decision on major sewage works.

With the outbreak of the Boer War, in 1899 there were a number of volunteers from the town to join the Army. Those wanting to undergo active service were tested and in January 1900 three members of the 'I' (Saffron Walden Company), 3rd Cambs Battalion of the Suffolk Regiment were selected. Sergeant A. Pitstow, Private F. King, and Private A. Ryan were treated like heroes, even before they had left. A large party was arranged at the Cross Keys, the night before they were due to go, with much merriment taking place. The next morning a large crowd 'including several ladies and gentlemen' assembled at the railway station complete with the Excelsior Band (the Town Band). As the train left large cheers followed the men and the band played 'Auld Lang Syne' and the National Anthem . Sadly, King was to die after six months in South Africa when he contacted enteric fever and dysentry. He was invalided home but died on 5th July 1900. Over 500 people attended his funeral at Walden Cemetery where he was buried in the north east corner.

Major events of the war such as the relief of Ladysmith and Mafeking were celebrated with patriotic fervour. When the news of Ladysmith reached Walden, flags and bunting immediately appeared. Dorset House, (the Mayors house) and the Town Hall were decorated with the Royal Standard, and Union Jacks appeared in shop windows and private houses. Strings of banners were run across roads, and the St Marys Company of change ringers rang a quarter peal of 'Ladysmiths Prize Major'. School children were given a half holiday, and in the evening a

Long serving medallists of the Saffron Walden "I" Company c.1900.

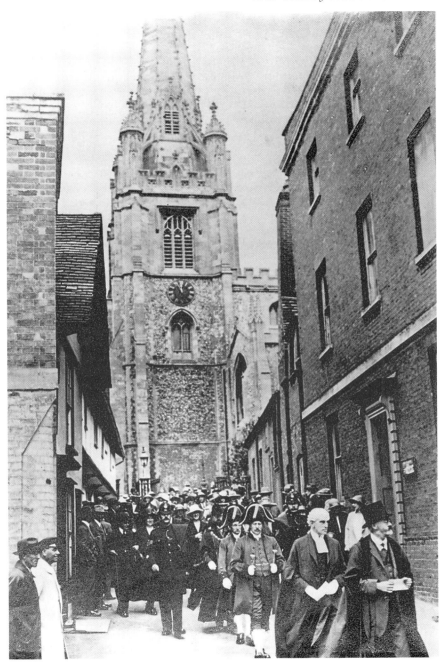

Dorset House and Church path c.1920.

torchlight procession was held around the town, with cheers being given for the Queen, General Buller and the Troops. The only disappointing note was that there was no band to lead the parade as the Excelsior had become defunct.

The missing band was rectified however, and by the time of Mafeking, in May 1900, a new band had been formed. The celebrations for the relief of Mafeking were, if possible, even more joyous. The news was received on Saturday 19th May, 1900, and immediately decorations, flags and bunting appeared. Crowds gathered in the evening expecting a demonstration, but it had been decided to leave the main celebrations until Monday night. The National Anthem was sung heartily in the Church on Sunday, and arrangements made for the Monday parade. On the Monday afternoon the children at Sewer's End School were given a half day and they marched into the town waving flags and singing 'Rule Brittania'. In the evening a procession about half a mile long lined up in Hill Street, by the Fire Station and proceeded to the Market Square. Amongst other floats there was one of 'Brittania and her subjects' which comprised of Brittania elevated on a pedestal, with representatives of the Army, the Navy, India, Australia, and others. The Saffron Walden Cycling Club appeared on their bikes 'attired in grotesque costumes', and the Fire Brigade carried a large gun on their old ladder carriage. The procession route was from the Market Square to King Street, High Street, through the Hospital grounds, London Road, Debden Road, Mount Pleasant Road, South Road, Station Road, Debden Road, High Street, and the back to the Market Square via Castle Street, Church Street, the High Street, George Street, and Market Street. During the procession £14 13s. 6d. was collected for charity.

Another General Election took place in September 1900. The towns standing member, Charles Gold decided to stand down, and the election became a straight fight between his successor as Liberal candidate, Armine Wodehouse, and the Conservative candidate, Charles Wing Gray. Wodehouse was elected gaining 3,247 votes to Gray's 3,137 votes, a majority of 110.

Chapter 12
Walden 1901-1914

Hardly had the new century started, when Queen Victoria died. In Walden the event was marked with a day in which all business was stopped, even the hotels and pubs closing from 10 am to 6 pm. A special memorial service was held in the Parish Church at which over 1,700 people attended. The new King, Edward VII was proclaimed from the Town Hall. Edward was probably the last monarch, until our present Queen, to visit the town in a private capacity, visiting Walden on several occasions.

The Town Council were still conscious of the need to provide a new sewerage scheme following the rebuke by the Local Government Board. In March, 1901 following a lengthy report the Council decided to proceed with a new scheme at an estimated cost of £16,000. However problems were to be encountered with this scheme which was designed to use Swan Meadows as the main disposal works. Following his own report commissioned from another firm of consulting engineers, Lord Braybrooke felt this scheme was inadequate and was not therefore prepared to sell the land. Much discussion followed, and by February, 1902 the Council were in a position to ask the Local Government Board for

Proclamation of Edward VII in the Market Square.

sanction to borrow £18,600. Following an inquiry in July, 1902, permission was given to borrow the necessary money. However agreement still could not be reached with Lord Braybrooke, and by 1904 the Council were considering compulsory purchase of the necessary land. For unspecified reasons the Council chose not to proceed with this. By May, 1905 the scheme was estimated to cost about £20,000, but further delays occurred whilst negotiations continued with Lord Braybrooke.

In 1910 it was finally agreed to use the existing site of Swan Meadows for the sewerage works and to dispense with the land treatment. When the new works were completed the existing works would be dispensed with. The effluent would be disposed by pipes into the Cam, discharging it downstream of Audley End House. Lord Braybrooke agreed that the pipes could go through the park, and the necessary land would be purchased at a cost of £820. Loan sanction for £23,000 was sought and obtained and in September 1910 the tender of Mr D.T.Jackson of Barking of £18,754 18s. 11d was accepted. The new sewerage works were opened in 1912.

In May, 1901, Sergeant Pitstow and Private Ryan the two surviving volunteers who went to fight in the Boer War, plus Private Lindsell, who went out at a later date, returned to a hero's welcome. Their train was met by a large crowd and the route from the station to the Church, where a special service was to be held was lined with people three or four deep. A large scarlet banner had been erected across the northern end of the High Street with the words 'Welcome Home' in white upon it. After the Church service the men went through the cheering crowd to the Town Hall where they received a formal address from the Mayor. A few days later they were provided with a special Homecoming Banquet in the Corn Exchange.

The town was forced to hold a by-election in May, 1901, when the sitting member, Armine Wodehouse suddenly died. It was a much publicized contest, and on 14th May, the famous politician, Austen Chamberlain visited the town. The Liberals chose as their candidate, Joseph Albert Pease. He was opposed by Charles Wing Gray for the Conservatives. Pease held the seat for the Liberals gaining 3,994 votes to Gray's 3,202, a majority of 792.

Pease was the first member for Walden not to have any local connection. He had previously been Member for Tyneside, Northumberland from 1892 to 1900, but lost his seat in the 1900 election. It is not clear whether Pease ever resided in the Walden area, but it is known that he had a house in London, as well as one in Yorkshire. He was returned again in 1906, with 4,203 votes against 2,935 of Sir W.D.Barttelot for the Conservatives. (57)

In January, 1902, the new Girls' British School was opened in South Road by Sir Thomas Fowell Buxton. It became attached to the Training College and was used by the College for teaching practice for many years. The school now forms part of the buildings of the Bell College.

For many years, probably since the 16th century the town had had a fair on the first Saturday in November. This was usually in the form of a horse fair. However in January, 1902, the Council met to consider its future. The demand for the fair was rapidly declining, and there was very little, if any, genuine sale of horses. The fair itself was described as to have 'so fallen away from its original character as to be reduced almost to an encampment of travelling shows and other attractions of the like nature', and it was considered that the amount of tolls were insufficient to meet the labour and expense involved as well as proving economically detrimental to the trade of the town. In addition complaints were made by neighbours of unkempt animals, non-existent sanitary conditions, and noise from steam organs, roundabouts and shooting galleries.

In the face of this the Council therefore decide to seek the abolition of the November Fair. However application to the Secretary of State for the Home Department was met with an immediate refusal and for the time being the fair had to continue.

Probably one of the towns more notable landmarks were created on 7th March, 1902. On that date Mr Edmund Birch Gibson gave to the town the trees which are planted down the High Street. According to Adams (1) Gibson made the memorable quote 'Plant as tho' you live for ever and live as tho' you die tomorrow'. Following the planting Gibson then entertained about 30 of the Corporation employees to dinner at the Temperance Hotel at the corner of Abbey Lane and the High Street.

The trees in the High Street c.1910.

THE . .
Abbey Temperance Hotel,

✦ ✦

51, HIGH ST., SAFFRON WALDEN.

EXCELLENT ACCOMMODATION

For Commercial Gentlemen. Visitors, Tourists, Boarders, etc. :: Good
Restaurant and Private Room for Ladies.   Hot Luncheons Daily.

LARGE ROOM TO LET for Meetings, Parties, Dances, etc.

Bath Room and Lavatories, *(Hot and Cold)*. : : A Half-size
—— Billiard Table for the use of Guests. ——

STABLING.   LOCK-UP FOR MOTORS AND CYCLES.
Horses and Traps, Waggonettes, etc., on Hire.

CATERING undertaken in all its branches, in or out of the Town
Balls, Parties, Club Spreads, Wedding Breakfasts and Receptions
School Treats, Fetes, Garden Parties, etc., etc.
To Let on Hire. Marquees, Tables, Chairs, Portable Coppers,
Cutlery, Crockery, Urns, etc., etc.   **Terms on Application.**
Proprietor—A. G. EDWARD.

1

In May of that year the town geared itself up for the celebrations for the Coronation of the new King, Edward VII. Numerous decorations were erected, but on the morning of the celebrations a telegram arrived postponing the events because of the King's serious illness. The celebration committee decided, however to proceed with the children's sports and teas so as not to disappoint them!

The celebrations were only delayed until August, 1902, when the town again excelled itself in decorations. The following description of the street decorations is from the Saffron Walden Weekly News of 15th August, 1902:-

'In the work of the official decorations 1,150 fairy lamps and 2,500 candles were used. There were 270 Japanese lanterns lighted. Seven hundred yards of cloth were used, also 470 yards of coloured wreathing and over a mile of coloured streamers on ropes, besides quantities of rose garlands etc. On the Market Square a three pole mast was erected over the fountain and suspended from these to poles on either side of the square were eight strings of roses etc.in various colours. On all sides of the Square were scarlet clothed venetian poles and masts which were continued on both sides of King Street, all gaily decorated. At the south end of High Street, from a pole in the centre, strings of floral wreathing were stretched across to side poles similar to the Market Place. . . . Large chinese lanterns were also hung between the poles. . . .'

In addition all the buildings were heavily decorated. The Town Hall had a large Union Jack. On the front there was a large gas jet crown with 'VII' underneath it and 'E.R.' on either side. The triangular ridges were illuminated with fairy lamps. The Corn Exchange was festooned with lamps. The pillars at the entrance were entwined with evergreen and fairy lamps, and on the clock and parapet there were gas jets. Barclays Bank, the museum gates, the Conservative club and the Rose and Crown were all similarly decorated, as were virtually all the shops, and numerous houses. A visitor to the town said that he thought it was the best display outside of London.

The day-began with a fanfare at 7 o'clock, followed by a Coronation peal on the Church bells. After a Council meeting where a loyal resolution was passed, a Church Service was held following which a large procession wound through the streets. Over 4,000 spectators then watched the numerous sports events on the Common, including running, wheelbarrow, sack, bicycle obstacle and donkey races, as well as Messers Thurston and Barker with their 'Monster Fair'. Certainly Saffron Walden gave the new King a grand welcome!

The following year was to bring Walden into the national limelight, with the magistrates court in the Town Hall, being the scene for the first stages of the trial of Samuel Dougal, the infamous murderer. Dougal had been a soldier with the Royal Engineers and was now retired living on his army pension of £50 a year. He married or lived with a large number of

Coronation of His Majesty King Edward VII.

SAFFRON WALDEN CELEBRATION

NOTICE.

The following Programme will be observed :--

WEDNESDAY, JUNE 25th :--

3 to 8. Treat to the Children, and distribution of Medals in the Deer Park,

By the kind permission of the Rt. Hon. The Lord Braybrooke.

THURSDAY, JUNE 26th :--

7 a.m. Fanfare, and Coronation Peal.

10.45. Assembly in the Market Place to take part in the Mayor's Procession to Church.

11.15. Service at the Parish Church.

12.0. Public Reading of the Address of Congratulation to the King and Singing of the National Anthem in the Market Place.

12.30. Dinner to the Aged Poor at the Town Hall.

2.30. Sports on the Common.

6.0. Distribution of Prizes by the Mayoress.

8.0. Procession to form upon the Common.

8.30. Procession to start.

9.55. Signal Rocket to be fired.

10.0. Lighting of the Bonfire.

10.15. Fireworks and Dancing on the Common.

ROUTE OF PROCESSION.

The Route of the Procession will be as under :--

Cates Corner. Hill Street, Market Street, Market Place, King Street, High Street, Church Street, Castle Hill, Castle Street, High Street, London Road, Borough Lane, Debden Road, High Street, George Street, and Hill Street to the Common.

DECORATIONS.

The Committee cordially invite the Townspeople to decorate and illuminate their Houses on this auspicious occasion. In placing Streamers across the Streets along the route of Procession, precautions should be taken for preventing the same BEING LOWER than 18 feet from the surface of the Street.

Suspension of Vehicular Traffic.

In order that the Procession may be as little obstructed as possible, the Committee earnestly request that all Vehicular Traffic along the Route of Procession, be suspended between the hours 8 and 10 o'clock on the evening of the 26th, June, and that the centre of the Streets be kept as clear as the circumstances will permit and that the By-standers will refrain from breaking into the line of Procession. The Committee confidently appeal to the Public to assist them in the observance of this rule.

Town Hall,
Saffron Walden,
June 16th, 1902

W. ADAMS,
C. H. TAYLOR, } *Hon. Secretaries to the Committee.*

HART AND SON, PRINTERS, SAFFRON WALDEN.

woman; In 1869 he married a Miss Griffiths who died in Nova Scotia in June 1885; In August 1885 he married Marie Boyd who died two months later in October 1885. He then lived with a third woman from Nova Scotia, who gave birth to his child in England. However both she and the child returned to Nova Scotia. In 1887 Dougal met a fourth woman, who bore him two children before leaving him. In 1892 he again married in Ireland, but it is not known what happened to this marriage.

What all this did prove however was that Dougal was a notorious womanizer. Camille Holland whom he met in September 1898 was almost totally innocent of such a character, she herself being a maiden lady of fifty-six. She appears to have been relatively well off, and on meeting Dougal they initially set up house at Hassocks, near Brighton. Later, Dougal spotted a farm for sale at Clavering; having no money of his own Camille agreed to purchase it. While the sale was taking place, the couple moved to Saffron Walden, taking rooms with a Mrs. Wiskens who lived in the last house in Market Row, although the address is sometimes given as Cross Street.

In April, 1899 they moved into Moat House Farm. Camille was last seen alive on May 19th, but Dougal was to continue writing cheques on her account, forging her signature. A new servant, Kate Cranwell was employed by Dougal, and in December 1902 she gave birth to Dougal's child. Meanwhile, Dougal was seeking a divorce from his wife in Ireland and in August 1902 had made application for an action against his wife in the divorce court. The divorce was due to be made final in March, 1903,

Dougal arriving at Saffron Walden station.

but the decree was quashed, by the intervention of the King's Proctor who was able to prove that Dougal was guilty of misconduct as Kate Cranwell had sought an affiliation order in the Courts. It was during these proceedings that the forgeries came to light.

Dougal first appeared in court in Walden, on the 20th March charged with forging and uttering a cheque for £28. 15s. payable to J.Heath and purporting to be drawn by Camille C. Holland. The police not being able to find Camille immediately started a search. Her body was found in a shallow grave at the farm and Dougal was arrested for her murder. He was ultimately tried at Chelmsford High Court, found guilty and hung at Chelmsford Prison on 14th July 1903. Legend has it that his initials were engraved by him on a window in Walden Police Station where he was held prior to his trial. Camille Holland was buried in the north east corner of Walden Cemetery, where her grave can still be seen today.

During 1904, the Council gave serious consideration to providing electric lighting for the town. However there was some objection, mainly by people who considered the existing gas lighting was quite adequate. The proposals involved siting a generator at the water works site in Hill Street. These objections were again raised later and as a result the scheme was dropped.

The early 1900's saw considerable activity in house and road building. During this period, houses in Victoria Avenue were being built, and in 1904-05 the Council created Fairycroft Road by widening a narrow lane

East Street showing the entrance to Fairycroft Road shortly after road widening.

previously known as Foundry Lane. In 1906, Peaslands Lane was widened and called Peaslands Road, and similarly, in 1907 Borough Lane was widened.(1)

Each year the Medical Office of Health gave an annual report to the Council. That of March, 1904, gives a good idea of the type of accommodation in the town at this time:-

'(The housing) accommodation for working classes in this district may be said to be fairly adequate, there being 4.3 persons per house at the last census as against 4.5 at the previous census. About most of the cottages there is a sufficiency of open space and cleanliness of surroundings is enforced as far as possible. Of the total number of inhabited houses, about 5% had less than 3 rooms, and about 10% less than 4 rooms and 30% less than 5 rooms. The total number of tenements in the last census was 1,382.'

In February, 1905 following a meeting at the Rose and Crown, a Walden Volunteer troop of the Essex Imperial Yeomanry was formed. This, along with the 'I' volunteer company of the Cambs. Battalion of the Suffolk Regiment, and the 'D' Company, Essex and Suffolk (Cyclist) Battalion which was formed in 1909 were to form the volunteer forces from which Walden men were to march to the First World War.

For some time Sewards End had experienced difficulties with its water supply. But in April, 1905, the Mayor, W. Favill Tuke was able to inaugurate the new water supply to Sewards End. The hamlet required approx. 5,600 gallons a day, or 15 gallons per head of population. The new supply was provided by extending the existing 2½ inch main at St. James Workhouse for about ½ a mile to Long Meadow. Here a sunken brick tank was kept supplied by gravitation from the town reservoir. An engine then pumped the water up Pounce Hill to a new water tower, 35 feet high built adjacent to The Towers. On top of this was a cast iron tank capable of holding 5,000 gallons of water. The Council had even taken the trouble to plant varigated ivy plants alongside the tower! The tower still exists as a working landmark today. This scheme was again partly attributable to the munificence of the Gibson family, Miss M.W.Gibson giving £105 to the scheme.

Following the successful coronation celebrations of 1902 the coronation committee had a sum of £119 left over. A number of suggestions had been made as to what this should be spent upon, including the idea that it might be used towards the purchase of the Dutch Gardens at Bridge End. But after consideration it was decided to provide a new footbridge across the Common, as the old bridge had fallen into decay. The money was offered to the Council who undertook the work. The steelwork for the bridge was supplied by Mr. C.B.Smith of Glasgow, the brickwork was undertaken by Messers Fairclough Brothers, and the iron work by Mr C.S.Blyth.The bridge was declared open on 27th March 1906, by the Mayor cutting a blue silk ribbon, after which, to the crowd's delight, he gave the school children of the Boys' British School a half day holiday.

On September 13th, 1906 the new Catholic Church of Our Lady of Compassion was opened in Castle Street. In about March, 1906, the Westminster Diocesan Missionaries had purchased The Close at the junction of High Street and Castle Street for their Headquarters. An article in the Walden Weekly of 14th September, 1906 relates details of the Church's use of this attractive building:-

'Although The Close is supposed to have existed prior to Queen Mary's reign, the only traceable date within its walls is the year 1554. The house is very rich with old oak, the value of which has been greatly increased since the Fathers have resided there; in fact the interior has been overhauled and repaired from attic to cellar. and many points of interest, both interior and exterior, have been brought to light. The only place in the house which it was found would serve as a chapel for the few Catholics of the town was what was previously known as the old Baronial Hall, which was restored for the purpose, and this place of worship suggests that in the earlier period it had been used for a similar purpose. The building would only accommodate about seventy to eighty persons.'

When the services first started this was of sufficient size, but as the Clergy gained a reputation as great preachers the services became more popular. To cope with this the services moved outdoors, but this was obviously unsatisfactory. To overcome the problem, the Church acquired the adjoining stable block. Again the Walden Weekly provides the description:-

'It consists mainly of what has been, appropriately the stable block, a building five bays in length, and of a height which comprised ground storey and loft. It is constructed for the most part of stout rough hewn-out timbers, weather-boarded outside. The roof is covered with old tiles and has a charming turret, with vane outside the ridge. . . . The whole height of the old portion has been opened out by the removal of the old loft floor; the rough-hewn timbers stained. . . . The clerestory and aisle windows are glazed with simple leaded lights. The floor is covered with a warm-tinted jointless flooring material. . . .'

The Church was opened with a solemn High Mass, and the building continues in use today.

The cause of Womans Suffrage came to Walden first in 1904 when a meeting was addressed by a member of the Central Society for Womans Suffrage. As a result of this a public meeting was called two years later in November, 1906 and a Saffron Walden committee was formed. In December, Miss Edith Palliser, the Secretary of the Central Society spoke to the committee. There was considerable support for the cause in Walden and even the Mayor, Joseph Bell whilst regretting that he would not be able to attend the meeting, expressed the belief 'that the time must come when the franchise will be given to woman'.

A major fire swept through the warehouse and stores of Messrs. Joseph John Robson and Sons, in King Street, in January 1908. A passing man spotted smoke and called the fire brigade, but despite a good supply of water from standpipes in High Street, George Street and Abbey Lane, the fire quickly took hold, with the roof eventually collapsing. Robsons' were a wholesale and retail provision merchants and the coffee roasting chamber and machinery were all destroyed, as were other floors containing soap, sugar salt and other dry stuffs. The upper floor contained over 700 gross of matches, and these must have contributed to the severity of the blaze! The damage was estimated at over £5,000 and the building had to be completely rebuilt.

Two other major events occurred in 1908. The first was yet another magnificent gift to the town by the Gibson family. The Council had for some time been discussing the possibility of the provision of public baths in the town. On the 10th July, the Mayor, Joseph Bell, reported that Miss Mary Gibson had agreed to give the site in Hill Street for the new baths as she did not think that it should be left to the ratepayers to pay for the site. The work started on the site in 1909, the contract for the new baths being let to J.L.Glasscock of Bishop's Stortford for the sum of £1,290.

The second important event was the opening of the Liberal Club on the corner of Hill Street and Gold Street. Having acquired the building, the Liberal Association carried out various structural alterations. The new building comprised of an agents office, a large hall with a gallery for meetings, and a reading room. Arrangements were also being made for billiards, bagatelle and other table games.

During 1908, Lloyd George had succeeded in steering his Old Age Pensions Act through Parliament. This act, which was important as one of the first steps towards a welfare state system, gave single pensioners five shillings a week and married couples 7/6d a week. The idea of something entirely 'free' to a generation used to the hard ways of either the workhouse, or considerable poverty was completely new, and people reacted in different ways. A report on the payment of the first pensions in Walden in the Saffron Walden Weekly News of the 8th January, 1909 shows how this novel event was received:-

'There was no small amount of excitement over the advent of old age pension day in Saffron Walden and the villages roundabout. . . . In Walden there are 100 pensioners. On Friday morning a Mr. List of Walden was the first to present his book at a Walden Post Office counter. During the morning about a dozen and a half received their pension. Some did not draw their money until the Saturday . . . the applicants in these cases being styled as the 'better classes' who have deliberately wished to avoid the first day crowd. . . . One instance of the first payment of pensions is worthy of special notice. One of the recipients (said to be a female) dropped her five shillings into one of the offertory bags in the Parish Church on Saturday as the collection was being taken for the assistant clergy fund.'

Buildings in Hill Street demolished for the swimming baths.

One suspects that members of the 'better classes' wanted to avoid recognition, as many people initially regarded pensions as charity and were reluctant to accept them.

To celebrate the introduction of pensions, the Saffron Walden Men's and Women's Liberal Association held a special dinner at the Victorian Cafe (now 5, King Street). The Chairman remarked that 'it was a grand day . . . (to see) so many who had stood the storm and stress of life and whose services to the state had at last been recognized by the Liberal Government, and (that) provision had been made which would enable them to keep the wolf from the door'.

The General Election to be held in January, 1910, was the first in which the womans suffrage movement were to take an active part locally. Their meetings were peaceful, the suffragettes giving speeches and a lantern slide lecture in Debden, Chesterford, Clavering, and Widdington as well as Saffron Walden. A petition was organised and signatures sought outside polling stations The Walden Weekly reports that nowhere was any antagonism displayed to the principle that everyone who paid rent, rates and taxes should have the vote. At Walden, the number of signatures on their petition exceeded their expectations and it was reported that workers at polling stations were finding cases of men, who at first refused to sign, but when the position was explained actively encouraged others to sign.

The new member was to be Colonel Douglas J. Proby, the Conservative candidate, who defeated the sitting Member Joseph.A.Pease by 4,283 votes to 4,011 votes. a majority of 272. Proby had been educated at Eton and Oxford and then had a full military career. He lived at Little Walden Hall. There was not a little acrimony after the election, with Pease claiming that his defeat was due to the advantage his opponent had over him of being able to speak in the constituency whilst he had been attending to his duties in the House. Pease felt that his opponents had 'wilfully mislead' the electorate and said that he had always thought that 'amongst gentleman it was generally expected that honest motives were attributed to their opponents'!

Such accusations obviously caused no concern to Peases' supporters who, according to the Walden Weekly, took to the street in their thousands on a torchlight procession after the announcement of the result.

The new swimming baths were finished on April 21st 1910 and formally opened on April 30th. The site of the swimming baths in Hill Street had previously been occupied by Messrs. T.C. Nunn and Son who sold furnishings, ironmongery and earthenware goods, and was purchased through the generous donation of Miss Gibson. The building was 72 feet by 37 feet wide, and 26 feet high. It was constructed of old red brick, with cast cement ballasters on the front elevation. The roof was slated with a

The Hill Street swimming baths in 1912.

glass lantern, 33 feet by 12 feet. The baths themselves consisted of the swimming bath, 59 feet by 25 feet varying in depth from 3 feet to 6 feet 3 inches at ground level, and four slipper baths on the first floor. There were changing rooms on the west side. A spring board and diving board were also provided, and it was illuminated by an eight light incandescent gas pendant in the centre, with brackets on the wall. The water supply was pumped from the old well adjoining the baths (this would have been Jabez Gibsons' original well) and was circulated, and heated, by the exhaust steam from the waterworks.

In May 1910, the Saffron Walden Pageant was held. This was a musical event arranged to celebrate Walden's history, with music specially written for the occasion. Little cameos of Walden life were enacted in the Town Hall over three nights, featuring such events as 'Ansgar's Banquet', 'the funeral procession of Geoffrey de Mandeville' and 'Cromwell and the Generals at the Sun Inn'.

Sadly the day before the pageant started, the King, Edward VII died. The event was marked in the town by the tolling of the tenor bell in the church from 11.45 am to 12.30 pm, and that evening the town band played solemn music in the Market Square. The proclamation of the new King, George V was announced to a large crowd in the Market Square on Tuesday 10th May.

A traditional Saffron Walden event held on 27th June 1910 was Great Ringing Day. This was in fact the 287th Anniversary of the event which had started in 1623 following a bequest from Thomas Turner. In his will, Turner left:-

'. . . thirty three shillings and fourpence . . . [to] be bestowed yearly upon such persons which shall ring the Bells of the Church of Walden upon the Day of the Year on which I shall be buried.'

The money was wisely invested and the proceeds from it used to provide a dinner for the ringers. Ringing of the church bells started at 9 o'clock, a Church Service was held at 12.45, and following a dinner at the King's Arms, ringing resumed until nine in the evening.

The year, having began with a General Election was also to end with one. Asquith in his struggle with the Lords was forced to call an election and Walden went to the polls. On this occasion the Liberals recovered the seat. Their candidate was Mr Arthur Cecil Tyrrel Beck who was born in 1876. He had been educated at Haileybury and Jesus College Cambridge, and qualified as a barrister. He had been Mayor of St. Ives, Hunts. in 1905-06 and had been M.P. for Wisbech from 1906 to 1910. In a close election he polled 4,071 votes, to Colonel Proby's 4,031 votes, a majority of 40.

The coronation of the new King did not take place until June 1911, and this gave the town ample time to prepare. As with Edward VII's coronation the town was elaborately decorated with a considerable

View from the water tower, 1913 showing Debden Road and Borough Lane.

View from the water tower, 1913 showing Mount Pleasant Road and the common.

number of flags, bunting, streamers and flowers. According to the Walden Weekly:-

'To some this might seem incredible, but it is nevertheless a fact that the town is ablaze with colour. Bunting and flags have been very largely used and there are fairy lamps by the thousands, to say nothing of the scores of crowns, stars, devices and initials in gas. It is not within the recollection of the oldest inhabitant that Saffron Walden was ever so gay before. In their loyalty everybody has expressed their sentiments in the best way they could.'

All the town's principal buildings were decorated, with shops, banks and businesses all joining in. The day's programme began at 7 am with a fanfare of trumpets followed by a Coronation peal on the Church bells. At 10 am a mayoral procession led the way to a Church Service after which the town's address of congratulations to the new King was read from a proscenium erected in the Market Square. Local school children were then presented with medals, and this ceremony concluded with the singing of the National Anthem. In the afternoon there was a band concert, and a dinner in the Town Hall for people over 65. In addition a dinner was to be held on the Common. This was very carefully organised. The admission ticket stated:-

'Each person and family to come neatly dressed and all to bring their mugs knives forks and plates for their own use and to replace their knives forks and plates into their baskets as soon as dinner is over and send them home. Silence is to be observed at the sound of the bugle when grace is to be said . . . the parties to retire at 5 o'clock, notice to be given by the sound of the bugle. Families are requested to keep together and go as orderly as possible to their respective place.'

About 1500 children were catered for with a special treat in the Deer Park comprising of tea, games and fireworks, and special dinners were held in the hospital and workhouse. A cricket match was held on the Common and the day closed with a large procession around the town, and dancing on the Common in a decorated enclosure.

During the early part of the century there had been some building work in the south of the town, in particular, Mount Pleasant Road, South Road, Victoria Avenue, Borough Lane and Mandeville Road (which was made up in July 1911). However this was beginning to take its effect on the town's water supply and it was becoming obvious that something would have to be done. The Borough Surveyor presented a report to the Town Council suggesting that a water tower should be constructed on land at the side of the reservoir at Debden Road. He proposed a cast iron tank 20 feet square by 12 feet deep with a capacity of 30,000 gallons, be placed at the top of the tank, 65 feet above the level of the ground or 353 feet above Ordnance Datum. The height of the tower should be 87 feet with the width at the base 25' 6" by 26' 6". The cost of this was estimated at £2,205. The Council accepted his recommendations and the foundation stone was laid on May 9th, 1913. The tower was opened in October 1913, having cost a final total of £2,469.

In fact water was in great demand throughout the summer of 1911, as an exceptionally hot period was experienced. A large number of stack fires occurred and it was fortunate that the fire brigade had acquired a new engine that year.

The following summer, 1912, saw the town at the centre of army manoeuvres. It was during these, on September 16th that the first aircraft to land in Walden came down in fields near Peaslands Farm, approximately where the Leisure Centre is now. The children from the towns schools were given a special half day holiday to enable them to see this new marvel!

The Saffron Walden Cinema opened on the 11th November, 1912 at the top of the High Street. It had been designed by Mr. A. Edwards, an architect, and was built by Messrs. H. Rooke and Sons. Initially it opened every evening with matinee performances on Tuesday, Thursday and Saturday afternoons, for 'Projection of high class pictures'. The 1914 Saffron Walden Almanac tells us that 'It is considered by most people to be an ornament and useful addition to the town. No longer can it be said: There is nowhere to go on Winter evenings! It is fitted with upholstered

The High Street showing the Saffron Walden cinema in 1924.

tip-up seating and is lighted throughout by electricity, is heated by gas radiators and has ample ventilation including two electric fans'. Certainly it must have been a rarity for a town as small as Walden to be able to boast a cinema at such an early date.

The proprietor, Mr. E.E.Smith gave an open invitation to the town for the first show, and the cinema was packed out. Films on show that day included:- 'Rapids of Kivaitch', 'The Bugler of Battery 'B'', 'An Unforbidden Guest', 'Pandora's Box', 'Nippers lullaby', 'The Gamblers', 'Lena and The Geese' and 'Deep Sea Fishing'.

It was rather ironic that the Walden Weekly reported:-

'Great attention has been paid to ensure the safety of the public. The building is of fireproof construction with half a dozen exits. Powerful hydrants are ready for immediate use and the engine and projector are of an especially constructed fireproof chamber 30 feet from the main building'

– for the building was to be burnt down in 1950.

Chapter 13
Walden 1914-1918

There was no obvious evidence in Walden during the early months of 1914 of the tumultuous events about to overtake the world. Locally two main events occupied the political agenda. The first was a proposal by Councillor Ernest Tanner to introduce electric lighting to the town. An attempt had been made to do this before, but it had failed. Councillor Tanner now thought that the time was ripe. A committee was set up by the Council to investigate this matter. The second matter was the question of the expenditure of £3355 on the Isolation Hospital (situated in what is now Hill Top Lane). A public meeting was called to protest at what many people thought was unnecessary expenditure. The Mayor, David Miller, proposed 'That the Borough of Saffron Walden and the Saffron Walden Rural District area strongly protest against the extravagant costs of the alterations of the Isolation Hospital and suggest small extra accommodation to be provided'. The view was expressed that the necessary enlargements and improvements could be carried out for about £1,000. It was also said that the hospital was quite sufficient as it was as it was never overcrowded. The matter was subsequently considered at a Council Meeting where it was pointed out that the present hospital, was not properly equipped, there were no proper conveniences, no proper disinfecting room and that people were consequently being discharged still infected.

But these parochial matters were shortly to be disrupted by the outbreak of the Great War in August 1914. The war was greeted at Walden, as elsewhere, with tremendous patriotic fervour and delight. The Walden Weekly for 7th August 1914 illustrates this clearly:-

'Walden. The War. Exciting Evening Scenes.
Wednesday was a somewhat exciting day for Walden. It was the day of departure of the Cycling Company [This was 'D' Company, 8th Essex

(Cyclist) Battalion a Walden volunteer force with a strength of 56 NCO's and Men] . . . to mobilise at Colchester. It was also the general day for reservists to leave for their respective Headquarters. A great number of people were in the street and the crowds surrounded the local Headquarters of the Company to see the men depart. There were many tears among the wives, children, sweethearts and touching scenes were witnessed. However the men went off in good spirits and were given a hearty cheer at the railway station.

At about half past seven on Wednesday evening the group 'Peace at any Price' party endeavoured to open a meeting but were met with somewhat hostile reception, the Market Square being packed. Any attempt to speak was futile and the motor car with the speakers in it was forced away from the square and the chauffeur quickly drove off. There was much excitement in the streets and a large procession was formed up and, with Union Jack banners marched through the streets of the town singing 'Rule Brittania' and other tunes.'

Men were quick to flock to the colours – some being saved from other fates – Arthur Woodley and Frank Barker who were both due to be in Court for being drunk and disorderly on 4th and 5th August did not appear because they had gone to join the reservists. Their cases were adjourned.

Public recruitment meetings were held in the Market Square. Patriotic slogans were used. A meeting held in September was typical. The Chairman told the crowd that from the Saffron Walden district:-

'they wanted the broad shouldered Essex Men who could go onto the field of battle and give a good account of themselves . . . (they would) be fighting for the very existence of their Country. They were not going to be discouraged by setbacks . . . and . . . they were going to win this war!'

In fact men from Walden and district were already flocking to the colours. The first batch of recruits (as opposed to reservists) left the town on 11th August just one week after the outbreak of war, and by the end of August another 80 had followed. By early September 265 men had enrolled including sundry tradesmen, railway officials, solicitors clerks, shop assistants, mechanical engineers, butlers, foremen and gardeners. The majority were farmhands whom enlisted as soon as the harvest was completed.

The general euphoria was accompanied by a conviction that it would all be over by Christmas. A letter quoted in the Walden Weekly in October reflects this view. The letter was sent by Private H.E.Dally to his mother living at North End:-

'Just a line in answer to yours of today to thank you for the splendid parcel. . . . When we arrived over here we entrained for the front and were denied our first shot . . . the next day there was a tremendous hustle against big odds. . . . Don't worry about me or the rest of our lot. We hope to finish this game before Christmas because everyone has arranged to be home by then and we shall win by a few runs.'

But the realities of the War were soon to hit Walden, when the first wounded soldiers arrived on Tuesday 29th September. Long before the train was due, a huge crowd, including the Mayor had assembled at the station. The wounded men were not apparently seriously injured as they were all able to walk to the waiting motor coach. However a number of the men were lame, or had arms in slings and some had heads bandaged. Three cheers were given to the men as they left the station.

There was strong anti-German feeling in the town, and this was to lead to an attack on a Councillor's house. Councillor Arthur Midgely lived in Larchmount, a large house opposite the General Hospital in London Road. Two German friends had been staying with him for a while, and news of this was circulating around the town. With the news of the German Advance (probably the First Battle of Ypres) Councillor Midgely's guests began to become the major item of conversation in the hotels and inns of the town. He was advised to get his German friends to leave the town as quickly as possible, and although reluctant to agree to this he arranged for them to catch the 5.40 train on the Saturday afternoon.

However this was too late too appease the town. It was the practice of Councillor Midgely and two or three other people to hold a small religious meeting in the Market Square on Saturday evenings. Although being made aware that if he appeared he was likely to be attacked, he nonetheless took up his usual stand. A large crowd was already in the square, and no sooner did the service start than the crowd started shouting and booing. There was a certain amount of pushing and shoving, but the police intervened and advised the Councillor and his accomplices to go home. They decided to leave, but a crowd of over 500 people followed them up the High Street to Larchmount. A force of police, under the local police chief, Superintendent Boyce were there, but the mood of the crowd was angry, and stones and missiles began to be thrown from a pile which had been assembled at the side of the road. Several windows were smashed as well as a greenhouse at the rear of the property, and even with the police presence the situation threatened to get out of hand. However another Councillor, Ernest Tanner, stood on the railings at the front of the house and addressed the crowd. He said that he had no sympathy, especially at the present time with the idea of bringing Germans into the town especially as they were staying in a house opposite the hospital containing wounded British soldiers. He felt that all enemy aliens should be imprisoned even if it meant 99 honest people had to be confined in order to capture the one spy in a hundred. He said that he had told Mr. Midgely not to hold the meeting in the Market Square that evening and that there would have been no riot had he agreed. He then asked for three cheers for the wounded soldiers which was given and the crowd gradually departed. There seems little doubt

London Road in the 1880s.

that but for the action of Councillor Tanner, an even nastier situation would have occurred.

At the end of 1914 a detachment of troops were billeted in Walden. The Boys' British School was hurriedly commandeered by the military authorities, the building being used to accommodate over 100 soldiers of the S. Staffs. Regiment. The Boys' British hastily set up a temporary school in the gallery of Abbey Lane Congregational Church.

The Friends' School was also taken over, with just two days' notice by 350 troops. 160 children were sent home with just 24 hours' notice, and although protests were made they were to no avail. The soldiers remained for 11 weeks, but gave no cause for complaint. (59)

Rifle ranges were set up in local chalk pits, and special sports events arranged on the Common. However the influx of a large number of troops presented some problems as neither the Town Hall or the Friends' School were big enough to provide entertainment for the troops in the evening. In February, a new YMCA hut was opened for the troops in Station Street. The building was designed to accommodate 600 men and included a post office and a savings bank. At the opening ceremony over 500 soldiers and public were present. The building cost £495 of which two individuals gave £100 each, the remainder being raised from the town. Sadly the troops did not always respond in such a kind manner. When the Boys' British School were allowed back into their building in March 1915 they found that the school had been subject to considerable damage – desks smashed, cupboards forced open and a general scene of destruction.

The town and district continued to respond to the call for volunteers. By November 1914, 518 men had enrolled at the Town Hall and in January 1915, the recruiting office was able to report that men were still signing on at the rate of about seven a day. Recruiting rallies were a regular feature in the town throughout 1915, often with army bands, and on one occasion an address by Private Godley, the man who won the first Victoria Cross of the War. In June 1915, a Walden Company of the Essex Volunteer Regiment was formed. Until then, most volunteers went into either the 2nd Battalion of the Essex Regiment or into Lord Kitchener's Army.

Personal tragedies inevitably occurred as the war progressed. In October 1915 the towns Vicar, the Rev. J.J.Antrobus heard that his brother, Capt. Antrobus of the 6th Cameron Highlanders had been killed in action in October. He had already lost another brother at the Dardenelles in April and by the end of 1915 reports were becoming quite regular of local men being killed or injured. But alongside this there were also reports of heroism. Sub Lieutenant Viney, who was born in Saffron Walden in 1891 was a member of the air service. Whilst on flying patrol he bombed a German submarine and broke its back, the submarine sinking within a few minutes of the bombing; and a former Walden school boy, Noel Mellish, became the first Chaplain to win the Victoria Cross. Mellish attended Walden Grammar School from 1894 to 1896, and was later on the Board of Governors. He later became the Vicar of Dunmow. A dormitory at the School was named after him.

The position of conscientious objectors is always a difficult one in a time of war. Walden's connection with the Quakers and particularly the Friends' School meant that the problems soon had to be addressed. After conscription was introduced, the Saffron Walden and Rural Tribunal met regularly to consider cases for military exemption. The problem was considered at a tribunal held in March 1916. The tribunal first considered a number of cases of local people seeking exemptions. A farmer from Audley End was exempted as he was the only man on the farm who could milk, and a similar exemption was given to a local poultry farmer. Then the tribunal had to consider the cases of Mr. John T. Whitlow, Mr. David Pearson and Mr. Philip Bradley, all assistant masters at the Friends' School and members of the Society of Friends, and all of whom had applied for exemption as conscientious objectors.

Mr. Whitlow, speaking on behalf of all three of them, said that the principle of the Society of Friends with regard to war was clear: all war was contrary to the spirit of the teaching of Christ, and he believed that it was wrong to take life. The Chairman of the tribunal asked him whether, if a man ran a bayonet into him he would not try to kill him. Mr. Whitlow replied that he might hit him, but he would rather lose his life than kill him. The military representative then asked him if he would be prepared to live under German rule. Mr. Whitlow said that he would rather that than be a conscript. He went on to claim that he was already in important national service and therefore exempt. He had been on relief work in France for eight months helping to repair war damage.

The tribunal decided to relieve these three from combatant service and leave it to the military authorities to give them non-combatant work. However this did not satisfy the teachers who said they were not prepared to undertake any work under military authority, and they gave notice of appeal.

However not all conscientious objectors were treated so lightly. Herbert W. Starkey claimed he had to live at home because of his mother's ill health. The military representative was almost disdainful of this saying that they would be better without this class of man, and the chairman castigated him for refusing to help his country. His application for exemption was refused.

The Tribunal also gives an indication of the effects the war effort were having on the towns manpower. In June 1916, Mr. A. H. Forbes, the Borough Surveyor applied for exemption for the manager and the stoker at the gasworks. He pointed out that of a pre-war staff of 44, he was now left with only 31 including women and a boy and they had an increased workload. In this case exemption was allowed.

By 1916, the war had reached mainland Britain. With Zeppelin raids along the east coast, it was realised that Walden could suddenly find itself in the front line. As a result blackout regulations were introduced and this inevitably caused complaints and confusion. Unlike the second World War there were no sirens to alert the public and the suggestion of Councillor Miller that the gas at the gas works be lowered on the approach of a Zeppelin was adopted. This would have the twofold effect of warning the townsfolk, and ensuring that any lights exposed were dimmed.

Despite this there were people who forgot, or refused to comply with the blackout. In March, 1916, the matron of Walden hospital, Miss Emily Fawcett was fined £2.5s. on two charges of not screening certain windows at the hospital. Sarah Sage, a widow of West Road, refused to comply with the blackout and was fined £2.

The air raids were also having an effect on the school children of the town. In October 1916, the headmaster of the Boys' British School wrote:-

'We find that the air raids of late are having a very bad effect on the children who are kept up all night, in a state of great fear. We have to go very quietly with our work.'

The large number of men away from the town in the forces was beginning to have a devastating effect on the town's economy. On 15th June, 1916 a largely attended meeting was held in the Town Hall. The meeting, which had been called by a number of prominent Town Councillors, had as its purpose a proposal to petition the War office to send troops to the town, not so much for patriotic as economic motives! As Councillor Williams made clear, the town and district had been large enough to accommodate a brigade and could do the same again. He remarked that Walden had been loyal throughout and he saw no reason why they should not have some return by the placing of troops in the town.

Little thought seems to have been given to the logic of this argument, which carried to every town, would have seen troops billeted every-where, with none left to serve in France! Notwithstanding this the following motion was passed and a copy sent to the Rt. Hon H.J.Tennant, the Under Secretary of State for War:-

'That this meeting of townsmen of the Borough of Saffron Walden respectfully desires the War Office to give its favourable consideration to the advantages of this town for the purposes of billeting troops if this can be done without interfering with military necessities. Attention is called to the fact that we have no munitions or similar character and, with the advent of compulsory service the earning capacity of the town is so reduced that great hardship will ensue.'

The petition was unsuccessful and there were no large number of troops billeted in the town.

Until 1916, Walden had been lucky in receiving relatively few deaths to its men, although in June 1916 one particular tragedy occurred when, Corporal Brand, one of the Walden Cycle volunteers, was accidentally shot by a comrade whilst on duty on the east coast.

But all this was to tragically change. On 1st July General Haig commenced his Great Advance on the Somme. This long attritional battle was to drag on till November, and on the first day in particular there were tremendously high casualties. The Walden men who had joined Lord Kitcheners Army (the fourth) or the Essex Regiment, were involved in the big push, many on the first day. At least two Walden men, Private William Dewberry and Private George Cornell, both from Castle Street were killed on the 1st July on the Somme. A third Castle Street man, Private G. Melbourne survived the initial attack and on the 9th July wrote to his parents of his experience. It is worth repeating that letter as it gives an indication of the terrible conditions that many Walden soldiers had to experience:-

'I am sending you just a few lines to let you know that I am alive and well. . . . I have come through the first big battle absolutely unscathed except for a few scratches and a bullet straight through my steel helmet and quite near enough to remind me of it. It was a terrible scene such as one can never forget and it will live forever in my memory. We went over the top at 9 a.m. on Saturday after a terrific bombardment which lasted three or four days. It was indeed a veritable hell on earth, the last three or four hours being the worst. Everyone was excited until the appointed moment came when the order was given to fix bayonets and over the ladders we went. However how I managed to get out onto the top of the trench I am at a loss to say. I was mad I believe. It was a fine sight to see the boys advancing and the glitter of the bayonets in the sun. But then it was so terrible, the exploding of the mines, the deafening roar of the artillery. Hardly had I gone five yards than down went two of my chums by a whizz bang and others were going down all around me. How on earth I escaped is marvellous but I went on with the rest until I found myself in the German trenches under terrific shellfire all the time. The Germans were lying on top of each other dead and we got any amount of them prisoners being only too glad to be taken out of it . . . we were pushed onto a village and here a Corporal and a Private were shot dead either side of me.'

Others killed in the early stages of the battle included Private Frederick Boyce, son of the Walden Police Superintendent, who was killed on the Somme on 20th July.

The casualty list was now, sadly, becoming a regular feature in Walden life and from now until the end of the War the Saffron Walden Weekly News records two or three deaths of Walden soldiers every week. One week typical of virtually every other week is that of Oct 27th 1916. In this week the Weekly News reported that Albert Kidman of the Essex Regiment from Mill Lane, Saffron Walden died in hospital in France. He had received a shell wound in the back during the 'great advance'. He was 35 and had been a maltster at Barnard's. Private William John Baker, aged 22 of High Street Saffron Walden, from the Royal Sussex Regiment was killed in France. He was formerly employed at Carnation Nurseries. Another employee of Carnation Nurseries, Private William Bouch aged 21 and serving with the Royal Fusiliers was killed in action, and Private F.G.Perkins, aged 20 was killed in France. He had formerly been a clerk at Messers Barclays and Cos. bank.

Lists like these continued until well into 1918. With these fatalities

Troops recovering in Walden Place Red Cross Hospital in about 1915.

followed the wounded. At the start of the war the hospital authorities had placed twenty beds at the disposal of the War office, at no cost to the nation. The hospital was established as a sub hospital to the military base at Colchester. In 1915 Walden Place had been taken over as a Red Cross hospital, with thirty beds. In November over fifty casualties arrived in the town with about thirty of these being stretcher cases. The troops that the townsfolk had asked for were arriving, but perhaps not in the condition they had in mind.

The treatment the patients received was obviously of first-class standard. At the annual general meeting of the hospital in March 1917, the hospital was able to report that of 142 military patients treated only one had so far died.

Rest and recuperation were a key requirement for the wounded, and in February, 1917, Lord Braybrooke was able to open a new wounded soldiers recreation hut which had been erected in the grounds of the hospital.The building, which was 40' by 20' and furnished and heated, had been paid for by local subscription.

In March, 1917, the newly formed detachment of the 3/2 Essex Volunteer Regiment first met in Saffron Walden, following a public meeting the previous November. The purpose of this regiment was to act as a 'home guard' for the town. The regiment comprised of 150 men from the town and villages. They were inspected by Colonel Colvin the Commanding Officer, and were reassured that there was no likelihood of them being called away from their immediate homes. It was the intention that they should be organised to defend their own homes.

The summer of 1917 saw one of the severest storms to hit the town. In August following heavy rain the Slade burst its banks. The flood gate near the entrance to the tunnel beneath the town was washed away, and the fire brigade had to pump water out of the cellars of The George in George Street and the Greyhound on the corner of George Street and the High Street. The worst flooding was at Bridge Street, where the water reached depths of three to four feet and stayed for some hours. Householders were trapped, with the furniture they could rescue, in upstairs rooms, and when the waters eventually subsided there were several inches of silt left in the rooms. The water also reached areas of Radwinter Road and Gold Street.

On the railway line the rain caused a chalk bank to slip and the line was closed by several tons of chalk which required a gang of navvies to clear it, and in Chestnut Avenue the depth of the water reached seven feet at the dip by the railway bridge. Probably the strangest occurrence happened in a garden in Pleasant Valley. Here a well of 150 feet depth was suddenly brought to light. The owner had, that morning been pulling carrots from the same spot! The well quickly filled at the height of the storm, which gives an indication of its intensity, but it equally quickly subsided after the storm abated.

Walden soldiers were decorated throughout the war. Perhaps one of the most suprising awards was that given to Capt. Edmund Walker the

ROLL OF HONOUR

THE MEN OF WALDEN TOWN WHO DIED FOR ENGLAND

These answered their King & Country's Call in the Great War 1914 ✠ 1918

Borough of Saffron Walden.
To The Mayor Aldermen and Burgesses
GREETING

... the members of the Committee appointed by the townspeople and charged with the duty of raising a Memorial to commemorate the deeds of one hundred & fifty eight men of this Borough, who either on land or water laid down their lives in the fight for Liberty against the enemies of England, having with your consent erected at Tuckingstool End in High Street as a symbol of their glory, the most worthy of all signs, a Cross, on which is inscribed in letters of bronze the names of those Sailors Soldiers and Airmen who made this supreme sacrifice, commit to the perpetual care and keeping of you the Mayor and People of Saffron Walden this record of honour in the sure hope that it will be preserved and maintained as a Continual remembrance to this & successive Generations that the great townsmen whose names live thereon died in youth or manhood for their happiness & freedom and so in grateful thankfulness inspire in them at all times a high standard of honour & Duty and a complete Devotion to Public Liberty, Order and Peace.

Given under our hands on the day of Dedication and unveiling by General Lord Horne, formerly in command of the Army in France & now of the Eastern Division of England, the ... day of May in the Year of our Lord, 19... ...

Adams William
Andrews Charles E.
Andrews Walter William
Archer Albert
Archer Alfred
Archer Charles Henry
Archer Walter
Auger Albert
Bacon Albert Edmund
Bacon Ernest George
Bacon Daniel Jabez
Badman Francis R.
Baker John William
Barker Frank
Barker Arthur Horace
Barker Sidney
Barrett David John
Bassett Albert Edward
Bassett Frank
Bassett George Joshua
Beard John Percy
Beavis Arthur George
Bird Sidney
Bouch William
Boutle Henry John
Boyce Frederick John
Brand Arthur
Brand Herbert John
Braybrooke Albert
Brown Arthur John
Chance Robert
Chapman John
Chipperfield Arnold Henry
Chipperfield Hubert
Clarke Harry
Clarke Simon
Coe Frank
Cornell George
Cornell George S.
Cornell Harold George
Cornell Thomas
Courtney Arthur George
Cox Alfred William
Crabb Walter Arthur
Davies Fred
Day Frank Douglas
Dewberry William
Downham Ernest
Downham Ernest Hubert Charles
Downham George A.
Downham Stanley William
Ellwood William
Elsom Frank
Elwood Charles
Erswell Horace
Everett Stanley
Fairecloth Rowland J.G.
Finch Ernest
Finch George
Francis Sam
Galley Victor Alphonse
Gardiner Charles Lewis
Gilbey William S.
Gilling Ernest Harold
Gilling Reginald
Goodwin William
Green Charles William
Green Horace Stanley
Grime Arthur
Guy William Norriss
Hailstone Dudley W.
Hailstone Arthur John
Halls Arthur William
Halls Benjamin Thomas
Halls James John
Hawes Frederick
Hewson William Matthew
Hill Walter Edward
Holland Walter Charles

Hopkins Reginald
Housden Charles John
Housden Peter Richard
Housden Sidney George
Howard George Henry
Jackson Julius
Johnson Donald Frederick Goold
Johnson Oven Bennett Goold
Ketteridge Bert William
Ketteridge Charles E.
Ketteridge Charles Herbert
Ketteridge Joseph Ernest
Lidman Albert Thomas
Lidman Harry Arthur
Ling Alfred George
King Charles
Lofts James
Mallion Jesse
Mallion John
Mansfield Ernest James
Markins Frank
Marks William Alfred
Martin Charles Douglas
Martin George Henry
Mascall Frederick
Meadows Arthur James
Moore George Edward
Moule Leopard
Munk Charles John
Norman Errington H.
Parsley Walter
Pearson Charles Stephen
Pearson George Stephen
Pearson Joseph
Penning Arthur William
Perkin Alexander
Porter Andy
Porter Bertram Alfred
Porter Henry Sidney James
Porter Joseph John
Pursey Douglas Charles
Reed Frank
Reed Frank Wilfred
Reed S.W.
Reed William Charles
Richardson Arthur
Richardson George
Ridgewell William James
Rushforth Arthur Samuel
Rushforth William Walter
Sauard William Henry
Searle Geoffrey
Searle Victor
Simpson Charles James
Smith Frederick Henry
Smith Tom
Start Samuel Charles
Start William
Start William Frank
Swan Eustace Isaac William
Swan George William
Swan George Roy
Swan William Dudley
Taylor Herbert Hampden
Taylor Walter William
Thorpe Walter George
Walker George
Waters Arthur
Wells Frank E.
Whitehead Archibald James
Whitehead Osborne
Wills Frederick George
Wilson Stanley George
Wisken William
Wren Charles
Wren George
Wren Hubert
Wright Ernest William
Wyatt Alfred John

son of Mr. J. Walker, the headmaster of the Friends' School. He was one of the first members of the Society of Friends to voluntarily join the forces for combatant service, and in January, 1918 was awarded the Military Cross for gallantry. Sadly his brother, 2nd Lieutenant Stephen Walker was killed whilst flying in May 1918. He had just completed 20 hours solo flying, and graduated as a Flying Officer. A number of Walden men joined the emergent Royal Flying Corps, and he was probably the first Walden aviator to be killed.

During the 4th to 9th March 1918, there was a War Bond week. Walden was set the objective of raising £15,000 and succeeded in actually raising £63,400. This marvellous effort is reflected by the fact that Cambridge was aiming to raise enough for a destroyer, estimated to cost £150,000.

As the War dragged onto its fourth year, with its long casualty lists, the concept of remembrance began to capture the public imagination. In Walden it was decided to hold a remembrance day on August 4th 1918, the fourth anniversary of the outbreak of the war. By this time 111 men from the Borough had been killed. There was as yet no war memorial, and so it was decided to use the fountain in the Market Square as the centre for the ceremony. According to the Walden Weekly of 9th August 1918:-

'The fountain . . . was transformed into a war shrine and effectively adorned with flowers and evergreens. At the summit there was a display of Union Jacks. Wreaths and garlands of evergreens were hung and brought down to the four corners of the base of the structure. Rising from each corner were pyramid foliage plants in large pots, and on the steps of the fountain and on the four sides were large pots of scarlet geraniums. Around the whole, and forming a rail were a row of evergreens. On the south side of the fountain was hung the Roll of Honour. The frame is of gold and black and the inscription at the head of the list of names is as follows: To the Glorious Memory of the men of this Borough who have fallen in the war 1914-1918. On the north side of the fountain was another large framed illuminated list inscribed with the ships and regiments in which the men named on the Roll of Honour were serving. Then followed the names of five warships and thirty-five Regiments to which the men belonged. At each of the four corners of the shrine, sergeants and local volunteers were on guard with fixed bayonets.'

What was almost certainly the first Remembrance Day Ceremony in Walden started with a procession in King Street at 10.30 a.m., where about 500 people walked past the shrine on the way to Church. A member of each of the organisations represented dropped within the enclosure by the fountain, a wreath or a posy of flowers. Church ceremonies were then held in all the town's churches, and following the services, the procession reformed and marched back to the Market Square. Here, in front of the Town Hall, a large platform had been erected, with seats for wounded soldiers. Loyal addresses were given, grateful thanks expressed and the ceremony finished with songs and the National Anthem.

The town understandably gave a sigh of relief when the armistice was finally signed three months later on 11th November 1918. Rumours of the signing reached the town at about 9 a.m. that morning, and despite the bad weather people began congregating outside Messrs. Hart and Sons premises in King Street, where traditionally telegrams were displayed. Then at 12.45 the crowd spotted the Mayor, Alderman Myhill, making his way from the Post Office in King Street to the Town Hall, and they quickly followed him. He reappeared at the first floor window of the magistrates room and read out to the crowd the following telegram:-

'Armistice signed at 5 o'clock this Morning. Hostilities ceased on all fronts at 11 o'clock. Official.'

Flags began to appear everywhere, and there was considerable excitement. On the Tuesday evening a service of thanksgiving was held in the Parish Church, which was well attended by a large crowd. However there were undoubtedly many sad memories, and the crowds dispersed relatively quickly in a subdued, if happy mood.

Today 158 names of dead from the Great War are recorded on the War Memorial. Wounded would have probably been double that figure, and at a time when the towns population was little more than 6,000 there could have been very few families who were not touched by the war's tragic consequences. Walden's almost euphoric welcome of the war was echoed all over the country and we must not let ourselves judge our predecessors from the position of hindsight. The Walden men who fought and died on land, sea and air did so for many reasons. Undoubtedly one of those was to ensure that a town which had nurtured and raised them was defended so that generations such as ours could live freely and safely.

Harts shop from which Walden learnt of the end of the war.

Peace celebrations in the Market Square, July 1919.

Chapter 14
Walden 1919-1929

The post war period started with a General Election. In Walden, the sitting member, Arthur Cecil Tyrrel Beck, stood for the Liberal coalition. He was opposed by J.J. Mallon, the official Labour representative. The poll was declared on the 3rd January, 1919, with Beck retaining his seat with 10,628 votes to his opponents 4,531 votes, the increase in votes cast being due to the success of the womans suffrage movement in obtaining votes for women over 30. In January, 1920, Beck was knighted.

Although the war had ended in November, it took some time for prisoners to be repatriated. Once they were home however the Council decided to greet the men with a welcome-home dinner. Twenty-three former prisoners were entertained at the Victorian Cafe (now 5, King Street), in January 1919, with the Mayor proposing a loyal toast.

On 19th July 1919, the town formally celebrated the peace in style. The town was decorated throughout, with the fountain in the Market Square being treated as a war shrine. Large portraits of Admiral Beatty and Sir Douglas Haig adorned the Corn Exchange, and the usual bunting and flags were seen everywhere. A laurel wreath hung over the Boys' British School with the inscription 'To our 80 dear British school boys who have fallen' which perhaps best symbolised the poignancy of the occasion and brought home the large loss of life.

The actual celebrations started with a victory march of about 450 discharged and demobilised men who assembled at the top of the Common and marched to the Market Square via Castle Street, the High Street and King Street, where the Mayor took the salute. A formal address of thanks on behalf of the Council was read out, and the officers and men then proceeded to the Town Hall and the Corn Exchange for dinner, loyal toasts and speeches. Meanwhile sports were arranged on the Common for the children, and after this they were given tea at their schools. In the evening, there was a procession of floats through the town, and dancing was held in Bridge End Gardens. Finally at 10.00 p.m. a large bonfire was lit on the Common and effigies of the Kaiser were burnt.

However with such a heavy loss of life it was inevitable that peoples thoughts turned to how these men could be commemorated. In March, 1919, the Town Clerk had reported that the War Office had written to him offering the town a 77 mm field gun and this was later presented to the town in February, 1920 by the 9th Battalion of the Essex Regiment. So when a meeting was held in the town in May, 1919 a number of people suggested that the gun could be incorporated into some form of memorial. Others however felt that the memorial should be in a more practical form, such as housing or financial assistance to widows or children. The Mayor was not prepared to entertain such ideas as this as he felt that this provision should be made by the Council and not from money voluntarily raised. The gun itself was later kept in the museum grounds for safekeeping.

A committee was established to look at fifteen different suggestions, and in December 1919 they reported back with their conclusions. Their decision was to erect a 25 foot high War Memorial of octagon shape made of portland stone at the southern end of the High Street, and to place a Roll of Honour in the Town Hall. Any surplus funds were to be spent for the benefit of the dependants of the dead, or for assistance to the hospital. The meeting endorsed this decision and work commenced on the memorial.

But the question of housing was not forgotten. In a report made to the Council in June, 1919, the Borough Surveyor identified the need for about 70 more houses in the town. He considered the shortage was due to the growth of the town, the fact that a number of 'air raid exiles' now wished to remain in the town, the return of servicemen, some of whom had now married, and the absence of any building for the previous five years.

The Borough Surveyor recommended that the Council acquire a site on either side of the Debden Road above Isolation Hospital Lane (now Hill Top Lane). It was felt to be a suitable site because of industry in that area, and because the land lent itself to 'a garden city model'. The Council agreed to proceed and by the end of 1921 work had started on building what is now Landscape View.

The Post Office moved from King Street to its existing site in the High Street in 1919 opening there on Saturday 21st June. The old site had proved to be too small.

Despite the sorrow of the war, life continued and a number of Walden institutions opened in the years after the war. On the 10th September, 1919, the Golf Club was opened, and on 14th October 1920 the United Services Comrades Club opened in premises in Church Street. The Club was formed for ex-servicemen, and started its life in Dorset House before moving to its present location in the High Street. In December, 1919, the Council decided to confer on Alderman Addy Nunn Myhill the Freedom of the Borough. The award was principally for the 'splendid patriotism shown by him during the war 1914-1918' as well as for his services to the Mayoralty during the latter part of the war. Alderman Myhill had been closely associated with the local charitable war enterprises, had done much work for the hospital in assisting the wounded, and had helped on numerous war and peace time committees.

Two major controversies occurred in the town in 1920. The first was the application by the Vicar and churchwardens for a faculty to place five statues in niches in the north and south walls of the Church. Amidst allegations of idolatry and popery, Sir Alfred Kemp, the Chancellor of the Diocese held an inquiry to consider the matter. The Vicar, the Rev. Hughes, explained that the Church was considered the finest structure in the Diocese of Chelmsford, but it was considered slightly defective in ornamentation. Opponents, led by Ernest Tanner, considered it was a

'Superstitious reverence' and presented a petition of over 600 parishioners objecting to the statues. However after hearing both sides, the
faculty was granted and the statues erected.

The second controversy, surprising for the war was only over for two
years, was the suggestion that the town did not show proper respect on
Armistice Day. According to the Walden Weekly, beyond the flying of the
Union Jack at half mast on various buildings, there 'was nothing of a
public character in commemoration of the day'. Allegations were also
made that the average man and woman in the street carried on driving
their horses and cars, and made no attempt to honour the dead. A couple
of weeks later, the paper printed a letter from the newly formed United
Comrades Club and sent to the Council saying:-

'. . . It is a great pity . . . that a town like Saffron Walden should treat
Armistice Day in such a cold and off hand manner. . . .

The question also arose as to when something further will be done
towards the erection of the War Memorial. It is understood that Saffron
Walden is one of the few towns or villages who have not, as yet, erected
its War Memorial.

The general opinion is that Saffron Walden is endeavouring to
achieve the distinction of having been the last town in the country to
erect a memorial to the fallen.'

The opening of the War Memorial, May 1921.

Whatever the rights or wrongs, the town were attempting to erect a War Memorial as quickly as possible, and on 7th May, 1921, it was formally unveiled, by General Lord Horne, GCB, KCMG, General Officer commanding of the Eastern Command. A parade of 150 ex-servicemen and 14 Officers marched from the Market Square via King Street to the memorial, where the Council were assembled. Also present were Lord Braybrooke, and Sir Cecil Beck, the towns M.P. When General and Lady Horne arrived, there was a hymn, and then the General unveiled the memorial. Following this the last post was sounded and after a short vote of thanks by the Mayor, the ceremony was concluded. Hundreds of people were present and the bottom of the memorial was virtually obscured by wreaths and flowers. The carvings on the four sides of the memorial show:- a wreath of wild rose surrounding the shield of Saint George; a wreath of English oaks surrounding the shield of the County of Essex; a wreath of Saffron Crocus and a shield with an embattled castle enclosing three saffron flowers; and a wreath of bay leaves enclosing the old town seal, a lion rampant and a fleur de lys.

The Chairman of the organising committee also presented the Mayor with an illuminated Roll of Honour in a gold frame, and this the Mayor agreed to place in the Council Chamber, where it can still be seen today. The memorial was well tended and for many years new flowers would be frequently seen on its steps.

Later that year the town became involved in what was described as a 'Whitehall Scandal', when the town's M.P. Sir Cecil Beck was cited as a correspondent in a sensational divorce case. The application for divorce was sought by Capt. E.B. Charteris, a Private Secretary at the War Office. At the hearing evidence was given by the managing clerk of the solicitors acting for Capt. Charteris. The clerk had gone to a Paris hotel, where he saw Sir Cecil in his pyjamas. He also saw Mrs. Charteris in the same bedroom. A decree nisi was granted. Whether it was caused by the case, is not clear, but Sir Cecil decided to sit for another seat in the next Parliament.

Despite the promise of work for returning soldiers, unemployment remained high both nationally and in Walden. In December 1921 the Mayor reported receipt of a letter from a committee representing the unemployed, asking for the Councils assistance. The Highways Committee suggested two projects which could be undertaken to provide work, the widening of Thaxted Road at Peaslands Farm, and opposite Brick Kiln Farm. The acquisition of the land was quickly agreed and as it was a County road the consent of the County Council was sought. In addition work was also offered to the unemployed in assisting with the laying of nine new gas mains throughout the town.

During the early months of 1922 there was some debate about whether the area could continue to support two Grammar Schools at Newport and Saffron Walden. The County Council had carried out a review of educational requirements and felt that a solution might be to make Saffron Walden Grammar School a girls' school. Meanwhile, the Board of

Education announced its intention to withdraw the grant from Walden Grammar School as Newport was of sufficient size to take all the pupils from the area. In April 1922, the County Council announced that if it was the intention of the governors of Walden Grammar School to close the school they would be prepared to transfer the free place pupils to Newport. However the Governors made it quite clear that it was not the intention to close the school and after lengthy discussion a formula was reached to keep the school open. In July 1923, the school, celebrated its quin-centenary with a thanksgiving service, and a lunch in the grounds of Farmadine.

The town saw a number of lively meetings over the question of prohibition of alcohol. A meeting called by the town branch of the National British Womens Temperance Association in March, 1922 was broken up by hecklers, who objected to both the theme of the speaker and the fact that she was a foreigner! A meeting was then held in the Market Square under the auspices of the Fellowship of Freedom and Reform, which unanimously passed a resolution condemning prohibition. Of course the prohibitionists then claimed that it was the effect of drink that had resulted in the breaking up of the meeting!

We have already seen the numerous donations made to the town by the Gibson and Tuke families, but one further donation remained. In April, 1922 Mr. W. Favill Tuke wrote to the Chairman of the Vestry expressing his wish to place something in the Parish Church in memory of his wife. He suggested a Chancel screen which it was estimated would cost about £1,000. He wished to know if the erection would meet with the approval

Interior of the Parish Church before the rood screen was installed.

of the Vestry, although added, perhaps mindful of the controversy with the statues in 1920, that he had decided to omit from his proposal a roof beam with figures carved upon it. The Vicar supported the scheme, adding that there was evidence that there had been a chancel screen before as was evidenced by marks on the stonework. He believed it had probably been removed by Cromwell. The Vestry accepted the proposal, and the screen was eventually erected in 1924. The screen is made of best English Oak and is 25' 3" high, and 23' 3" long. It was dedicated at a special service on 10th October 1924 at the same time as the opening of the Church organ following its reconstruction.

The most wide ranging decision made in 1922 was to bring electricity to the town. A special report commissioned by the Council was undertaken by Mr. H.P.Girling. Mr. Girling had carried out a survey to determine demand and had found an overwhelming support for the introduction of electricity. The report, presented to the Council in October, recommended the establishment of an electricity plant on the site of the Gas works in Thaxted Road. It was pointed out in the report that as the town was already favourably placed by owning the gas and water undertakings, the Council would be in a position to supply a large additional amount of gas to power the electricity supply in the event of a coal strike. The estimated cost of the initial scheme was about £6,000. The report was adopted by the Council, and in November, 1922 application was made by the Council to the Electricity Commissioners for a special order enabling the Corporation of Saffron Walden to supply electrical energy for both public and private purpose in the Borough. Permission was granted and on 1st April, 1925, the electricity supply was officially switched on.

As predicted the electricity supply proved extremely popular. Initially there were 29 consumers, but by July 1927, the Council had completed additional works because of the demand which, by then, had reached 160 consumers. The extra work involved increasing the capacity of the station to 160 KW and installing new engines.

At the end of 1922, there was a General Election. The sitting member, Sir Cecil Beck had decided to chose another seat, and so the Liberals chose Dr. Robert McNair Wilson as their candidate. However there was to be an upset in the Walden seat, and William Foot Mitchell captured the seat for the Conservatives. The full result was:-

William Foot Mitchell (Con) 9,844
William Dawson Harbinson (Const. Dem) 3,097
Robert McNair Wilson (Lib) 2,853
William Cash Jnr. (Lab) 6,797

Mitchell was a director of the Shell Oil Company, and lived at Quendon Hall. He remained the towns M.P. until 1929. In December 1923 at the General Election he received 9,652 votes, William Cash finishing second for Labour with 6,398 votes, and Wilson polling 5,752 votes for the Liberals. In the 1924 election he polled 12,289 votes to 6,340 for William Cash (Labour) and 5,195 for A.N. Mathews (Liberal).

Early in 1923, the Council were successful in obtaining Central Government grants for unemployment work. As a result of this work was carried out in road widening on Ashdon Road, Little Walden Road, Debden Road, and at the chalk cutting on Newport Road and Butlers Corner. A tragic death occurred in 1924 when a workman was killed whilst working on the chalk cutting on Newport Road. The bank slipped and he was buried under the chalk.

For some years the Council had been concerned that the two fairs held on the Common had deteriorated into a gypsy encampment and numerous complaints had been received about their behaviour. The fairs which dated back to the towns 16th century charters were normally held on the Saturday before and the Monday after Mid Lent Sunday, and the first Saturday and the following Monday of November. The primary purpose of the fair was to act as a horse fair, although there were also amusements as an adjunct to this. Matters came to a head in April, 1923 when the Superintendent of the Police wrote to the Council complaining that the action of the traders on the Common were virtually beyond his control. Some of the stall holders were arriving on the Thursday night, and as they were not allowed onto the Common until Midday on Saturday, they were blocking up the streets. Many of them refused to leave on time, and horses and other animals were allowed to roam causing complaints from farmers. Although latrine accommodation was provided the travellers frequently fouled the Slade, and the Borough Surveyor was concerned that the large number of traction engines now being used left the Common in a ploughed quagmire. Allied to all this was the fact that trading in horses, the primary purpose of the fair, was becoming negligible. The Council therefore applied to the Secretary of State for the abolition of the Mid Lent and November fairs. Abolition was approved and an agreement reached with the Showmans Guild over the running of the pleasure fairs which were to continue.

The abolition of the fair, perhaps highlights the gradual change the town was seeing from the horse to mechanised transport. By Christmas 1923, the question of parking was being considered by the Council. Cllr. Titchmarsh expressed his concern that there was nowhere to park and he felt permission should be given to park on the Common. Cllr. Tanner supported him and said that in the City of London there were places where cars could be parked all day long! Walden was obviously not ready for this yet, however, as the Council did not feel the problem was sufficiently pressing to take such action. By 1925, though, parking was being allowed along the top of the Common despite complaints that nobody would use it because it was too far from the Market – shades of Swan Meadow in the 1990's.

A Saffron Walden branch of the National Union of Society for Equal Citizenship was formed in the town in February 1924. The Society's aim was to ensure woman had a voice in all concerns that affected them and were working hard to achieve equality of the voting age. This was achieved in 1928. Despite the towns reputation as being slow and sleepy

Saffron Walden Corn Exchange c.1900.

Walden was in fact one of the first towns to have a woman elected as a Councillor, Mrs. Mary Midgley being elected on the 1st November, 1919.

From the number of building applications being received the town appears to have been recovering economically. The twenties generally saw quite extensive building both private and Council. In 1921 and 1922 the Council had built 32 houses in Landscape View, in 1927 they built 16 houses in Thaxted Road, and 8 in Little Walden Road and in 1930 another 22 houses in Radwinter Road and Thaxted Road. Private house building occurred throughout the town with roads such as Springhill Road, Summerhill Road, and Victoria Gardens all being developed at this time.

All of this, and new Government legislation was causing additional pressures on the Council staff and in July 1924, the staffing was reorganised and additional staff appointed.

The town had always supported a Volunteers Company, but this had folded at the end of the war. In April, 1924 a meeting was held for the purpose of raising a company of the 7th Battalion of the Essex Regiment (Territorial) Army in Saffron Walden. Before 1914, Walden had supported the Saffron Walden (Cyclists) Battalion, but unfortunately during the war the battalion had been found to be of no further use because of the nature of the war. The appeal was immensely successful and a new Company was quickly formed. The Company soon established itself, and by November 1924, had already won the Battalion recruit cup for Musketry, and were the best turned out recruits during the Regiments Summer Camp. It established its headquarters in Dorset House, where a number of recreation rooms were fitted out.

A Rotary Club was established in the town in 1925, and on 25th July, the Saffron Walden Rotary Club received its Charter of Membership to the Rotary Clubs of the World. The Rotary Club still continues to this day.

Inevitably, with narrow streets, dangerous turnings and an increase in car ownership, traffic was beginning to become a problem in the town. The town still had no one way streets, which did not come until the thirties and the Council concerned at the risk of accidents suggested a 10 mph speed limit should be imposed. However the County Council were not prepared to support an application to the Ministry of Transport, and the matter had to be dropped.

The Board of Management of the hospital launched an appeal in July 1925 for £6,000 with a view to improving the facilities offered by the hospital. No major works had been carried out at the hospital since its inception in 1864 and the Board wished to provide an anaesthetizing room, an ante room for staff, a sterilizing room, a new cubicle and dark room for the x-ray department, and further accommodation for the nurses and to house the various clinics. The appeal made a tremendous start with donations amounting to £2,123 almost immediately being paid.

On December 27th, 1925, a serious fire broke out in the vestry of the Abbey Lane Congregational Church. For a time it was thought it might burn down the church, but it was eventually brought under control, although causing about £700 worth of damage.

As we have seen improvements were made to the Electricity Under-taking during 1926 because of the demand. At the same time the Council also agreed to spend £10,570 on an enlargement scheme for the gas works, as a number of complaints had been made concerning the quality of the gas.

Before this work could start however, the General Strike occurred in May 1926. Its effect on the town appears to have been very little, although no doubt the foresight of the Council in providing a gas powered electricity system was appreciated. The only men on strike in the town were the railway staff. London newspapers were unpublished, but the Cambridge Daily News produced a special strike edition, and wireless bulletins were written down and pasted up in shop windows. According to the Walden Weekly the sale of wireless sets increased in the town. Rumours circulated around the town that building trade operatives might strike, but in the event these proved false. The Council held a special meeting to discuss the situation and acquired powers to restrict street lighting and to reduce gas pressure, but neither of these powers were used. They also appointed a coal controller and quickly acted to organise food supplies. The Council were later congratulated for their quick response which ensured that both food and coal were plentiful through-out. During the strike a number of lorries delivering food supplies to the town were stopped on the Bishop's Stortford road by pickets from the Transport Workers Union, but police intervention ensured they could continue to the town.

The strike lasted only a few days, and according to the Walden Weekly of 14th May, 1926:-

'The news that the great strike was over was received with general satisfaction in Saffron Walden. Those who had heard it over the wireless soon spread the glad tidings and it is not too much to say that within 10 minutes the news had reached every part of the town.Those who had posted bulletins on shop fronts soon displayed the windows with the magic words 'Strike over'. The general opinion amongst townsfolk appears to have been that the strike was a blunder on the part of organised labour and that the Government headed by Mr. Baldwin took a strong line throughout the crisis. Many people have remarked upon the inactivity of the local Labour Party. Not one public meeting was held during the strike. Whatever the consequences to those who come out on strike, Saffron Walden, although little affected from an industrial point of view, received the news that the strike was over with one of thankfulness and gratitude.'

It should not be thought that the strike was totally ignored in the town. In November 1926, two famous Labour politicians, George Lansbury and Ellen Wilkinson gave a talk at the Town Hall. Lansbury who was giving support to the miners still out on strike, met with frequent interruptions, and eventually two members of the audience had to be ejected. Ellen Wilkinson talked on the wastage of war.

As we have seen concern at housing conditions in 1925 had led the Council to consider a house building programme. Allegations of slum housing had resulted in the building programme and this appears to have been fairly successful. In August, 1926, the Medical Officer of Health made his annual report to the Council. He noted that the towns population had declined, from 5,874 in the 1921 census, to an estimated 5,574 in 1925. However he was able to report that overcrowding had been overcome to the extent that no small houses were now known to be occupied by more than one family – in 1921 there had been 150 such houses. It was still believed that about 104 houses were what was described as 'cramped and unhealthy'. The Council's housebuilding was to continue throughout the thirties.

But just as housebuilding was begining to increase in Walden the agricultural slump began to be felt. Reports in the Walden Weekly throughout 1927 and 1928 continued to show how the slump was affecting farm prices, and a poor harvest in 1927 did nothing to help the economy of the town. Even those things normally well supported financially began to feel the effects – the hospital appeal despite such a tremendous start was still £500 short of its target 18 months later.

Probably the major talking point of 1927 was the visit to the town of an Avro aeroplane and pilot. For ten days during April townsfolk had the opportunity to see the town from the sky. The pilot, Capt. D.P.Cameron, an ex- service pilot gave trips around the town taking off and landing from the field opposite Copt Hall Farm in Ashdon Road (now De Vigier Avenue). Hundreds of people flocked to the temporary airfield on the first day, although flying was not possible then because of weather conditions. But later during the weeks hundreds of people experienced their first flight.

The Masonic Hall in Church Street was opened in 1927. For many years a freemasons' branch had existed in Walden, but had no permanent home usually meeting in the Vergers House in the Churchyard. The new hall provided both a meeting place and a hall which could be let out.

At his election as Mayor in November, 1927, Dr. J.H.Swanton had suggested that a Development and Publicity Committee should be formed in the town with the object of making the town and neighbour-hood more attractive to traders and residents. The suggestion proved popular, and was taken up in particular by the recently formed Rotary Club. They considered a number of suggestions for ways to improve and promote the town at a meeting in January 1928. Amongst the suggestions made were to transfer the town to Cambridgeshire, thus relieving the town from the effects of being rated with Metropolitan Essex; bringing pressure on the Government to lift restrictions on house building; providing a new recreation ground; and providing roadside advertis-ments to attract visitors and businessmen to the town.

A publicity committee was set up to look at these suggestions and reported back in March 1928. Amongst other things they suggested advertising the town at places like Liverpool Street Station; encouraging traders to use material advertising the town in their correspondence; establishing a social reception committee whose duty would be to welcome new residents or visitors to the town, and encouraging the Railway authorities to provide a faster and more efficient service to the town. All of these suggestions were acted upon, although it cannot be said what effect it had on the town.

The Cricket Club were also interested in the possible provision of a new recreation ground. The Club had played on the Common since at least 1812, but this was now proving less than satisfactory. The Club was losing fixtures because of the state of the ground, and with the public having access to the ground problems sometimes occurred. During 1923, the Club had made an effort to obtain its own ground. An approach to Lord Braybrooke to use Audley Park had failed and although a field at Farmadine was under discussion, it had been rejected as there was no security of tenure.(58) So in 1928 the club approached the Council with the idea of buying a piece of land in Debden Road, close to the Landscape View development. The cost to lay out the ground was estimated at about £350, and the club offered the Council £50 for the ground. However the Ministry of Health, whose consent was required would not sanction the sale and so the scheme fell through.

The Common with the cricket pavilion c.1881.

During 1927 and 1928, work had been undertaken on the building of a Carmelite Convent on land at the top of the Common. The Convent was founded by the Reverend Mother, the Prioress of Notting Hill, and was built on the lines of the Carmelite Convent at Avila in Spain. When it was built, the Walden Convent was believed to be the only purpose built Carmelite Convent in England. The Convent comprised of about 80 rooms with choir, ante-choir and chapel and sitting accommodation for about 200 people. It occupied grounds of about 4½ acres, and was intended for a community of twenty four nuns.

The Convent was opened by the Archbishop of Westminster, Cardinal Bourne, on Monday 16th July, 1928. Sadly some controversy surrounded the opening as the Town Council refused to offer a civic welcome to the Archbishop, and this angered a number of people. The Convent closed in the late 1970's and the site developed for housing.

Undoubtedly, however, the major issue of 1928 was the sale of the Mazer bowl, famous if only because of its connection with Samuel Pepys. The idea of its sale was first mooted in April. The trustees of the King Edward VI Almshouses had decided, reluctantly, to sell the bowl to provide an endowment for the almshouses. Under the trust deed the trustees had to provide for 62 almshouse inmates, and they should have been able to appoint any poor person to an almshouse, subject only to residential qualifications. However because of the lack of an endowment, in practice the choice was restricted to those who had sufficient secured income, hence the need to sell.

The decision produced an uproar, with letters appearing in the press every week. Various suggestions were made to try and keep the bowl in the town, and the national press became embroiled in the controversy. There were suggestions that the Council might buy it, and one wealthy person offered to pay 200 guineas towards its purchase provided five other persons came forward to match this. In December 1928, the Council passed a resolution calling for a public inquiry into the sale.

But all this was to no avail. In January, 1929, the Charity Commissioners approved the proposed sale and authorised a scheme permitting the trustees to sell the bowl. It was eventually sold on 3rd July to a London Silversmith, Mr Percy Oliver of Regent Street for £2,900. This figure itself was a disappointment for it had been expected to fetch about £5,000. Eventually the bowl found its way to America, where it is kept in the Pierpont Morgan Library in New York.

In November, 1928 new rating assessments were made for the town. These caused an uproar and a public meeting was called. Councillor Tanner led the protest and suggested everybody appeal against the assessments. In the event an advisory committee was formed, but the protest subsided.

The hospital had proved remarkably successful over the years and had obtained a fine reputation, but the trustees had been concerned that it had been beyond the reach of poorer people. In May, 1929 they launched the Saffron Walden Workers Hospital Scheme. Its object was to obtain regular contributions from members and in return to provide use of the hospital, x-ray facilities and convalescent home, free of charge, when required. The scheme was open to all workers within the town and district, whose income did not exceed £250 per year. The contributions were:-

Man and wife and children to age of 14 – 2d per week
Adult 18 plus – 2d per week
Adult 14 to 18 – 1d per week
Widow, with or without a child to the age of 14 – 1d per week

The General Election of May, 1929 saw a new candidate, Richard Austen Butler, standing for the Conservatives, Foot Mitchell deciding to stand down. The Conservatives retained the seat with Butler polling 13,561 votes, William Cash polling 8,643 votes for Labour and A.N.Mathews obtaining 8,307 votes for the Liberals.

'RAB' Butler as he became universally known proved to be one of the town's most famous characters. In his long parliamentary career, in which he remained as Walden's member until his retirement in 1965, RAB held numerous high offices including Lord Privy Seal, Minister of Education, Home Secretary and Chancellor of the Exchequer. He was twice only narrowly passed over as Prime Minister, and despite all this was an excellent constituency MP who was to be frequently seen in and around the town.

Chapter 15
Walden 1930-1939

During the 1930's the Council continued its house building policy. In 1930, fourteen Council houses were erected in Radwinter Road, opposite the Cemetery, four in Thaxted Road, and four next to Springfield Cottages.(1) The debate concerning the siting of the houses which took place during the housing committee meeting of 10th January, 1930 is interesting as showing how attitudes have changed in respect of size of sites and their amenities. Some Councillors considered that the Radwinter Road site was not suitable, as the plots were only 150 feet long, had the cemetery in front of them, and the Slade at the rear. Compared to present day building, the plots were large. At least one Councillor was however quite perceptive in forseeing the rise of the car. According to the Walden Weekly: 'Councillor Englemann suggested that the houses be semi detached. In the future everyone would want a garage (laughter) and it would be easier to build.' Perhaps Councillor Englemann has had the last laugh. It was eventually agreed to proceed with the erection of the houses in Radwinter Road.

The Council completed the Radwinter Road houses during 1930 and decided to carry out a complete survey of the towns housing needs. This was to involve recommendations to remove a number of slum dwellings details of which are given later.

Radwinter Road and cemetery before the 1930 Council houses were built opposite it.

The economic slump and unemployment was begining to affect the town by 1930, and this was brought home to the Council by a demonstration during a Council meeting. A deputation, consisting of 60 unemployed men, led by Alderman E. Tanner, an Essex County Councillor marched unannounced into the Council Chamber and demanded the provision of work instead of the dole. The demonstration was orderly, and the men expressed their appreciation after assurances were given that the Council would do whatever was possible to ease their position. But what could the Council do? As in times past the Council fell back on providing employment by improving the local roads. Discussions took place between the Town Council and Essex County Council about the possibility of improving the Dunmow to Chesterford road. If permission for this could be obtained, the Council were prepared to act as agents for the Walden to Chesterford section. However the idea fell flat the County being unprepared to carry out the work as they did not consider there was excessive unemployment in the town, and the work was unbudgeted.

Some highway work was possible however, and improvements were made to the corner of Station Street and Audley Road during 1930, as well as to the footpaths surrounding the Battle Ditches. In addition some additional sign posting was erected to warn of dangerous corners in the town.

The first 'talkie' films reached Walden in 1930. The first film featuring sound was 'Blackmail' with Donald Calthrop and John Longdon. This obviously proved popular for within two years the town saw the opening of a second cinema, The Plaza, in Station Street. According to the Walden Weekly of 23rd December, 1932 the cinema was 'Designed specially for the use of talking pictures'. Its many features included seating for 467, as well as cloakrooms and up to date projectors. The paper adds 'From the outside the building presents an attractive appearance, being of modern design, and a noticeable feature is the neon lighting which here finds its first appearance in the town'. The Plaza eventually closed in the 1970's.

In August 1930, there was a fire at Raynhams Farm, Peaslands Road, which caused £500 worth of damage.The fire was allowed to get a hold because the fire brigade discovered once they started pumping, that the water pressure had failed. This was not the first occasion that this had occurred and it spurred the Council in its determination to provide new water works.

The Council had already decided, in November, 1929 to undertake a major new scheme for water supply to the town, and application had been made to the Ministry of Health for a loan of £15,000. The scheme which involved the provision of a new water supply, from new works built at Landscape View, required sanction from Central Government, and at one stage this looked unlikely, because of the national economic crisis. However the Council was able to convince the Government of the urgent necessity of the works, and the scheme was approved and adopted by the Council in 1932. The works were opened by the Mayor in

October, 1932. The new well bored at Landscape View was 512 feet deep with a 24' bore, and had cost £1,621; the pumping machinery and softening plant had cost £5,652; new mains, extending the system to Little Walden Road had cost £4,540 and the buildings and other works had cost a further £1,350, a total of about £15,000.

In 1931 a General Election was called. For the first time the Liberals decided not to fight it, and as a result RAB Butler romped home, polling 22,501 votes to Stanley Wilson's Labour vote of 6,468.

The slump in the British economy during the 1930's hit Walden quite badly. The agricultural trade on which the town depended was badly affected and in June, 1932 the National Union of Agricultural Workers held a mass meeting of farmworkers on the Common. The particular grievance which caused the meeting was the decision of a number of local farmers to cut the annual harvest bonus, but there were also complaints against the conditions of agricultural employment in general. The effects of the economy on the agricultural industry brought to a head the age old grievance of tithes. In April 1932 a mass meeting was held in the Town Hall to call for action against tithes. Speakers maintained that tithes were not in keeping with modern conditions and were an unfair imposition. In particular it was felt to be an unfair burden on British agriculture at a time of acute agricultural distress. The stated aims of the National Tithepayers Association, of which there was a strong and active branch in Walden were 'to achieve a remission of the existing high tithe charge in relation to the existing low return from farming'.

Tithes were a major issue of concern locally, and the correspondence columns of the Walden Weekly were kept busy with numerous letters throughout the early thirties. As the market town for a large rural area, Walden hosted a number of protest meetings. Ultimately the problem was solved in 1936 with the passing of the Tithe Redemption Act.

Unemployment became no better as the 30's wore on. Meetings to protest were held in the Town Hall, but of course did little to solve the problem. Two of the famous hunger marches of the thirties stopped over in Walden. The following report from the Walden Weekly of 28th October 1932 of the first of these marches gives a good example of the poor circumstances many of these people found themselves in:-

'Between 4 and 5 o'clock on Sunday afternoon there struggled into Saffron Walden the main body of the north-east coast contingent of 'hunger marchers' after their 15 miles march from Cambridge, where they had rested during the previous two days.

The men – or rather boys – for they were mostly about 18 years of age, presented a pitiful sight, having marched practically the whole way in driving rain. Many of them had no overcoats, and their footware was in poor condition, some of them even wearing canvas slippers. In spite of the miserable conditions the men maintained a buoyant attitude and were accompanied by an improvised band and several banners were carried high and proudly. One banner bore the emblem of the scythe and sickle and others the inscriptions: 'We want bread' and 'Down with the Means Test'.

The men, mostly drawn from Newcastle-on Tyne, are of the labouring classes, but their numbers include several clerks and men of similar occupations. . . .'

The men were accommodated in the Public Assistance Institution in Radwinter Road (now the hospital) and given a meal of thick meat soup, cheese and coffee with monies raised from townspeople, including the Mayor and Mayoress. The purpose of this march was to protest against the Government's unemployment bill, and it met with some limited success, forcing the Government to delay its proposals. The second march passed through Walden in February, 1934. On this occasion the marchers were again protesting at a new bill designed to impose a stricter 'means test'. About 100 marchers were put up in Abbey Lane Church Hall and were provided with blankets by the Friends' School. The Public Assistance Institution provided food with the assistance of local contributions.

Attempts were made by the Council to help the local unemployed through various schemes. In 1932, after the road scheme with the County Council had fallen through, the Mayor launched his Unemployment Fund, designed to raise money for work for the unemployed. The fund was well supported raising £300 by the end of the year. In an effort to provide work, the Mayor announced that the Council would purchase land at Catons Lane for a sports ground. The ground proposed was that used already by the football club, as well as some adjoining land. The football club agreed to join in a comprehensive scheme for a sports field. This would enable the unemployed to be put to work and receive the benefit of every penny raised from the Mayors fund. In 1945 the Council purchased additional land to add to this area and this now forms the Anglo American Memorial Playing Fields.

There were some successful enterprises in the thirties however. The cement works in Thaxted Road, were taken over as a derelict concern, but new management invested heavily in bringing in up to date plant, and created some considerable number of local jobs. This enterprise had been considerably helped by the decision of the Air Ministry to build the new aerodrome at Wimbish (later to become RAF Debden) and this in itself also helped local employment.

In July 1932 the Council conferred the Freedom of the Borough on John Dane Player (a descendant of John Player the first Mayor under the 1835 Municipal Corporation Act) and on William Favill Tuke (a relative of the Gibson family) on the occasion of the centenary of the Museum (1).

As communications and transport improved the town found itself less isolated. As a result it was inevitable that the County Council began to look at merging certain institutions. Thus in 1932, proposals were made by the County Council to close the Isolation Hospital when it was suggested that a number of independent hospital areas, including Saffron

Walden, be merged into a joint hospital board. The scheme which would have involved transferring patients from Walden's Isolation Hospital to Braintree was strongly and successfully opposed by the Town Council.

The County Council also proposed closing the Saffron Walden Poor Law (or Public Assistance) Institution, as part of their scheme to build a vast new institution at Takeley. Again the Town Council vigorously opposed the scheme and received support from Dunmow Rural and Saffron Walden Rural Councils. The town's MP RAB Butler also opposed the scheme because of the huge cost involved – about £300,000. This scheme was more difficult to defeat and was not finally laid to rest until 1936.

The increase in motorised transport meant the Council had to consider the towns first one way scheme in 1932. Not surprisingly it involved King Street and Cross Street, where the Council considered that the congestion of traffic was causing a danger to pedestrians. An order was sought from the County Council to make the streets one way but objections to this were made by a number of shopkeepers, fearful of a loss of trade. Some Councillors supported this view, feeling that an alternative scheme could be undertaken to relieve congestion. As a result it was decided not to proceed with the scheme.

In 1932 the Town Clerk, William Adams, in conjunction with the Society for the Preservation of Ancient Buildings launched an appeal to raise sufficient monies to enable the National Trust to purchase the Sun Inn. The appeal was successful and raised £1,500 and today the Sun Inn still remains in the ownership of the Trust.

The Sun Inn c.1910.

Perhaps this is an opportune place to look more closely at the Sun Inn, probably one of the finest examples of mediaeval architecture in the town. The building in fact consists of a number of cottages and is described in the Monuments of Essex (North West) thus:-

'The two cottages on the N.W. are of two storeys with a cellar and were built in the 15th century with a hall in the middle flanked by solar and kitchen wings. Late in the 16th or early in the 17th century an upper floor was inserted in the hall, and at a later date the upper floor of the S.W. wing was raised and a wagon way cut through underneath it.

The central portion of the building now used as a shop . . . was built late in the 14th century and the roof truss and doorway are most interesting. . . .

The house . . . has the date 1600 on the N. bessumer, but it is said to have been brought from elsewhere. The building is not apparently of earlier date than the 17th century, but a window in the W. end of the front is partly of late 14th century date, and suggests that the west end of the structure, though much altered in the 17th century, may be part of the late 14th century house which adjoins it on the S.W.'

The two figures over the gateway at the western edge of the building were probably meant to represent Gog and Magog, the fabled giants. References can be found to these figures as representing Tom Hickathrift and the Wisbech giant, but this appears unlikely because of the scale of the figures. No documentary evidence exists to support either claim.

The earliest documentary evidence of the building is a title deed of 1699, which shows that the property belonged to Henry Winstanley, very possibly the Winstanley of Littlebury who designed the Eddystone Lighthouse. It is known that the Sun Inn was used as the headquarters of Cromwell's army, so it is probable that Cromwell stayed there although no documentary evidence exists to prove this, his letters merely being addressed as 'Saffron Walden'. Certainly local tradition has always connected the Inn with Cromwell and in 1876 a set of Delft tile pictures, bearing Cromwell's portrait were found in the Inn.

The early thirties saw considerable change in the town. New housing and buildings were being erected, older buildings being condemned and demolished and shops changing ownership as chain stores began to take an interest in the town.

In March, 1933 the Territorials new headquarters opened in Station Street. The building, which today is used as the ambulance station, comprised of a large hall, a room for billiards, a restaurant, a lecture hall, a games room, a rest room and administrative offices. At the rear of the building a covered rifle range was provided. The hall was to be the home of the 'C' company of the Essex Regiment under the command of Captain Myhill. At the opening of the hall, the Union Jack that was unfurled was the same one used in the towns celebrations of the relief of Mafeking!

The Council were keen to continue their housebuilding programme, for it provided not only housing but local employment during the

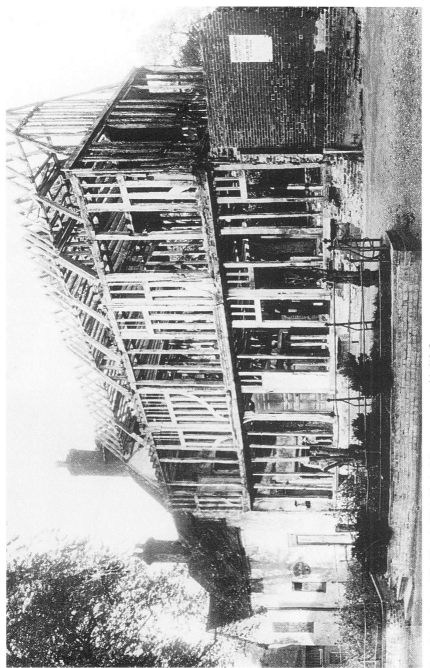

Demolition of part of The Close in 1934. The building was re-erected in W. Sussex.

construction works. In January 1934 the Council decided to proceed with the building of Council houses on a piece of land between Ashdon Road and Radwinter Road. The contract, for 42 houses, was let to a firm of builders, W.W.Parker of Ongar at a price of £538 per pair of Semi-Detached houses. This was subject to an unwritten condition that the builder would use some local labour, and there was much controversy later when it was discovered that in fact there were very few locals employed. The contract for the road, later to be named Hollyhock Road, was let to the local firm of F.W.Goddard for the sum of £754.

During 1934 part of The Close, the building on the corner of Castle Street and the High Street, was pulled down. This part, which adjoined the present building on its southern side, was brick and plaster faced, and during its demolition it was discovered that there was a 400 year old Tudor structure behind the facade. It is believed the plaster had been placed on the building in about 1700, and the brick work was added in 1854. The building was subsequently brought, restored and moved down to West Sussex. The removal of this part of The Close revealed an attractive and previously unseen view of the western elevation of the Church. Following correspondence in the paper, public subscription raised sufficient money to purchase the site. The Close Gardens were opened to the public in September 1938 by Mrs. Butler to commemorate the coronation of George VI.

Change in the ownerships of shops was becoming noticeable by the mid thirties. The editor of the Walden Weekly commented that '1935 was remarkable for the number of new shop premises'. There were some complaints at this, but little anybody could do to prevent some of the larger chain stores moving into the town and by the end of the 1930's Woolworths, the Co-op and Internationals all had shops in the town.

Sport thrived in the town during this period. The cricket and football clubs could hold their own against much of the local opposition, and in 1933 the towns first Rugby Club was formed. Like its successor, its big problem was where to play and it relied on the good will of local farmers to assist with a ground often playing on land owned by the Englemanns in Thaxted Road.

During 1933 the Council concerned itself with much discussion on the sale of the electricity supply works at Thaxted Road. Although the Council was reluctant to lose control of the supply it was recognized that a private company could supply electricity, much cheaper, and to the outlying villages. In August 1933 the decision was taken to sell the works to the County of London Electric Supply Company in return for paying off outstanding debts and giving certain guarantees in respect of future charges.

The Council, itself, needed new offices. For many years the Borough Treasurers and Surveyors office had been at no. 3, Hill Street, whilst the Town Clerk, William Adams, worked from his firm of solicitors in Church Street. In November 1934 they looked at three possible new options:- building new offices on the site of the old pumping station on the north side of Hill Street; purchasing Hill House, in the High Street former home of Miss Mary Gibson who had recently died, or purchasing no. 5/7, Hill Street. This building had previously been used as a private house and was owned by a Mr. H.J.Barrand. The Council decided to purchase no. 5/7 Hill Street, as it was the cheapest option and was in the centre of the town, and the house was acquired for £1,500.

National affairs were always in the back of people's minds during the thirties. In October 1933, the 1st Saffron Walden B.P. Scout Group held the celebrations for their 21st anniversary. This consisted of a ball at the Town Hall as well as a 'Camp fire' on the Common, but more surprisingly were the contents of a 'rag' held in the town. This comprised of a number of scouts dressed up in various costumes with several dressed as Nazis. The Scoutmaster dressed up as Hitler in what was described as a 'realistic, if somewhat robust impersonation of the German Dictator'. According to the Walden Weekly, the procession proceeded down King Street and 'when the Market Square was reached two 'Jews' appeared on the scene . . . an encounter between them and a horde of Nazis resulted in one of the Jews being so badly 'injured' that the ambulance men were given an opportunity of showing their abilities'. The obvious bad taste of this exercise to us with the the benefit of hindsight should not condemn those who undertook it. It merely reflected the circumstances of the time.

A more pleasant occurrence in 1935 was the silver jubilee of the accession of King George V and Queen Mary to the throne. Their early years had been scarred by the events of the Great War, but they had steadily gained the affection of their subjects. The economic crisis of the thirties meant that the country was ready for a celebration, and so in Walden, as elsewhere the town entered the celebrations with keen enthusiasm. In March 1935, the Council decided to dedicate the gardens attached to the new municipal offices at 7, Hill Street, as a rest garden for the use of the public. The gardens were to be equipped with seats, and a new gateway was made from Hill Street. The gardens were opened by the Mayor and named 'Jubilee Gardens' as a permanent commemoration of that event.

A public meeting held in the town in March 1935 decided to ask the Council to levy a 2d rate which would raise £264 for the local celebrations. This, the Council agreed, and a programme of events were swiftly put together. It was agreed that souvenirs would be provided for the children; there would be a united Church Service in the morning, with loud speaker arrangements for listening to the service from St. Pauls Cathedral; and there would be a sports meeting in the afternoon. In the evening it was proposed to hold a mass open air gathering with community singing and a dance on the Common, as well as a procession. Other plans included illuminating the War Memorial; providing tea for all the school children; decorating buildings, and providing monetary gifts for almshouse inmates, old age pensioners 'and those in distressed circumstances'. The events proved tremendously succesful, with over 2,000 people packing the Market Square for events, and over 500 children being given tea in the Corn Exchange, the Masonic Hall and Museum Street Infants School. In the evening a half mile long procession comprising of more than 50 vehicles and 20 horses passed through the town.

Following the silver jubilee the Council found that it had a balance of £23 left. Some members wished to use this to provide some swings on the Common. However a recent fatality on swings at Cambridge meant considerable debate followed. Eventually the Council agreed to use this money, and an additional sum totalling in all £110 to provide swings, a rocking boat, a joy wheel and a plank swing, and these were installed on the Common in May 1936.

Probably the town's first air display took place in April, 1935. The display featured Lieutenant Owen Cathcart-Jones, the England to Australia and back record holder. The event, which was held at Copt Hall Farm, offered the opportunity to take a flight, as well as stunt flying, and novelty items such as paper cutting, balloon bursting and a parachute jump from 1,000 feet.

Throughout 1934, and 1935, the town had been making a concerted effort to raise money for an extension for the General Hospital to provide a children's ward. A fete held in the summer of 1934, in the grounds of Shortgrove, had raised the phenomenal sum of £914, and during 1935 events were held to try to bring this up to the estimated cost of £2,000. Eventually with the aid of subscriptions and grants this amount was raised, and the extension was completed in October 1935. The flat roofed extension, (recently demolished in the conversion of the hospital to offices) was on the west side of the hospital and consisted of three private wards, an observation and nurses duty ward, as well as the children's ward which provided for eight beds.

The children's ward at the hospital shortly after its completion.

Great excitement gripped the town when it was learnt that the building was to be opened by the singer Gracie Fields, then at the height of her popularity. The hospital site was packed and the town band struck up with her famous song 'Sing as We Go' as she appeared. After the opening she entertained the crowd by singing to them.

Politically, 1935 was an active year in the town. The General Election of that year saw RAB Butler again returned as the member for Saffron Walden, polling 22,501 votes against 9,633 votes for his Labour opponent, Mrs. C.D.Rackham. In addition the town saw the visit of a number of fascists, culminating in talk at the Town Hall in May, by Mr. R.A. Thomson, the Director of Policy of the British Union of Fascists. This meeting was severely heckled by about 40 students who had cycled over from Cambridge. Despite this the meeting closed with the National Anthem and the Fascists gave their salute. The town flirted with fascism throughout the thirties, but it never found an extensive following.

Two major events occurred in the town during 1936; the Essex Show was held in Walden and the King died. The death of the King in January of that year, was marked with a memorial service in the Parish Church. The Church was packed for the occasion, and as it was on a Tuesday, the Council agreed that a market would not be held on that day. In addition a large number of shops shut for the day and social activities, including whist drives and dances were cancelled or postponed. All hunting in the district was temporarily suspended. Although George V had never visited Walden, Queen Mary had made a number of private visits to Audley End. The new King, Edward VIII, was proclaimed, as in the past, in the Market Square.

However the event which really put Walden on the map that year, was the Essex Show. The show had been held in the town in the past, in 1860, 1870 and 1884, on each occasion in the Deer Park at Audley End. But this was the first occasion in modern times, and it was decided to use a new site at Herberts Farm. The town had been chosen for a number of reasons, and particularly because for many years it had run a very large and successful Horticultural and Horse Show.

The site chosen, Herberts Farm, is at the southernmost point of the town off Debden Road, and close to the Claypits Plantation. The site occupied 35 acres on the eastern side of Debden Road, with a further 10 acres on the western side being used for car parking. A special grandstand capable of seating 1,900 people was erected, and a ring 500 feet by 250 feet created. As well as the usual livestock competitions, there was a large flower show, organised by the Saffron Walden Horticultural Society; an exhibition of the history of Saffron Walden, staged by the curator of the Museum, and a representation of an old English Farmyard provided by the curator of Colchester Museum. The show, which was held on the 10th and 11th June, 1936 attracted over 25,000 visitors, a record turnout, and the poor weather failed to spoil the occasion.

An aerial view of the 1936 Essex Show at Herbert's Farm.

The cattle ring at the 1936 Essex Show.

In 1936, the County Council Hospital Survey Committee considered the possible provision of a new hospital in Walden. Following a review of hospital facilities in North West Essex, it was felt provision should be made for additional accommodation for the acute sick, and that a further 50 to 60 beds should be made available for chronic cases. The County Medical Officer of Health felt improvements could be made to hospital accommodation under the poor law administration. He proposed asking the voluntary hospital (i.e. London Road Hospital), to help with additional provision by building an extension to provide for cases currently at the Radwinter Road Institution. If they would not do so he suggested a new hospital should be built. The trustees of the London Road hospital were willing to go along with this plan and agreed to extend the hospital once more to take the chronic cases from Radwinter Road. The County Council agreed to make an interest free loan of £42,000 to finance these works. This was to cover the cost of purchasing the land, adjoining the hospital, then in use as allotments, the erection of the buildings, and the provision of the necessary medical equipment. The extension, would accommodate 71 chronic and infirm cases. (Later in October 1938 the cost was revised to £55,332). However these proposals, which would have trebled the size of the hospital were prevented by the outbreak of the war.

These proposals cut right across the suggestion of building a huge new institute at Takeley, and so the County Council now dropped this scheme ensuring the survival of the Radwinter Road Institute.

Extensive work was undertaken in 1936 to the towns infrastructure. In January, three new gas mains were laid. The first main was from East Street, along Audley Road to the hospital; the second ran from the High Street to Abbey Lane and the almshouses, and the third from the junction of Debden Road and Borough Lane along Mount Pleasant Road to the boundary of the Friends' School. The work, carried out by the Council, also included a sum for a new gas showroom, designed to encourage the towns residents to use more gas appliances. The total cost of all these works was £3,500.

In April, 1936, the Council considered a report by the Borough Surveyor on the unsatisfactory condition of the town's sewerage works. Although the works had only been completed in 1912, the growth of the town, the difficulties involved in disposing of sewage in a valley and the long lead time in building new works meant careful consideration had to be given to the possible provision of new works. The loan charge on the existing works expired in 1940, and it was estimated that even if new works could commence in 1941, it would take 7 – 8 years to construct. For the time being, however the Council could do little and no action was taken on the report.

The housing survey, originally started in 1930, was now being undertaken in connection with the Governments overcrowding regulations. Its results show that Walden had a considerable amount of low rateable value housing. There were 1,217 houses with a rateable value of £15 or lower, of which 122 were Council houses.

A Council Meeting held on 10th July, 1936, considered the housing survey in depth and came up with two schemes, one to deal with overcrowding, the second defining nine clearance areas where the Medical Officer of Health considered the houses were unfit for human habitation. It was considered that 28 houses in the borough were overcrowded and the Council agreed to build 30 houses under the Housing Act, 1935. Fourteen of these were to be three bedroomed, twelve four bedroomed, and four four bedroomed with a parlour and living room, for families of eight or more.

The clearance areas provided the Council with a bigger problem, for occasionally there would be a serviceable house amongst unfit houses. After debate however it was agreed that the only viable solution was to demolish all the buildings. Nine areas were identified, involving a total of 57 houses:-

High Street Place – 6 houses (Between Nos. 64-68 High Street).
Ingleside Place – 15 houses (Between Nos. 92-94 High Street).
Museum Court – 2 houses (Between Nos. 52-54 Castle Street).
Chapel Row – 5 houses (Between Nos. 69-71 Castle Street).
Long Row – 9 houses (Adjacent to 62 Thaxted Road).
Cates Corner – 5 houses Oxbarrows Yard – 2 houses.
Sarah's Place – 8 houses (Between Nos. 25-27 Castle Street).
School Row – 5 houses (Between Nos. 91-93 Castle Street).

Derelict cottages in Castle Street.

To rehouse the residents of these it was agreed to build 40 new houses and 16 flats on land purchased from Lord Braybrooke on either side of Little Walden Road, and to the east of Catons Lane. The land was acquired for £1,200 and tenders sought. However only three tenders were received for the work, the lowest being £23,900. As this was £4,662 more than the original estimate the Ministry of Health insisted the Council readvertise. This was no more successful with the lowest tender being £22,914, and the Ministry still objecting. Eventually, in January, 1938 after negotiations with the tenderer and the Ministry, the Council were able to accept a revised tender of £21,637. There was also quite a lot of private building taking place in the late thirties, particularly in the south of the town. Twenty-six semi-detached houses were built at the corner of Borough Lane and Newport Road, in 1937, and in the same year the necessary works, for the adoption by the Council of Summerhill Road and Springhill Road were carried out.

In 1938, the North West Essex Regional Planning Committee produced a town planning scheme for the Borough. A public inquiry was held to consider this, because of objections to proposals concerning street widening, and new building lines. At the inquiry, the Town Clerk pointed out that since 1931, 144 houses had been erected in the town by private enterprise, and the annual number being built was increasing. The housing waiting list was about 250 people.

The County Council also looked at the towns educational facilities in the 1930's. In November 1934, the Education Committee agreed to proceed with the reorganisation of elementary schools in the town. They realised that the town required a senior school to serve both the town and the outlying villages, and therefore agreed to acquire a triangular site of 8 acres at the junction of Audley End Road and Newport Road (the site of the current Saffron Walden County High School). Lord Braybrooke was reluctant to sell, but after looking at alternative sites, the committee decided this was the only suitable location. This was despite an objection from the hospital committee who thought the noise of the children would affect their patients! The matter dragged on until 1938, when following the Haddow Report it was decided to compulsory purchase the 8 acre site, as well as an additional 4 acres of land to provide for senior education of children over 11 as distinct from the elementary schools. However the war interrupted and it was not until 1955 that the Saffron Walden County High School was to open.

Another aspect of the town's infrastructure that the Council had to consider was the traffic difficulties. As we have seen several attempts to introduce one-way streets stumbled on the resistance of shopkeepers. As late as December, 1937, the proposal to introduce one way traffic to Market Hill was rejected for that very reason. So it became necessary to consider a radical solution, that of a bypass. In March, 1938 the County Council proposed two bypasses for the town, one following a northerly route, the other a southern route. The northern bypass was to start just below the top of Windmill Hill, go past Bridge End Gardens, join Catons

The Market Square during the 1930s.

Lane and then proceed via Little Walden Road, to the Common, Chaters Hill and Thaxted Road. (This scheme was to continue on Town Plans until as recently as 1976.) The southern bypass was intended to link Newport Road and Radwinter Road. It was to start the town side of the chalk cutting (approximately where Rowntree Way now goes), run across Debden Road on the southern side of Summerhill Road over fields to Thaxted Road. From here it would go north up Thaxted Road to approximately where Shirehill is now and then running parallel to the railway join Radwinter Road at the Sewards End side of the bridge.

The Town Council approved both of these routes, and recommended that the County Council proceed with the construction of the northern bypass as soon as possible, so as to relieve the traffic passing through the centre of the town, and more particularly the corner of High Street and George Street – a problem still not solved in 1991.

A public inquiry was held in August 1939 to hear objections to the proposed bypasses. The County Council spokesman pointed out that Walden was a very congested town, being at the junction of no less than nine county roads. The fact that the town had over 150 buildings dating from before 1700 meant road widening was not a practical proposition, and the construction of the airfield at Debden and the oil dump in Ashdon Road, had resulted in a considerably increased traffic flow. Between 1935 and 1938 traffic had increased by 60% according to the County Council's figures. Objectors were concerned that the routes proposed would be very expensive and would involve some demolition of building in particular at the top of Chaters Hill. However the Inquiry Inspector was not able to produce his report. War broke out just 10 days later and like so many other projects the bypasses were shelved.

All this change meant concern began to be expressed about maintaining the character of the town. In December, 1937 a new Saffron Walden Society was formed, 'to preserve the picturesque charms of the town'. The formation of the society followed a meeting in the Town Hall which was addressed by Clough Williams-Ellis the famous architect. He expressed his particular concern at the demolition of old cottages condemned as unfit for human habitation. He felt that many of these would be better modernised than replaced with modern buildings. He felt it was important to prevent what he called 'this distinguished town' from being a no mans land, spoiled by speculative building. The meeting agreed to 'approve the formation of a Saffron Walden Society for the protection of the urban, rural, historic and architectural amenities of the town and neighbourhood'.

But above all this the spectre of war lurked throughout the late thirties. Following the events of the Spanish Civil War when the Luftwaffe had shown the possible awesome effects of aerial bombardment, the Government began a massive air raid precaution programme. As early as 1936 there was considerable discussion and debate on this matter in Walden. In particular, concern was expressed as to the effectiveness of any precautions, especially if gas should be used. In September 1936, the

Council were asked to set up a local air raid precaution organisation. This consisted of representatives of the Borough Council as well as the Walden Rural and Dunmow Rural Councils. However confusion as to whom was responsible for financing the organisations activities meant that its work was inefficient initially. Even by November 1937 it had not been possible to appoint a paid organiser for the North West Essex area due to insufficient finances. Such actions as were taken had to be on a voluntary basis – for example the local traders were approached to see if they would be prepared to act as dispatch riders in the event of phone lines being cut by bombing.

In July 1937 a huge British Legion rally was held in the town. Branches of the Legion came from all over Essex, and nearly 3,000 members marched from the Common through the town and past the War Memorial to the Deer Park. It was the biggest rally of its kind to be held in Essex. It also served as the forerunner to large scale army manoeuvres which were held in the town throughout August and September 1937. These were the first manoeuvres of their kind in the area since 1912, and perhaps warned the town of the things to come.

The Walden Weekly reported on 13th August:-

'Saffron Walden has taken on the atmosphere of a garrison town. Aeroplanes roar overhead, military motor transport and guns pass through the streets and at weekends the khaki of the troops camping in the district for manoeuvres mingle with the blue of the RAF from Debden. On two occasions already some officers have imbibed to freely and caused disturbances. . . .'

The Royal Artillery were encamped at Sparrows End, with their headquarters at Audley End. During their stay they were visited by the Minister for War, Mr. Leslie Hore-Belisha. Other troops were also camped on the outskirts of the town.

The purpose of the manoeuvres, to ensure the troops met with real combat type conditions meant some 'fighting' occurred in the town centre. Two such incidents occurred in early September. The first was when a troop of Cavalry from the 5th Royal Inniskilling Dragoons entered the town from Newport Road. They advanced down the High Street with the support of machine gun and anti-tank detachments, but at the corner of George Street they met resistance from two armoured cars manned by the 12th Lancers. With much authenticity the two cars were 'disabled' and the crews captured.

Then, later that day the Dragoons were attacked at the junction of Newport Road and Debden Road, and on this occasion they lost one of their armoured cars. Such excitement was not unanimously welcomed. In October 1937, the Peace Pledge Union held a meeting in the Town Hall, which was addressed by Canon Dick Shepherd, the leader of the Union.

Indeed the divisions between the two factions of this debate were perhaps best illustrated by the arguments between the League of Nations Union, and the British Legion over the hiring of the Town Hall on

Armistice night. The Council were called upon to act as arbiters after the British Legion complained when the Town Hall had been let to the League of Nations for an armistice celebration. The Mayor, Ellis Rooke, himself a member of the British Legion tried to arrange a meeting with the two organisations, but the British Legion refused to attend. The Mayor promptly resigned his membership of the Legion, and then, acting with the judgement of Solomon announced that in future the Town Hall would be used for a town function on Armistice night under the patronage of the Mayor.

Meanwhile the threat of war continued. In March 1938 the Mayor, Ellis Rooke called a public meeting in the Corn Exchange. He was now able to report that following meetings with Essex County Council and the Home Office, it had been agreed that the County Council would bear all of the cost of the organisation of air raid precaution works, and the Home Office would bear the cost of all additional fire appliances. This now cleared the way for the air raid precautions to be quickly established. Above all, the main requirement were volunteers for posts such as Air Raid Wardens, First Aid Parties, Ambulance Drivers, Rescue Parties, Decontamination Squads and such like. The Mayor called for 590 volunteers from the town saying:-

> 'I call upon you to stand by your Country and unite, and help one another in case of need. . . . I feel so confident in this old loyal town of Saffron Walden that you will come forward to your utmost to help us deal with this matter.'

The number of 590 volunteers might sound high when the town's population was barely 6,000, but it should be remembered that following the bombing of Guernica during the Spanish Civil War huge casualties were expected. Captain Ballantyne-Evans, the newly appointed Air Raid Precaution organiser for the Saffron Walden and Dunmow area warned in July 1938 that the country could expect 600 tons of bombs daily, and on that basis there would expect 72,000 casualties per week.

Demand for volunteers was such that it was difficult to fill all the posts and in January 1939, the Mayor was still appealing for more Air Raid Wardens, and drivers for the Auxiliary fire brigade.

At the same time the Council put other preparations in hand. The fear of fire spreading quickly amongst the towns narrow streets with its old timbered buildings is ever present. With the possible advent of war the Council became very concerned at its water supplies. It was reported that if damage should occur to the main water supply from the pumping station, then the supply of water in the Debden Road Water tower would only be sufficient for normal usage of four to six hours. For this reason and the risk from incendiary devices the Council placed a number of static water tanks in strategic places, including the Common. In August 1939 the Borough Engineer, came up with an alternative suggested water supply. Councillor Englemann who owned the Nurseries in Radwinter Road, was prepared to permit a connection to be made to his borewell. It

Saffron Walden Territorials c.1935.

was found that this was a practicable suggestion and a lot cheaper than
the alternative schemes for additional water supply. Arrangements were
therefore made to take a supply from this well in the event of an
emergency. At the same time the Council agreed to undertake a complete
survey of all valves and hydrants in the town.

The Munich crisis of September 1938 tested the system to its fullest. As
the very real threat of war loomed at the end of September, Walden's air
raid precautions swung into action as the following report from the
Walden Weekly of 30th September shows:-

'At Walden air raid precautions are rapidly becoming established.
Arrangements are being completed as soon as possible. The distribution of gas masks starting on Wednesday (September 28th) has been
undertaken at the various schools and other suitable depots in the
Borough. Fairycroft House has been used for installing gas masks for
the district . . . Walden is considered fortunate in having works that
can be readily converted into air raid shelters. The Slade on the
Common, and at Little Walden Road and the Battle Ditches have been
turned into shelters. Gas proof chambers will be prepared for mothers
with babies, and it will be to these that all mothers must take infants in
the case of emergencies. Tonight (i.e 30th September) or Saturday
morning about 3,000 children are expected to arrive from London in
three train loads. If need arises they will be billeted in the town and
district. A house to house survey has already been carried out, and
available quarters have been ascertained. More children will be coming
later and altogether it is expected that 10,000 will come into the town
and district. . . . Between 7 and 10 p.m. tonight the warning signal will

be given from the gas works siren followed later by the all clear. It is imperative that everyone should be alert and prepared.'

The impact of 10,000 children descending on the town and district would have been colossal, but even as the Walden Weekly went to press Chamberlain was returning from Munich with his legendary 'piece of paper' which brought Britain a further year to rearm. The worst was yet to come.

Life in the town continued normally despite the worsening international situation. The Town Council were applying pressure to the County Council to address the urgent need for a secondary school. Councillor Stanley Wilson accused the County of shamefully neglecting education in rural areas. He was given an assurance that work on Walden's secondary school would start by 1943.

In February, 1939, the annual meeting of the Literary and Scientific Institute had to report a decline in numbers, but this was perhaps made up for by the creation of a National Fitness Council for Saffron Walden, the following month.

Car parking and traffic congestion were proving a problem in the town at this time. A meeting of the Chamber of Trade in March, complained that the police were being 'aggresive' towards motorists, to the detriment of trade in the town. The Chamber felt it was unreasonable to expect a traveller to carry his samples backwards and forwards, and they should be able to stop outside the shops they were visiting. The Town Council later decided to introduce limited parking places in the High Street.

A public meeting was called in March 1939, by a Mrs. E. Tennant, and supported by the Mayor. The purpose of the meeting was to assess the townspeoples views as to whether they wanted bomb-proof shelters in the borough. Mrs Tennant was concerned that whilst an adequate ARP system had been organised there was no proper provision for bomb shelters. She felt shelters should be made in surrounding hill sides, and suggested the cement works pit in Thaxted Road, the football field and the chalk pit in Little Walden Road as examples of sites which could be used.

However it was pointed out to the meeting that the Government were endeavouring to ensure that every household had a shelter, and that these were in the process of being issued. There was some cynicism expressed about the effectiveness of these 'Anderson' shelters but it was explained that this was Government policy. However there was nothing to stop the town from pursuing its own shelters, and a committee was set up to investigate possible sites for bomb shelters.

By April 1939 the Air Raid Precaution service was getting into full swing. Fairycroft House had been purchased and converted as a centre for the ARP activities. It now contained a lecture room for volunteers, a storeroom for protective clothing, an office department, and a section for the Womens Volunteer Service. Twelve Warden posts had been established at the following locations:-

1. Little Walden Road
2. Castle Street
3. The Rose and Crown, Market Square
4. The Police Station, East Street
5. The Grammar School, Ashdon Road
6. The Abbey Hotel, Abbey Lane
7. Saffron Lodge, Mount Pleasant Road
8. 'Bannold', Borough Lane
9. Pleasant Valley
10. Stanleys Farm, Thaxted Road
11. The Fox Public House, Sewards End
12. The Estate Office Audley End.

A total of 115,000 sand bags intended for the whole ARP area of North West Essex were delivered in April, and further appeals for firemen were made. Meanwhile 'B' Company of the Essex Territorial Regiment were able to report that during the week of 28th April 53 new recruits had signed up, of which 29 were from Saffron Walden.

During July 1939, the Council were concerning itself with what it perceived as a housing shortage. The Council had recently completed the development in Little Walden Road, but Councillors felt that the town still had an acute shortage. The new houses were fine but had only replaced slum dwellings and had not added any additional units to the housing stock. Councillor Rowntree was particularly concerned at the effects this was having on rented accommodation and gave examples where rents had risen from 3/6d per week to 13/- in a period of a couple of years. The increased activity caused by Debden aerodrome was also affecting demand. It was agreed that the Council must look at the question of further housing provision, but the war intervened before anything was done.

A practice blackout was carried out on August 9th as part of an ARP exercise which was designed to test the services in as realistic conditions as possible, in an effort to find weaknesses in the system. All lights had to be covered between midnight and 4 A.M. The practice was only just in time; on 3rd September war was declared.

Fairycroft House, home of the ARP during the war.

Chapter 16
War in Walden 1939-1945

Before beginning this chapter it should be pointed out that much of the information relating to the War has been taken from the Saffron Walden Weekly News. The newspaper as with every other paper of the time, was subject to censorship, and therefore some of the details may have been distorted.

With the outbreak of war obviously imminent, sandbagging of public buildings took place. The Police Station was the first building to be protected and later other civic buildings were suitably covered. Captain Ballantyne-Evans the ARP organiser announced that in the event of the outbreak of war all casualty services, decontamination squads and rescue parties had to immediately report to Fairycroft House. The organiser probably thought that aerial bombardment would commence immediately or even prior to the declaration of war. Evacuation started on 1st September, 1939. There were approximately 1,000 children, 200 blind people, 300 mothers and a large number of teachers due to arrive in Walden, with a total of 6,000 evacuees assigned to the town and district. Billeting officers had already identified homes and the evacuees were efficiently met and housed.

The speed with which these operations were undertaken show the very real concern at the time that bombing and possibly invasion would come almost immediately. This was also reflected at Walden Registry Office. The Walden Weekly of 8th September 1939 reported :-

'Owing to the war there has been an unusually large number of weddings at Saffron Walden Registry Office this last week. Nine couples have been married since the end of August and in most cases the bridegroom has been a member of the services.'

The Council were also quick to move into action. A food control committee, and a war emergency committee were appointed, and appeals made by the Mayor to the townsfolk to be careful and frugal with their use of water and fuel. However the main concern of the Council was the large influx of evacuees, the vast majority of them coming from Tottenham. The Mayor appeared to be concerned about the effects that such a large scale immigration would have on a town of barely 6,000 population.

On September 28th he called a meeting at the Conservative Club for the evacuees. Here he appealed to the evacuees to give due consideration to their hosts. At the same time he helped to set up a club for the evacuees so they could meet on a regular basis.

As we shall see Walden was to be a pioneer in making the evacuees welcome, and indeed made national coverage for their hospitality to the parents, but initially, perhaps inevitably, there was some hostility. A letter in the Walden Weekly of 13th October said:-

'. . . I hope that those responsible [for the billeting] . . . may at any rate take some notice, and seek to minimise the inconvenience which many of us have been suffering for some weeks, and may have to suffer for a good many more, if something is not done.

To board and lodge, provide bed linen, do washing, etc., for girls of 16 on a pittance of 8s.6d per week is bad enough in itself, but one hardly expects to be looked to for providing hospitality to fathers, mothers, grandmothers, uncles, aunts, brothers and sisters, who are taking advantage of being relieved of the maintenance of their children, to take a week-end jaunt to the country every Sunday or two.'

It was perhaps this valid point that resulted in the Mayor issuing an invitation to over 1,000 parents to come to the town. Whatever the reason it proved extremely popular, and on 22nd October about 500 of the parents arrived in nine large motor coaches, and a long procession of private cars.

The Council had made the Town Hall and Corn Exchange available so that the parents could meet the children and foster parents. Conscious of the complaints of the hosts, the Council had arranged for light refreshments to be available at a small charge. The staff and pupils of Tottenham High School had decorated the buildings, and both the town band and the Tottenham Girls' School choir performed.

Various dignitaries attended including the town's M.P. RAB Butler, the Mayor and Deputy Mayor of Tottenham and the Director of Education for Tottenham. The visit was seen as a pioneer of its kind and Miss Florence Horsbrugh M.P., the Parliamentary Secretary to the Minister of Health declared it was the best day she had had in connection with the evacuation scheme. It made the national newspapers, and the idea was later followed by scores of other towns. Further visits were arranged for November and December.

Ideas were also considered for entertaining the evacuees, and following discussions, a football league, and a folk dancing group were established by the Council.In addition a play scheme and nursery school were started at the training college for the youngest evacuees.

The success of these schemes can be seen from the following letter from Councillor S. Halford, the Chairman of the Governors of Tottenham High School for Girls and Tottenham County School. The letter was published in a local Tottenham newspaper:-

'The Girls' High School is in Saffron Walden. Both the town and its surroundings seem exceedingly attractive. The parents of Tottenham whose children have been evacuated there are to be congratulated on the happy place selected to place their youngsters out of danger.

The impression of the attitude towards these children of the usual inhabitants of the town was that they were very helpful and hospitable.

But apart from the attitude of the townspeople and the beauty of the town's situation there was the question of what is being done to secure that the pupils of the Tottenham Girls' High School continue their education. That is now assured and the parents need no longer fear that while evacuation saves them from air raid danger it deprives them of the teaching that the school is intended to give. The Town Council is very active in helping towards the efficiency of the arrangements. I came away feeling easier in my mind about the Girls' High School as far as it has been evacuated.'

Further mass visits by parents followed in November and December, and by Christmas two-thirds of the evacuees were still in Walden, whereas nationally only about one-third of evacuees remained. Perhaps the Walden Weekly was entitled to pat the town on the back when it said:-

'Ours was the first reception area to invite parents down in a mass visit to let town meet country and tackle the problem man to man. Much was done in this way to clear up difficulties and our effort was national news. We led and others followed.'

As the 'phoney war' progressed, the only danger to the town, seemed to be natural ones. In February 1940, the railway line was blocked by a heavy fall of earth. The fall took place about one mile from Walden Station, in a 30 feet cutting on the Audley End side of Beechy Ride. There were two falls of earth, about 40 tons in all, and covering about 50 feet of the track. All trains had to cease running and it took over a morning to clear the track.

The initial flurry of activity once war broke out had included banning all dancing at the Town Hall after 10 p.m. This was resented as little appeared to be happening during this period, and the Council relented in January, and permitted the hall's use until midnight. A series of dances and concerts were organised by the Council and these proved very successful.

The first locally reported casualty of the war was a 23 year old man, Sergeant Pilot Percy Thurgar, who was killed in February, 1940, just three weeks after being married in Walden Parish Church to a local woman.

Reclamation schemes for wastepaper, and later metal were very successful in the town. By March 1940, the town had collected over 9 tons of paper and later that year schemes for collecting metals were also well supported. In August a three-ton lorry was filled with aluminium collected in a depot in South Road, and even a German Field gun presented to the town by the 9th Battalion of the Essex Regiment after the first world war, and kept in the museum grounds was sent away for scrap! It was also at this time that the railings around the church yard were removed for scrap.

As we have seen evacuation had worked very successfully in the town, so it was perhaps not surprising that in March, 1940, a new evacuation scheme allocated an additional 400 children from the Stratford area to

Saffron Walden. The Council expressed alarm at this. Apart from the difficulties of accommodating such a large additional number it was felt it would be in everyone's interest if additional children came from the Tottenham area. Stanley Wilson, a Councillor and then the town's chief billeting officer, the Mayor, Hubert Collar, and the Town Clerk visited the House of Commons to point out the difficulties. In particular they stressed the near impossibility of providing adequate educational facilities for such a large number. As it was the Tottenham children were having to be educated in the Boys' British, the Girls' School in South Road, the Castle Street National School and the Walden and Newport Grammar Schools alongside Walden children, and other accommodation was also having to be used. The Friends' School also took a large number of evacuees. For some time the training college acted as hosts to the Tottenham Girls' High School and other buildings had to be quickly adapted. Fortunately these arguments won the day and only Tottenham evacuees were sent to the town.

A survey of provisions for evacuees was carried out in March, 1940. It was noted that every billet had been visited by one of the towns 40 billeting officers. The children had generally become absorbed into the life of the town and had been encouraged to join the local scouts and guides, churches and other organisations. A new scout troop had been formed especially for the evacuees, a local football league with six teams of both local and evacuee boys had been formed, and the English Folk Dance society were teaching the evacuee girls their rural craft. In addition, the Council had established the first Nursery School specifically for evacuees, in Essex, and various bodies were on hand to provide free clothing, shoes etc. where it was required. There seems little doubt that the town carried out its duty to its evacuees in a praiseworthy way.

Meanwhile Walden men were doing their bit in the services. Gunner Frank Smith, from Little Walden Road, was captured at Dunkirk, having been one of a small party detailed to cover the retreat. However he escaped, by knocking out his German guard with a 'straight left' to the jaw, and was back in Walden by the end of June.

Another Walden man to escape from imprisonment after being captured at Dunkirk, was Lance Bombadier J.Dixon of East Street, who had been reported as missing, but after escaping eventually reached Spain by crossing the Pyrenees.

Roy Housden of Audley Road was involved in an even more daring adventure which made the men concerned national heroes. Roy was an 18 year old merchant seaman and one of the crew of the San Demetrio a ship carrying a large consignment of petrol in convoy across the Atlantic. The convoy was attacked, and the San Demetrio was set on fire. In a famous incident, the escort ship, the Jervis Bay, deliberately steered for the raider, and drew her fire. Meanwhile Housden and the crew of the San Demetrio had abandoned ship. After being adrift in heavy seas for two days and nights, they sighted the San Demitrio still on fire and after voting decided to reboard her. The crew succeeded in putting out the fire, then negotiating a hurricane before bringing the ship and its cargo home to port. Sadly Roy Housden was killed later in the war.

With RAF Debden just down the road the skies above Walden during the summer of 1940 must have seen considerable action. During June and July there was some debate about whether the chimes of the Church should be silenced. The debate centred on whether the chimes could be heard in the air and so assist the bombers in locating the town! On a more serious note, however there was concern that enemy parachutists might find the chimes helpful were there to be an aerial invasion.

No doubt because of the Battle of Britain overhead, considerable work went into providing public air raid shelters during July and August. Even the front of the Town Hall was sandbagged to provide cover for those caught outside in the Market Square. Shelters were provided at Park Place at the rear of the Post Office, the top of the High Street at the entrance to Margaret Way, the tunnel under the Battle Ditches on the Gibson Close estate, in the Borough Market, at the Rose and Crown, and on the Common.

RAF Debden was often the object of German attacks and this inevitably affected Walden. At the end of August, 1940 the aerodrome was seriously damaged in two raids, when a total of over 200 high explosive and incendiary bombs were dropped on the base. Four RAF men and one civilian were killed, and the operations room had to be transferred. It was decided to move it away from the base, and it was relocated in the disused chalk pit in Thaxted Road (now opposite the Leisure Centre), where it remained until moving to the gymnasium at the requisitioned Grammar School. (20)

The General Hospital bricked up to protect against bomb damage.

During the raids, one of the bombers, a Dornier DO 17 was shot down by a Hurricane and exploded on Highams Farm, in Thaxted. Two of the crew baled out and were captured, but two more, Oberlt. Heidenreich, and Fw. Panczak were killed. They were buried in Walden Cemetery. (39)

The town and its defences were also fighting back. The Walden Weekly reported that in the same attack, residents of the town watched a German plane being shot down by anti-aircraft fire. The plane was seen to wobble after being hit whilst flying at about 1,200 feet, and parachutes were seen as the occupants baled out. Later three German airmen were taken to Walden Police Station having been captured by a local farmer. One of the Germans was wounded.

The town also came under attack. During the night of 17th August, 36 high explosive bombs were dropped close to the town, one of which failed to explode and had to be defused. A number of unexploded bombs also fell near the town four days later, and as one was thought to be close to the Friends' School, the surrounding area had to be quickly evacuated. Although this bomb proved to be a false alarm, another unexploded bomb did come down in what was called 'Maltings Field' in Station Road, and several bombs exploded in Audley Park. (7)

In September, 1940 there were more attacks in the area. A Heinkel 111 was shot down by AA fire at Thorley Wash near Bishop's Stortford, and three of its crew killed. Like their earlier counterparts, the three, Uffz. H. Pohl, Uffz. W. Goliath, and Fw. T. Alper, were buried in Radwinter Road Cemetery. (40)

Bombs were again reported in the area from a big raid of over 350 enemy aircraft on the night of the 29th November. 17 Bombs, including 2 unexploded bombs were dropped close to the town, and more fell close by on the night of the 9th December. (7)

Amongst the pilots involved in the Battle of Britain were Flying Officer R.F.Smythe, who was married to a Saffron Walden girl. He was awarded the D.F.C. for breaking up a formation of six Messerschmitt fighters near Folkestone, and destroying one of them. Another pilot was Sergeant Harry Perry of Little Walden Road, who, sadly was the last pilot to be killed in the Battle of Britain when his plane crashed on 30th October, 1940.

With the warm summer and the Governments 'Dig for Victory' campaign, the Council negotiated with the landowners of land to the south of Summerhill Road (now the Rowntree Way Estate) and in Newport Road (now Beeches Close) to acquire the land for allotments. The Council agreed to provide the land and plough it free of charge to any person who wished to have an allotment.

Possibly some of the money saved by people growing their own food went into savings for, as in the first World War, a National Savings scheme was launched and a target of £36,100 set for the town. A giant 'thermometer' on the side of the Town Hall registered the town's progress. Along with this scheme, the Saffron Walden and Dunmow licensed victuallers set up a Spitfire fund with the aim of raising £5,000 to

Saffron Walden Grammar School, headquarters of the USAAF 65th Fighter Wing.

buy a plane. This was less than successful however only raising £314 5s 10d which was sent to Lord Beaverbrook in February 1941.

As we have seen the majority of the child evacuees were able to be educated in local schools and other buildings. But in September, 1940, the Military Authorities requisitioned the Saffron Walden Grammar School buildings in Ashdon Road. The school, whose origins went back over 500 years looked for alternative accommodation, but were unable to find any, and on the 25th September, the governors decided to close the school for the duration of the war. Pupils were sent to other local schools, but the Grammar School never reopened. From 1943 to the end of the war, the building served as the headquarters of the U.S.A.A.F. 65th Fighter Wing, under the command of Brigadier-General Jesse Auton. Today the building is used for a private school.

Townspeople were very concerned at the possibility of 'fifth columnists' existing in the community. This fear, reflected a national feeling that certain continental countries had been undermined by German sympathisers. An editorial appearing in the Walden Weekly of 4th October reflected that concern in what was probably no more than a school boy prank:-

' 'Down with England'. These words written on chalk in block capitals appear in the wooden gateway at the Littlebury turning corner of the Park this week above a swastika crudely drawn in chalk. Was this the work of silly school boy bravado or has the message more sinister implications? The Police do not know. The chalk marks were removed the same day.'

The blackout regulations, as in the first world war, were rigorously enforced. In October, 1940, five people were found guilty of breaching the regulations, and fined between £2 to £5. Amongst those fined were Father del Olma the towns Catholic Priest, and Harold Woodward, a local auctioneer. In announcing the fines the Mayor said that the authorities were trying to make the blackout perfect. If one bomb dropped that would be enough for Saffron Walden.

Enemy action on the town again occurred on Monday 16th December, 1940. A German plane swept over the town at a height said to be lower than that of the church spire. It machine gunned Audley End railway station and injured the fireman of a train. The Walden Weekly reported:-

'The plane made about nine runs over the station and dropped several bombs in the vicinity, but only slight damage was done. One of the station staff who is in the Home Guard, seized his rifle, rushed from his office and fired two rounds at the plane. . . .

A bullet passed straight through the body of an unoccupied motor car standing in the station yard, and some bullets came through the roof of a nearby hotel, [presumably the Neville Arms]. Another smashed through the roof of a house and penetrated the wall on the far side of the room, puncturing a picture.

A number of boys cycling on their way to a village Grammar School [Newport] were machine gunned by the plane. They had to fling their bicycles in the road and scramble into ditches. Two of the boys – 13 years old John Walker and 12 years old Roy O'Brien – ran behind a haystack. When bullets began to fall close they sought shelter in a cottage. Another boy, an evacuee named Schooling, ran behind a tree. Bullets hit the tree behind which he was sheltering.'

Although a horse was killed elsewhere it was a miraculous escape.

It was not surprising that the railway line and station were attacked for the branch line was begining to play a significant role in the town. Armaments for the airfields at Debden, Duxford, Castle Camps and Little Walden were being transported via the line, and in 1939 petrol sidings had been installed at the new petrol dump in Ashdon Road. This dump and pipeline had been built to serve the airfields and contained high octane fuel. Many of the trains made a circuitous route to it via Shelford and Bartlow because of the risk to the town if a train were attacked whilst it was passing through. (36)

A second attack by a single plane appears to have occurred again in February 1941. As the Walden Weekly merely refers to 'an East Anglian market town' one must assume it was Walden. The report said:-

'A lone German plane which swooped out of the clouds and seemed to skim the rooftops dropped three bombs on the outskirts of an East Anglian market town on Tuesday afternoon.

The bombs fell in fields near a farmhouse. There were no casualties and apart from some panes of glass blown out of a nurseryman's greenhouse no damage was done.

It was market day and when the noise of the explosions were heard people crowded around the stalls on the town square, rushed to the shelter. The plane, a Heinkel bomber was flying so low and appeared to be moving so leisurely that although many people in the market-day crowd saw it overhead they thought it was a British plane. Even when the bombs fell some thought it was gunfire as the bombs were of light calibre. Some people actually saw the bombs leave the plane.'

The town again reported bombing in the area on the night of 23rd and 24th April, 1941.(40) It was at this time and perhaps due to incidents like this, that an additional siren was installed at Debden Road, and a census taken of stirrup pumps. Additional sand piles were also provided around the town for use against incendiary bombs.

RAB Butler, the town's MP helped to launch a War Savings week to run from 9th to 15th March 1941. The idea was that people would put their money into National Savings so that the money could be invested for the war use. A target was set of £60,000 but by the Wednesday the total had already reached £103,245. Various promotions were used to encourage the town to save even more. On the Wednesday, the RAF brought a long trailer into the Market Square containing a German fighter plane which had been brought down. It was displayed in the Corn Exchange along with some unexploded incendiary bombs, High Explosive bombs and different types of guns. On the Sunday, what was described as the largest procession of military units ever seen in the town took part in a church parade and march past.

Certainly the War Savings week was a success. The money invested by Walden residents in either Savings Certificates, Defence Bonds, National War Bonds and Savings Bonds came to a massive £181,645.

Rationing brought with it the problem of ensuring an active workforce were adequately fed. A scheme, started by the Ministry of Food and which became known as the British Restaurants, was introduced to encourage communal feeding. These restaurants ensured that there was a guaranteed food supply at a reasonable cost. The Borough Council established a British Restaurant in Cambridge House on the corner of the High Street and Church Street, in December 1941. The scheme was very popular – by the following December the restaurant was serving an average of 800 meals a week with 200 of those being served to school children. Another requirement of war time was the need to resalvage as much material as possible, particularly metal. To this end dumps were established at Thaxted Road, Catons Lane, the sewerage works, the Councils depot in the Borough Market, Audley Road, Pleasant Valley, and at Sewards End and Audley End. Old metal bike wheels, fire fenders, tin cans and iron bedsteads all found their way to these dumps.

Mention has already been made of the need for additional sand and stirrup pumps because of the risk of incendiary bombs. As the town was not a proscribed area, fire watching had to be on a voluntary basis. Appeals for volunteers produced a rota of about 200 volunteers.

Ironically when fire did hit the town it was accidental. On Saturday 12th July 1941, a fire broke out in the maltings at the top of Gold Street, next to The Sun public house. The maltings were used as a food depot by Messrs. Sainsburys, who had evacuated one of their grocery warehouses from London. Consequently it contained many tons of foodstuffs. The fire started at about 9.00 p.m. and the alarm was quickly given. The brigade arrived almost immediately, but the building which was made of old timber and plaster was very dry, and the flames spread rapidly. The top of the building contained a dormitory for staff, and this was quickly gutted. The fire brigade found the water pressure was very low and this hampered their efforts. A human chain of soldiers, airmen and civilians was hastily organised and managed to salvage several tons of food. Others helped dampen the fire with stirrup pumps and garden hoses.

However the fire was not easily quelled. Flames reached over 50 feet into the air, and the firemen had to concentrate on protecting the adjoining buildings. The fire was eventually brought under control by about 11 p.m. There were several casualties amongst the helpers, with four people being detained in hospital. Fortunately much of the food was salvaged, and the adjoining pub and cottages were only slightly damaged. The malting was completely destroyed. Later the Council was to investigate the water pressure difficulties. They were also concerned that this one fire had consumed over 100,000 gallons of water, and that a larger fire would use up the town's total water capacity.

In August 1941 the Council started negotiations with the Ancient Buildings Trust Ltd., over the possibility of acquiring a 45 year lease on the old Maltings on the corner of Myddlyton Place and the High Street. The Council wanted to use the building for a school and youth centre for some of the evacuees. Initally the negotiations fell through but eventually a temporary arrangement was made with the Middlesex Education Committee to provide accommodation for some of the evacuees. In August 1942 the Youth Hostel Association were able to announce that they had acquired the lease and accommodation for up to 60 people was provided. The malting has continued as the town's Youth Hostel ever since.

Voluntary financing of the war was to play a major effort in the War's success. In December 1941, the Saffron Walden Borough and Rural Councils decided to amalgamate for Warship Week which was to be held in February 1942. The aim was to raise £120,000, sufficient to adopt a Corvette. If the money was raised a ship would be allocated to the area and the town's coat of arms would be placed on the quarter deck as a tribute to the town.

The appeal was a tremendous success, with a total of £253,507 being raised, through a concert, dances, a darts competition, whist drives, raffles, etc. A 510 ton ship, the Marjoram was allocated to the area, but in June 1942, the admiralty announced that HMS Lapwing would be allocated instead. The Lapwing was a convoy escort vessel, and there had been previous 'Lapwings' in the navy since 1763. The original Lapwing had in fact sunk in 1764 with the loss of all hands! A brass plaque was fixed

HMS Lapwing, Saffron Walden's adopted ship.

to the ship recording its adoption by the Borough and Rural District Councils. HMS Lapwing was built at Scotts Yard on Clydebank in 1941, and commissioned at St. Stevens Yard Govan on 10th March 1944. She was involved with the Normandy landings between 6th June and 10th Sept 1944 and for the rest of her life she was attached to the Russian convoys in the Western Approaches. Sadly on 20th March, 1945, she was sunk by enemy action, whilst escorting a Russian convoy, with the loss of over 150 lives.

Another financial appeal, this time in the form of savings was the Tanks for Attack appeal during August 1942. Walden was set a target of £48,500 to raise and only fell short by a few pounds.

On 10th August, 1942 Little Walden Airfield was opened as an operational base for the American 8th Air Force. The base was quickly built with prefabricated buildings and three runways varying in length from 4,200 feet to 5,700 feet. It remained operational until the end of the war. One of the runways now forms part of the Little Walden to Hadstock road.

A number of Walden men were killed in Malaya and Singapore during their fall in April 1942, and several other casualties were reported from the Western Desert, although thankfully casualty rates were not as high as during the first world war.

By the middle of 1942, the bombing of London had eased and a large number of evacuees were returning home. In July the Tottenham High School for Girls decided to return en bloc. A letter from the Headmistress in the Walden Weekly showed their appreciation of the towns efforts:-

'Not only were our staff and girls received into your houses with a warm friendliness which cheered them, but that spirit has continued while we have lived amongst you. . . . To have welcomed into your homes these girls from an evacuation area, to have fed them and cared for them daily, to have entered into their lives with kindly understanding and sympathy over a period of three years is a noble contribution to the country's war effort. . . .'

With the threat of invasion apparently over some changes began to occur. Evacuees began to return home in large numbers – by December 1942, there were only 126 adults and 222 child evacuees left in the town – and in the following month road signs also began to reappear with signs being replaced at the High Street/George Street Junction, as well as at Common Hill, Thaxted Road and Newport Road.

In January 1943, Richard Henry Cornwallis, the 8th Lord Braybrooke, was killed in action. Tragically his younger brother had already been killed, and the title passed to their cousin, Henry.

The arrival of American forces into the area, resulted in a plea from the Mayor for families to act as hosts to the soldiers to make them welcome. A concert party was held to which American troops were invited. As the war progressed more and more Americans appeared in the town, particularly when the Eagle squadron took over RAF Debden.

240

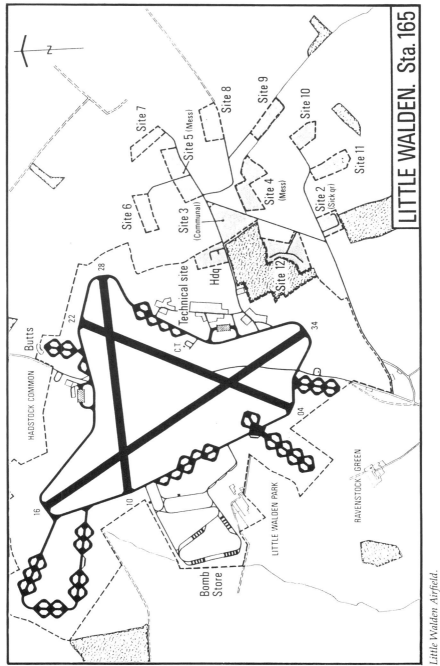

LITTLE WALDEN. Sta. 165

Site 7
Site 5 (Mess)
Site 8
Site 9
Site 10
Site 11
Site 6
Site 3
(Communal)
Site 4
(Mess)
Site 2
(Sick qr)
Hdq
Site 12
Technical site
C.T.
28
22
Butts
HADSTOCK COMMON
16
34
10
04
Bomb Store
LITTLE WALDEN PARK
RAVENSTOCK GREEN

Little Walden Airfield.

Large buildings in and around the town became used for a number of war-time purposes. The Grammar School has already been mentioned. The Town Hall was used as the billeting office for the town, and later used by the Military High Command for the Eastern Region (32) and Audley End Mansion was used as a training centre for Polish troops on underground missions to their homeland. Little Walden Hall became a women's training school for the National Fire Service, Eastern Region, and accommodated up to 46 women on regular training courses.

The major event in Walden in 1943 was the Wings for Victory week. Designed to be a national fundraising event like those of previous years, the Walden area was set a target of £200,000, with the town expected to raise £58,392. The week was to be held from 8th to 15th May and a series of events were arranged consisting of a concert given by the towns Hot Spots concert party, church parades, a band concert, darts and table tennis tournaments, whist drives, dances, an open air boxing competition, and film shows. Perhaps the most unusual event, influenced by the recent arrival of the Americans, was a soft baseball match to be held at Catons Lane football ground.

As with the Warship week the event was a marvellous success. A total of £322,096 was raised of which the town contributed £116,661, double the amount expected. According to the Ministry, the money raised was sufficient to purchase 33 fighter planes, and two bombers.

In November, 1943, the town learnt of another act of heroism by one of its former inhabitants. Captain R. Mead, formerly of Sewards End was on operational duty over the Atlantic, when his bomber, was shot down. He, and five of his crew took to a dinghy where they were adrift for eleven days. They were eventually rescued by a destroyer.

During the latter part of the war Italian prisoners were brought to Walden. They were housed in huts erected in Thaxted Road. Many of the prisoners volunteered to work on local farms, and they enjoyed a certain amount of freedom – indeed so much so, that in September 1944, the Council actually had to ban them from attending dances at the Town Hall as some of the American troops objected to their presence.

The large number of Americans in the area, from the air fields at Debden and Little Walden as well as army troops on manoeuvres, meant the town took on a distinctly 'American' air. In January, 1944 the Council agreed to make the Corn Exchange available to the U.S. Forces for basketball and volleyball games, and in the same month the Anglo American Canteen and Club was opened in Abbey Lane. This large well appointed building, had been paid for by war charities, and had an entertainment hall approx. 120 feet by about 30 feet as well as a canteen and other rooms. The building was opened by Colonel Mallinson, the Chief Army Welfare Officer for Essex and according to him it was a model for other Essex towns to follow.

With the war gradually turning the Allies' way the Country began to look to the future in peace time. It was the towns MP, RAB Butler, who as Minister for Education introduced the Education Bill to Parliament in

January 1944. The bill which eventually became an act created the present education system and has often been regarded as one of the most important pieces of legislation to have come out of the war.

Locally the Town Council was also concerned with the need to look ahead particularly in respect of future housing needs. The Ministry of Health had recently announced that between three to four million houses must be built in the first ten years after the war. In the light of this the Council made application to the Ministry, late in 1943, for permission to build 200 houses in the first year after the war. However the Ministry wanted to ensure that scarce building materials went to the blitzed towns and cities first of all and Walden was told it would not be permitted to build more than its average between 1920 and 1939. As this amounted to only seven houses a year, the Council were less than satisfied, and decided to lobby the Ministry.

The Council's efforts met with some success, and in May, 1944, consent was given by the Ministry for the Council to purchase 26 acres of land for housing to be built after the war. The land was intended for temporary as well as permanent housing. The Council were also given consent to buy additional building land at Little Walden and Sewards End. In July, 1944 the Council approved the purchase of 15 acres in Little Walden Road; 9.5 acres in Ashdon Road (this site is the present Whiteshot Way); 3.9 acres to the north of the Crown at Little Walden (now Petlands); and 2.7 acres in Cole End Lane (now The Dreys). The housing problem was undoubtedly acute. In the Walden Weekly of 27th October 1944, there was a report of a Walden family who had to live in a poultry shed in Thaxted Road. They had been ejected from their cottage at Byrds Farm because it was required for an essential farm worker, and this prompted the suggestion that the huts in Thaxted Road, which housed Italian Prisoners of War could, with a few alterations be used to house upwards of 40 families.

This idea was acted upon and in December, 1944 consent was obtained from the Ministry of Health to convert the hutments camp in Thaxted Road into temporary housing. Plans for the conversion of eight huts into dwellings were drawn up in January 1945 and submitted to the Ministry for approval.

As in previous years, 1944 saw a major fundraising initiative, this time the Salute the Soldier Week. The Saffron Walden Borough and Rural District were set the target of £250,000, the proceeds of which were to be used to equip two battalions of the Essex Regiment. The week, held in June saw all the usual fundraising events and succeeded in raising the phenomenal sum of £302,521, of which the town raised £110,585, an average of £13. 3s and 8d per person.

Heroism occurred both at home and abroad. During 1944, a large number of Walden men serving with the Essex Regiment were in action in Italy and reports of medals being awarded were a regular occurrence. One such example was the Distinguished Conduct Medal awarded to Sergeant W.J.Swan of Hollyhock Road for his conduct for fighting on the 8th Army front in Italy.

At home, Len Crickmore of the town's fire brigade was awarded the British Empire Medal for his actions when an ammunition dump exploded at Great Chesterford in June 1944. The blast, which meant that the whole of Great Chesterford had to be evacuated, was felt in Walden. According to the Walden Weekly a publican in a 'neighbouring town' was putting his takings into the bank, when the blast hurled him against a wall, blew the notes off the counter and filled the bank with dust. However perhaps one of the bravest acts was that of an Ashdon woman, Mrs. Betty Everitt of Puddle Wharf Farm. She witnessed two planes from Little Walden Airfield crashing in mid air, and dashed to the scene of the crash. She helped rescue one of the airmen, but, whilst going back to rescue another, was killed as the plane exploded. For this act of bravery she was posthumously awarded the Albert Medal. Sadly her husband had died five months previously, and their four year old son, Tony was left an orphan. A fund was set up to raise money for him to which the American airmen based at Little Walden contributed handsomely.

Death in action also came to the enemy. On the night of the 18th/19th April, the only plane to actually crash in the Parish of Saffron Walden, was brought down. The plane, a Heinkel 177 was shot down by a Mosquito flown by Flying Officer S.B. Huppery and Pilot Officer J.S. Christie, and crashed at Butlers Farm in Ashdon Road at 1.03 a.m. Two of the crew, Uffz. G. Speyerer and Oberg. F. Kopf were killed and four others taken prisoner. The aircraft disintegrated on impact. (41) The Walden Weekly reported that the two German airmen killed in the raid were buried in an 'East Anglian' cemetery, with formal military honours. The service was conducted by an RAF Chaplain, and flowers were sent from an RAF station 'in the district'. The graves of the two airmen are still in the military section of Walden Cemetery today.

On 16th September, 1944 a V1 flying bomb landed in fields to the south of the town, probably roughly where the Fairview estate is today. The Walden Weekly still restricted to keeping the town anonymous because of the censorship requirements, gave the following report:-

'Shortly before dawn on Saturday morning a flying bomb fell in the open country on the outskirts of a small town in the South of England. Its arrival and fall was seen by a large number of people. It came in low with its tail a mass of orange flame, putting along like a traction engine. After hitting the tops of tall trees it fell in a field, making a crater of about eight feet deep and 20 feet in diameter, scattering metal and debris in all directions.

Fortunately no one was killed or injured, but a few people had cuts and scratches. An Isolation Hospital [at what is now Hill Top Lane] suffered damage and the patients and staff were shaken, one of the staff suffering a cut lip.

At a well-known mixed secondary school [i.e. Friends' School] over 200 window panes were smashed. Fortunately the pupils which number nearly 300 . . . had not returned from the summer vacation.

At a young ladies training college about a hundred windows and panes were broken. . . . In the vicinity many houses also lost windows and doors came off and ceilings fell. Building trade workers have since been very busy rendering first aid repairs to the buildings.'

By the end of 1944, the realisation that the war was won was becoming obvious. At the beginning of October the street lights were relit, and the townspeople could move more safely at night; plans for the long awaited County Senior School were drawn up by the County architect and submitted to the Town Council for approval and in December the Saffron Walden 'D' Company of the 12th Essex Battalion Home Guard were stood down at a special parade. In addition perhaps with the advent of peace, reports were becoming commonplace of Walden girls marrying American servicemen from the local bases.

Thoughts were also turning to the forces homecoming. A public meeting held in the town in December, 1944 agreed to attempt to raise £6,000, £1 for every person in the town, and three schemes were considered:-

1) The engraving on the 1914-18 War Memorial the names of those killed.
2) The setting aside of £1,000 until at least 50% of the forces return home so that they could suggest how the money could be spent, and
3) The provision of a playing field comprising a cricket ground, bowls green, tennis courts, car and bus park, kiddies playing pens, band stand and ornamental gardens.

All three schemes were devolved to a special committee to consider, but, in March 1945, before any positive action had been made, the 65th Fighter Wing of the U.S.A.A.F. intervened by offering £4,500 towards the provision of a community recreation ground, a hall and a canteen, provided the Borough raised a similar amount. A letter from the Mayor, Joseph Custerson, in the Walden Weekly explained the intention behind the Americans suggestion:-

'. . . They were not interested in stone columns or anything of this kind; they wanted a memorial that the living could use, and they would like to ally themselves with a permanent body. The question he put to me was: Had I any ideas. . . ?

My reply was that I had very definite ideas, and I had had them for some years – for a social centre for Saffron Walden.

Also if they wished to ally themselves with a permanent body, the Borough Council had a history going back to the days of Henry VIII . . . I told them of a scheme that was started 13 years ago, when the town purchased the land in Caton's Lane for a football field and playing field for the children. To complete the scheme we needed approximately ten acres more land between Caton's Lane and Fry's Gardens for cricket, bowls, hockey, tennis courts, with a small hall in the grounds and a well fitted canteen.'

Architect's drawing of the proposed memorial playing fields.

The scheme unfortunately was not able to come to full fruition, as the town was not able to match the generous offer of the Americans in full. Nonetheless the Anglo American Memorial Playing Fields were to be opened in 1954 by Field Marshal Montgomery.

Peace came in May, 1945, with celebrations in the town, lasting for two days. Unlike the coronation celebrations of previous years this was a spontaneous event, but the town was still quickly decorated with flags and bunting. VE day was a Tuesday and also a market day, and during the morning the market and a number of shops were open. The church bells played during the morning and after lunch, people began to gather informally on the Common, and in the Market Square. Thanksgiving services were held in the Churches, and a number of people visited the cemetery where over 60 war dead of all nationalities now lay.

In the evening more formal ceremonies began. A dance was held at the Anglo American club in Abbey Lane, and then, at 9.00 p.m. a large crowd gathered in the Market Square to listen to the King's speech which was broadcast through a loudspeaker. Floodlights were then switched on to illuminate the square, and the drums and pipes of the King's Own Scottish Borderers (Airborne) Battalion beat the retreat. A torchlight procession, led by the town band followed and there was considerable merriment by both British and American troops with dancing going on until past midnight.

By 10.45 p.m., there were thousands of people on the Common, which was lit up by two large British searchlights and four American searchlights. There was other lighting around the town, including a large electric 'V' sign on the chimney of the nurseries in Radwinter Road.

The celebrations lasted officially for two days, although the children were allowed three days off school. On the second day sports and games were held on the Common, and again there was dancing in the Market Square until Midnight.

Perhaps surprisingly not everybody felt that such jollification should take place. A letter in the Walden Weekly of 18th May 1945 complained about the extension to licensing hours on V.E.Day and said:-

'Many of us are profoundly disappointed in the magistrates for pandering to the drink trade, at a time when their united help was needed to safeguard the public, and prevent our already overworked policemen from being taxed unduly. Did those magistrates responsible for the drinking extension until midnight on V-Day consider: 1)The further two or three hours disturbed rest of little children? 2) The encouragement to leave them unattended in homes? 3) The increased temptation for our young people in and out of the Forces, and for our visitors from overseas? . . .'

In the light of the celebrations this was probably a minority view!

With the peace came details of much of the secret work being carried on in factories in the town. In particular, the Tower Works plant in Debden Road (later the site for Acrow and now occupied by LPA) was involved in engineering works of the highest importance. They produced parts for Churchill tanks, and Mosquito aircraft, and also produced thousands of self-powered chainsaws which were used in Russia and Burma. They manufactured the majority of all the steel roadforms used for runways on airfields, and produced large quantities of scaffolding for repair work to bomb damaged buildings. But perhaps their two major achievements were the manufacture of a large number of Bailey bridges, used for numerous river crossings, and the production of steel shuttering used for the construction of the prefabricated ports, jetties and harbours known as the Mulberry harbours. The war effort of the Tower Works was a major achievement for the town and one of which all those employed there can be justly proud.

The town had come to be closely associated with many of the Americans serving in the locality, particularly those of the 65th Fighter Wing, and so it was fitting that on 8th June 1945 the Council awarded Brigadier-General Jesse Auton, the commanding officer of the wing the Freedom of the Borough. As the Brigadier recognised in his reply to the Mayor, the Council were not only honouring him, but were honouring all the Americans who served in the area.

Then came VJ day. Many Walden men had served in the Far East and the war to them did not end until August 1945. Again there was much celebrating in Walden. A church service, sports on the Common, including a womens soccer match, and dancing in the Market Square all took place. In the evening there was estimated to be over 4,000 people in the Market Square, as well as a dance in the Town Hall. The following day also saw sports, a fancy dress competition, and more dancing in the square.

With the ending of the war the town had to face a different world – but that's another book!

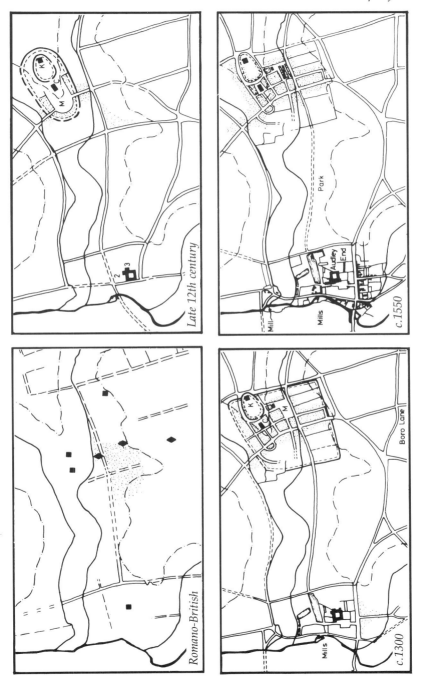

Late 12th century

c.1550

Park

Audley End

Mill

Mills

Boro Lane

Romano-British

c.1300

Mills

Development of the town from Roman times to the 16th century

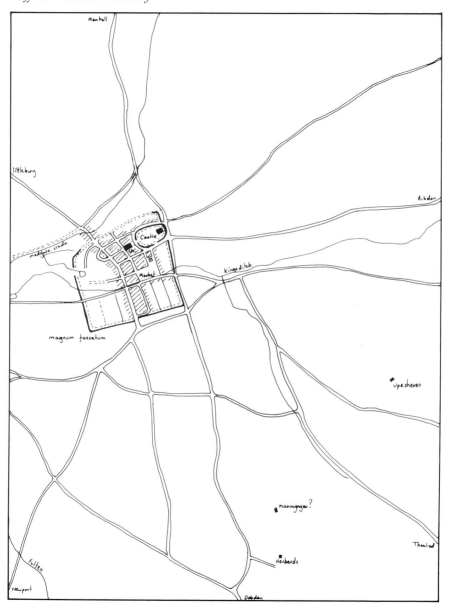

Manhell

littlebury

Ashdon

madgate slade

Castle

Ch.

Market

kinge ditch

magnum fossatum

upesheres

mannyngeo ?

Herberds

Thaxted

Fulfen

Newport

Debden

Chepyng Walden circa 1300

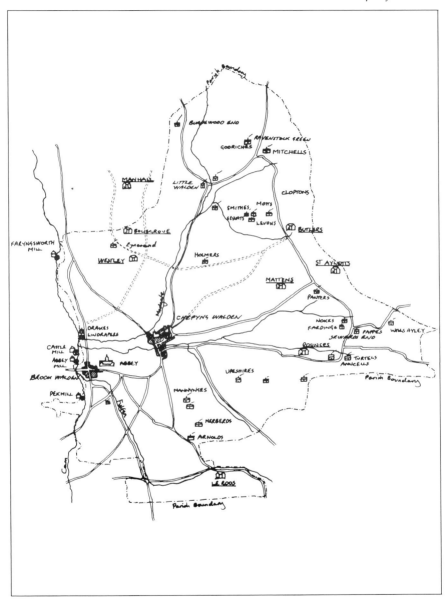

Walden circa 1400

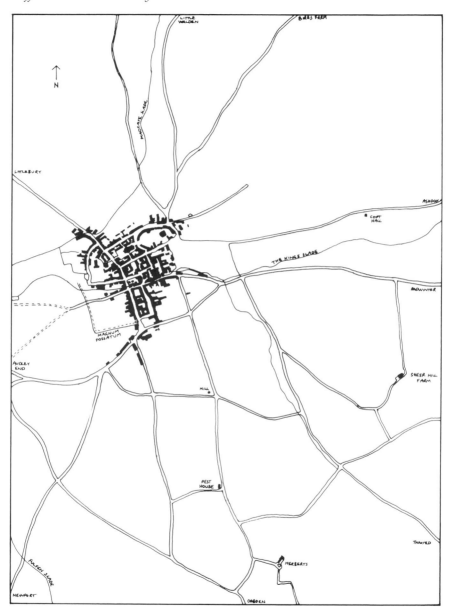

Saffron Walden circa 1750

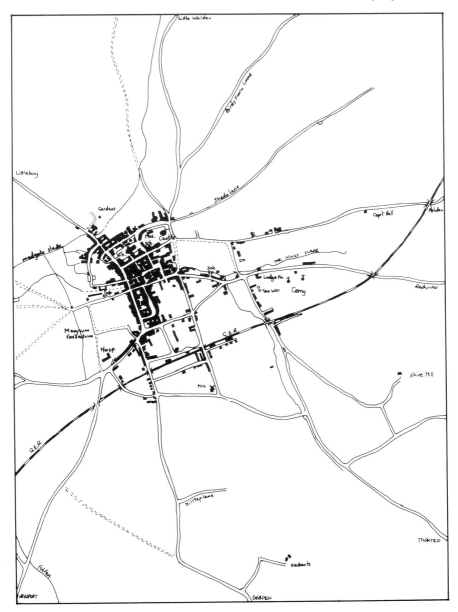

Saffron Walden circa 1877

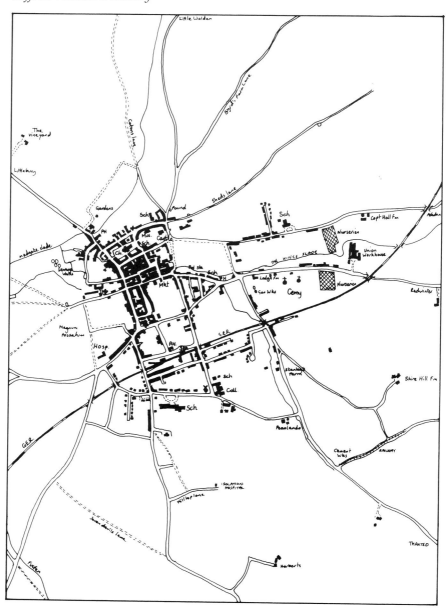

Saffron Walden circa 1921

Saffron Walden Town Centre 1921

BIBLIOGRAPHY

1. Adams, W: A short Account of the Corporation, its Members and Officers etc. 1932.
2. Barker, M.M: Ordnance Survey of England and Wales. Saffron Walden and District (Sheets 202 and 205).
3. Bassett, S: Report on site on corner of High Street and Gold Street.
4. Bassett, S.R: Saffron Walden : Excavation and research 1972 - 80.
5. Benton, Rev. G.M: Notes on Saffron Walden and its Church. Transcribed from a manuscript notebook.
6. Book of the foundation of the monastery of Walden, B.M. Arundel MS29.
7. Bowyer, M.F: Air Raid! The enemy air offensive against East Anglia 1939 - 1945. 1986.
8. Braybrooke, Lord: History of Audley End (1836).
9. Buchan, J: Oliver Cromwell, Hodder, 1934.
10. Cambridge University Library Manuscript. Add. 7090.
11. Carlyle, Thomas: Oliver Cromwell (Vol. 5) (Quoted in 'Scenes from Old Walden' - see 47 below).
12. Chambers, W.J: The Mystery of the Battle Ditches (Paper read to the Saffron Walden History Society on 17th April 1967).
13. Chisenhale-Marsh, T.C: Domesday Book relating to Essex.
14. Clark, Rev. A: Essex Review, April 1910.
15. Cromarty, D: 'Chepyng Walden 1381 - 1420, a study from the Court Rolls' Essex Journal Vol.2, 1967.
16. Cromarty, D: The Fields of Saffron Walden in 1400.
17. Darby, H.C: Domesday England. Cambridge University Press 1977.
18. Dickinson, P: Saffron Walden Guide (1969 Edition).
19. Dictionary of National Biography.
20. Douglas Brown, R: East Anglia, 1940.
21. Emson. C: A Calendar of Deeds relating to Saffron Walden and neighbouring Parishes 13th - 18th Centuries.
22. Emson, Frank: History of Saffron Walden, 1904.
23. Essex Archaeological Society Transactions New Series Vol.2.
24. Essex County Record Office: Essex Homes, 1066 - 1850.
25. Essex Review, 1932.
26. Essex Standard, 25th December, 1835.
27. Friends of Saffron Walden Parish Church : The Story of Saffron Walden Parish Church.'83.
28. Guild of Holy Trinity Accounts 1545.
29. A Handbook to the Parish Church of Saffron Walden With Illustrations and Notes upon Local Church History in Olden Times. 1884.
30. Humphreys, Dorothy: Saffron Walden Workhouse: the first thirty years of the new poor law (Saffron Walden History).
31. Lord, Roger: The Saffron Walden United Charities: an example of a local Charity. 1989.
32. Madonna, P.ed: Saffron Walden 1236 - 1986.
33. Monteith, D: Saffron Walden and its environs.
34. Morant: History and antiquities of Essex (1864).
35. Muir, Jane C: Saffron Walden in 1851: A study based on census data. Saffron Walden History, Spring, 1986.
36. Paye, P: The Saffron Walden Branch, 1980.
37. Player John: Sketches of Saffron Walden, 1845.
38. Plumb, Christine: The Economic activity of Saffron Walden, 1500 - 1780. 1983.
39. Ramsey, W. ed: The Blitz, Then and Now, Vol 1. 1987.
40. Ramsey, W. ed: The Blitz, Then and Now, Vol 2.
41. Ramsey, W. ed: The Blitz, Then and Now, Vol 3. 1990.
42. Reaney, P.H: Place names of Essex (1936).
43. The Register of Walden (Cartulary of Walden Abbey). Transl. from the original manuscript (B.M. Harlein MS 3697).
44. Report of the Committee appointed to carry into effect a plan for ameliorating the Condition of the Poor at Saffron Walden etc. 1830.
45. Rowntree, C.B: Saffron Walden then and now. 1950.
46. Rowntree, C.B: More Saffron Walden, then and now. Walden Cricket, 1954.
47. Scenes from Old Walden - hand book of the Saffron Walden Pageant, 1910.
48. Stacey, H.C: Saffron Walden in old photographs. 1980.
49. Stacey, H.C: Walden's Saffron - Crocus Sativus, 1973.
50. Stevenson: 'A contemporary description of the Domesday Survey'. English Historical Review xxii (1907) P.74.
51. Strickland, A: Lives of the Queens of England. Vol. 8.
52. Unstead, R.J: The Medieval Scene. 1962.
53. Victoria County History of Essex (5 Vols.).
54. Walden Castle. (Published by Saffron Walden Museum) (1986).
55. Ward, Dr. Jennifer: The de Bohun Charter of Saffron Walden.
56. Weaver, N: 'Life in an almshouse 400 years ago' Essex Countryside, August, 1965.
57. White, M.D: 'Members of Parliament for the Saffron Walden area.' (Newport News, Summer, 1987).
58. Woodgate, John: The Essex Police. 1986.
59. Woods, John C: Friends' School : A hundred years at Saffron Walden, 1879 - 1979. 1979.

INDEX

(S.W. = Saffron Walden)

Raymond, James 78, 80
Redgates Lane 23
Reginald (Prior of Walden Abbey) 17-20
Reynolds, Richard 66
Rickman, Thomas 99
Robinett, James 67
Roos Lane see Debden Road
Rose and Crown 58, 66, 74, 78, 79, 86, 87, 91, 108, 109, 113, 116, 132, 149, 161, 165, 227, 233
Rotary Club 199, 201
Rugby Club, S.W. 212
Rutland, Nicholas 33

Sack Making 90
Saffron Crocus 47-49
Saffron Walden Society 222
St. Aylotts 23
St. Mary's C of E School 100, 115
St. Mary's Parish Church see Church
Sarah's Place 219
School Row 219
Schools 100, 114, 115, 123, 145, 158, 165, 181, 183, 191, 220, 226, 232, 245
Searle & Co. 121
Semar, Katherine 33, 34, 45
Seven Devils Lane 74
Sewerage 151, 153, 157-158, 218
Sewards End 23, 93, 156, 165, 227, 237, 243
Shakespeare, William 49
Slade, The 1, 94, 186, 197, 205, 225
Slum Clearance 205, 219
Smyth, John 36
Smyth, Sir Thomas 36, 41-43, 44
South Road 100, 119, 140, 147, 158, 174, 231
Sparrow, Joseph 65, 67
Sparrows End Hill 106
Springhill Road 199, 220
Station Road 140, 234
Station Street 151, 181, 206, 210
Strachey, Thomas 33
Strachey, William 36
Suffolk, Earls of 39, 49, 67
Suffolk Regiment see 3rd Cambs. Battalion
Suffrage, Women's 166, 169, 191
Summerhill Road 199, 220, 234
Sun Inn 58, 209-10
Swan Meadow 2, 24, 157, 158, 197
Swimming Baths 123, 149, 167, 170
Symond, Geffrey 47

Tanner Cllr. E. 180-181, 192-193, 203, 206
Tanners Row 46
Territorial Regiment (Essex Regt.) 199, 210
Thaxted Road 133, 138, 153, 194, 196, 199, 205, 208, 212, 219, 222,226,227, 233, 237, 242, 243
Tottenham Schools 230-232, 240

Town Council, S.W. 78, 95, 109, 134, 136, 144, 149, 151, 153-154, 157, 158, 159, 164, 165, 167, 174, 177, 191-192, 194, 197, 200, 203, 205, 206, 209, 212, 222, 226, 227, 229, 231, 238, 243, 245
Town Hall 75, 78-82, 97, 101, 109, 111, 115, 118, 123, 130, 134-136, 143, 151, 154, 157, 161, 174, 181, 183, 188, 191, 200, 207, 213, 215,223-224, 230, 231, 233, 242, 248
Town Library see Literary and Scientific Institute
Tuke William Favill 195-196, 208
Tuke family see Gibson Family
Turgis d'Avranches 13
Turner, Thomas 56, 171

Unemployment 106-108, 194, 197, 206, 207, 208
USAAF 65th Fighter Wing 235, 245, 248

Victoria Avenue 119, 140, 164, 174
Victoria Gardens 199
Victorian Cafe 169, 191
Vincent, John 97

Walden (Name Derivation) 2-3, 16, 24, 25
Walden, Roger (d.1405) 28
Walden Abbey 13, 14, 25, 27, 37
Walden Place 25, 186
Waldensis, Thomas 28
Walker, Edmund 188
Walker, Stephen 188
War Memorial 107, 189, 192-194, 213, 245
Ward, Richard 93
Wastell, John 40
Water Tower 174, 224
Water Supplies 132, 164, 196, 206-207, 225
Weekly News, S.W. 139
West Road 119, 183
Westley Farm 23
White Horse Inn 89
Whitlow, John T. 182
William (Prior of Abbey) 14-17
Williamson, James 38
Williamson, Thomas 36
Wilson, Stanley 226, 232
Windmill Hill 1, 220
Winstanley, Henry 50, 70, 210
Winstanley, William 70
Wodehouse, Armine, M.P. 156, 158
Wolfe, Thomas 78, 79, 80
Wool 30, 45, 90, 137
Wooley, Hannah 70-71
Workhouse, The 75, 95, 106, 107, 108, 109, 150, 151, 165, 208

Youth Hostel 46, 238